# HOW TO LOSE
# $100,000,000

## and Other Valuable Advice

# HOW TO LOSE $100,000,000

## And Other Valuable Advice

## ROYAL LITTLE

Little, Brown and Company — Boston-Toronto

Fifth Printing

LIBRARY OF CONGRESS CATALOGING IN PUBLICATION DATA

Little, Royal, 1896-
  How to lose $100,000,000 and other valuable advice.

  1. Little, Royal, 1896-  2. Capitalists and financiers—United States—Biography.  3. Textron, inc.  4. Conglomerate corporations—United States. I. Title.
HG172.L54A34    332'.092'4 [B]    79-11628
ISBN 0-316-52786-6

VB

Designed by Susan Windheim

*Published simultaneously in Canada by Little, Brown & Company (Canada) Limited*

PRINTED IN THE UNITED STATES OF AMERICA

*Dedication*

To the future entrepreneurs of America whose courage to risk, whose ability to create, and whose determination to achieve will assure the survival of the free enterprise system in this country.

*"Success covers a multitude of blunders."*

—*George Bernand Shaw*

# Contents

## Acknowledgments

At age eighty-three, after sixty years in active business, I have finally broken the $100,000,000 loss barrier, hence the title of this book.

I am indebted to Harvard Business School's Dean Larry Fouraker, Professor Norm Berg, and second-year students Jerry Murphy, Bill McInnis, Rick Spillane, and Tom O'Neill, so if anyone should buy this book, half the royalties will go to Harvard Business School.

I am particularly appreciative of the work that Virginia Bowers has done in digging up facts and presenting copy in neatly typed form. Mrs. Bowers has done similar transcribing for other writers, so was unusually well qualified to work with me.

My special thanks go to Mary Young, my secretary of thirty years, for her help far beyond the call of duty. Besides research, advice and editing, she has had the boring job of doing a lot of typing.

Special thanks also go to Roy McKie, whose amusing cartoons have added a light touch to an otherwise dull book.

*"I understand you've written a book."*

## Introduction

Why did I write this book? During the last ten years at least a dozen authors and publications have urged that I let them write the story of my life. I have always refused. The personal histories of most businessmen are ego trips and of no real value to the business community.

On the other hand, when I am invited to speak to students and business groups I never talk about things that went well. The audience enjoys it much more when I tell about my mistakes. I have had meetings with business administration classes at Sloan (MIT), Tuck (Dartmouth), Carnegie-Mellon, Babson, Harvard, Duke, and Northeastern. I finally decided that by writing about my mistakes I might contribute something to our free enterprise system. Perhaps I can persuade others, both in school and business, to avoid some of the errors I have made. No businessman in the past has ever written such a book—possibly because no one else has compiled such an impressive record of mistakes.

## Foreword

I was born in Wakefield, Massachusetts, on March 1, 1896. My father died suddenly of typhoid in 1900, and two years later my mother married a man who was apparently the black sheep of a prominent family that controlled a large printing business in Boston. My stepfather took us from city to city across the country while he started printing shops first in Buffalo, then in Cleveland, Chicago, Sioux City, Denver, Salt Lake City, and finally San Francisco. Every printing business he started went broke, so we had to move to the next state to keep one jump ahead of the sheriff. As a result, I changed schools seventeen times before going to college.

In California I lived for a number of years on a ranch just below Mount Diablo about a mile or so east of Walnut Creek. While there I attended Oak Grove School, which was down the dirt road a few miles on the way to Concord. This was a small one-teacher, one-room, eight-class operation and at times had as few as seventeen students. From the ranch I rode bareback on a mule who was blind in his left eye. When anything crossed the road from left to right, he used to shy and throw me off as soon as his right eye saw what was coming. As a result I was often late for school.

Although I didn't learn much beyond the three R's at Oak Grove, one thing happened that probably helped extend my life span. The bigger boys used to take us out behind the carriage shed and make us smoke wrapping paper filled with straw. That experience cured any desire on my part ever to smoke, and I have never smoked anything since.

After getting my diploma in 1910 from Oak Grove School, I moved to San Francisco and entered Lowell High School for a few months. Then the most important thing in my life occurred. My uncle, Arthur D. Little, who was the founder of the prominent consulting firm of the same name, was married but had no children. He proposed to my mother that I should come east and live with them in Brookline, Massachusetts, so that I could have an excellent education, graduate from Harvard and MIT, become a chemical engineer, and join his firm.

Arriving in Boston in January 1911, I went to Brookline High

School and tried to transfer from the high school in San Francisco. I was advised that that would be impossible since the eight-grade grammar school standard in California was at least one year behind the nine-grade system in the East. I should have had languages, algebra, and other more advanced subjects. So I had to go back to grammar school and get a second diploma in order to be eligible to enter an eastern high school.

After four years at Noble and Greenough, a private school in Boston, I entered Harvard in the class of 1919. At the end of my first year, I was amazed, and my uncle was disappointed, to say the least, to learn that I was on probation and a dropped freshman. My grades were not adequate to move into the sophomore class. Spurred on by this shock, I worked very hard the next semester and rejoined my class the first of the following term. Then with the war in Europe going badly for the Allies and tremendous pressure on the United States to get involved, I joined the Harvard Regiment with many other students and left college. After some six months of infantry training and ninety days at the army's officers training camp at Plattsburgh, I was shipped overseas as a first lieutenant, where after finishing a French Officers Training School, I joined the Rainbow Division. I was assigned to the former 4th Infantry National Guard outfit of Alabama, which became the 167th Infantry Regiment. After serving in various sectors in France, followed by six months in the Army of Occupation in Germany, we returned to the States and were discharged from the service in May 1919. Mine was a truly distinguished career in the army, since so far as I know, I was the only officer in the American Expeditionary Force who never got promoted.

When I returned home from the war, my uncle proposed that I go back to Harvard and then take a graduate course at Massachusetts Institute of Technology in chemical engineering—a mere matter of five more years at the universities. To the disappointment of my uncle, I told him that I would make a lousy chemical engineer. I really wanted to go into business.

I then discovered that it might be possible for me to get what was called a War Degree from Harvard without returning to college if I could get credit for three-quarters of the courses required for a regular degree. When I went job-hunting it would be helpful to have a degree from Harvard.

Having anticipated three full courses before going to college, it would therefore be necessary for me to get credit for only another two and a half courses to graduate with my class in June 1919.

The college catalog listed full courses for Conversational French and German. The head of the French Department was a Frenchman. I told him all I needed was credit for two and a half courses to get a War Degree. "I've been in France helping to save your country from the Germans. I was the battalion billeting officer putting the men into French farmhouses and barns, so had to speak a little French. *"Parlez-vous français?"* *"Mais, oui, mon professeur, je parle très bien, n'est-ce pas?"* To my amazement he said, "Your pronunciation is fair, so I'll give you one full course in Conversational French."

Next I went to the head of the German Department, who had been born in Germany, and said, "I was in the Army of Occupation in Germany for six months and had to learn a little German. Will you give me credit for German 3 so I can graduate with my class in June?" *"Sprechen Sie Deutsch?"* *"Jawohl, Herr Professor, ich habe in Deutschland gewessen und ich kann ein wenig Deutsch sprechen."* *"Sehr gut,"* he said, and gave me credit for one full course in Conversational German.

It was now about one week before graduation. I was still a half course short of the required credits to get the War Degree. After studying the college's catalog again, I discovered a half course in map reading. Boy, could I read maps after leading troops all over France, Belgium, Luxembourg, and Germany! Getting an appointment with the head of the Engineering Department, I explained my predicament. If he would give me credit for the half course in map reading, I could graduate from Harvard with my class. He said, "This is a very serious matter. I will have to give you a test to see whether you are proficient in map reading."

Bringing out a large geodetic survey map of the eastern United States, he asked, "What are these brown lines on the map that never intersect each other?" To which I replied, "Contour lines, sir." He then asked "What is this black line running between Boston and New York?" "That, sir, is the New Haven Railroad." Then pointing to the map east of New England, he said, "And what is this large blue area?" "That, sir, is the Atlantic Ocean." Whereupon he said, "Young man, you have just graduated from Harvard."

I have gone into some detail about my youth and educational background to prove that one doesn't need an MBA from Harvard to lose $100,000,000.

# How to Lose Money on Personal Investments

# *Lustron*

*I*n spite of my uncle's disappointment at my decision not to go back to college and become a chemical engineer, he was most cooperative and helpful in suggesting possible job opportunities. He told me in June 1919 that it was most important for me to go to work in an industry that was going to have great future growth since, as he put it, I would be swept along with the tide. He mentioned two specific areas that he felt were particularly attractive. Explaining that the chemical industry before World War I had been dominated largely by the Germans, he predicted that there would be tremendous growth in the United States in the manufacture of a wide range of chemicals to eliminate the dependence on foreign suppliers for those products. He thought, however, that the synthetic fiber industry probably had even greater growth potential.

The American Viscose Company, controlled by Courtaulds of England, was the only major producer of synthetic fibers in the United States at that time, with annual output of about ten million pounds. He was certain that synthetic fibers would replace cotton, wool, and silk for many uses, with total production of such materials exceeding one billion pounds some time in the future.

My uncle then told me that he had invented the first process in the world for the manufacture of filament fibers made from cellulose acetate and that in 1914 he had given an exclusive license to Eliot Farley to form a company to produce these fibers. A meeting with Farley was arranged, at which I was tremendously impressed with his personality. I knew that he was the one I wanted to work for even though the company was tiny, producing only three hundred pounds per day of cellulose acetate filament yarn.

Before deciding to go to work for Eliot Farley at Lustron, my uncle persuaded me to meet with Bradley Dewey, the head of Dewey and Almy Chemical Company, which later became part of W. C. Grace. Although it was obvious that Dewey and Almy were going to expand rapidly after the First World War, my decision was based primarily on the personalities of the chief executive offi-

cers of the two companies that I visited. Eliot Farley's great charm won me over and I decided to join Lustron.

In early July of 1919, at my uncle's suggestion, I went to work for Cheney Brothers, the country's leading real silk manufacturer in South Manchester, Connecticut. My uncle's idea, to which Eliot Farley agreed, was that I could learn a great deal about the textile industry and all of the equipment used in various phases of it at Cheney Brothers prior to going to work at Lustron and that this background could be of great assistance to me later in the artificial silk business, as it was then called. I lived in Miss Quinn's boardinghouse at the top of the hill, just a block from the main street of Manchester, and I had only about a quarter of a mile to walk to the various plants which were located in the valley below.

The entire Cheney Brothers situation was most unusual. The family all lived in fine houses up on the hill within walking distance of their offices in the mill. There was an extremely friendly relationship between the workers and the Cheney family, and I was most fortunate in having the opportunity to participate in this environment for six months, and to learn so much in such a short time about all the various operations that the Cheneys carried on in manufacturing products from real silk. The Cheneys bought real silk in skein form from which they made filament yarns. They purchased cocoon waste which was used to make short-length spun silk yarns. Cheney Brothers' operations were completely integrated from raw material right through to dyed and printed finished products.

The Cheneys actually let me operate every type of machine in their mills, and since there were so many departments (at least twenty) I normally only stayed about a week on each job. For example, I ran winding machines along with the girl operators to transfer the fine filament yarn from skeins to spools, both in the raw state and after it had been dyed. I also had the opportunity to work in the dye house and see how the colors were mixed to match specified shades. For over a week I ran a loom in the weave shed where many of the fabrics had over a thousand individual ends in the warp. During my six months at Cheney Brothers I was exposed to practically every type of machinery that I would ever see in the textile business. Although I was an apprentice without pay, it was a most unusual opportunity for which I was always grateful.

During the summer and early fall, with work from seven to five, we got out of the mill early enough to go to the local nine-hole golf course and have some relaxation and fun. Most of my bosses at the mills were Cheneys, and almost every one of them liked to play golf. As a result the Cheneys often drove me out to play with them. Since I had first played golf in 1911 at age fifteen at the famous Ekwanok Club in Manchester, Vermont, it was only natural that I should take up the game again after the war at South Manchester. I entered the club championship that summer and beat all the Cheneys and other competitors except one. In the final eighteen-hole match my opponent was J. P. Cheney, who was head of the dye house and had been my boss. To me he was a real old codger—perhaps fifty-five years of age. If there had been a *Guinness Book of World Records* then I would have made it easily. At the end of eleven holes I was 7 up and 7 to go. Then I began to feel sorry for J. P. and let up, never to get my game back again. Believe it or not, he beat me on the first extra hole. Guinness would have considered that a record of sorts: nobody in the world had ever been beaten before who was 7 up and 7 to go on a golf course.

In addition to golf, all of the Cheneys made me feel at home and invited me to many of their social affairs. The president, Frank Cheney, Jr., had a summer cottage on a lake some ten miles south of Manchester. He had a good-sized houseboat with a small outboard motor that pushed it slowly around. We would all get on board and have lunch and invariably Frank Jr. would bring out his accordion and play "I'm Forever Blowing Bubbles." I was tremendously impressed with the kindness and thoughtfulness of all the Cheneys and with their wonderful relationship with their workers and the merchants in the village. To me this seemed like the ideal industrial complex where everyone was really on the same team.

Finally, just before Christmas, time came to go home. When I met with some of the Cheneys in the main office to say good-bye, they tried to persuade me to stay in South Manchester and work for the company. They thought it was dreadful for me to go to work for Lustron, which was making what was called "artificial silk" in competition with their real silk. They were determined never to use any "inferior" product such as Viscose, nothing but real silk would ever carry the Cheney name! I told them that I appreciated the compliment very much but, as I said to Frank Jr., "Mr. Cheney, you have thirteen members of the Cheney family working for the company. Every major department is run by a Cheney, and I have discovered that no one but a Cheney earns more than five thousand dollars a year. I therefore don't think I'd ever get very far in this organization unless I married a Cheney."

There is a most interesting story about the Cheneys, concerning what, in my opinion, caused their downfall. About 1926 the Cheneys were so outraged that Viscose and Celanese yarns were called silk, even though it had to be preceded by the word "artificial," that they got the Federal Trade Commission to force the synthetic yarn industry to pick a new trade name. The industry chose "Rayon" and no longer had to use "artificial silk" in advertisements. Thereafter synthetic yarns really boomed, and real silk took a beating because the synthetic yarn producers now had the "Rayon" name which they could promote without having to call their product "artificial" anything. Cheney Brothers never changed its point of view and, believe it or not, some years later this wonderful old firm, which made the finest real silk products in our country, went broke.

Returning from Cheney Brothers, I started work on the night shift at Lustron for $24 a week. After I had been there for a few months, the thing that amazed me was the enormous profit that Lustron was making in its tiny plant in South Boston. Although the company's total production was only about 110,000 pounds annually, the price of $7.75 per pound enabled the corporation, with only $400,000 of preferred stock and $40,000 of common equity, to earn a profit of over 200 percent after taxes on its common shares.

I had saved $2,500 from my army pay, and when an opportunity came along to buy a few shares of Lustron common stock I invested my entire savings in the company for which I was working, believing that I was going to make a great fortune investing in a company making such a high return on its capital. Unfortunately, the earnings were caused by the material shortages of fibers for the textile industry, which were caused by the enormous consumer demand for textile products after the government had taken so much of these products out of the market during the war.

After the Armistice in November 1918, price controls were taken off and practically every raw material used by industry doubled or trebled in price. For example, by 1920 some commodities increased thus:

| | |
|---|---|
| Silk | 300% |
| Leather | 200% |
| Pig Iron | 175% |
| Petroleum | 150% |
| Sugar | 275% |
| Oats | 175% |
| Wool | 280% |

The boom was short-lived, however, and by the second quarter of 1920 the entire commodity price structure collapsed, with the result that Lustron had to sell its products thereafter at $3.50 per pound instead of $7.75. From then on it was a real struggle just to break even.

Meanwhile the Dreyfus brothers of the Celanese Company had persuaded the government to convert the government-financed cellulose acetate plants from making dope for coating aircraft wing fabrics to spinning textile yarns. The Celanese Company's plant facilities were far larger than ours, their costs were lower, and they had millions in capital compared to our mere $440,000. When Eliot Farley went to a high-paying job in New York, Lustron was losing money and the situation looked hopeless. Being the only one left, I became president.

We finally sold the entire business including the patents, which were really all Celanese wanted, to Celanese for a price that paid off all of Lustron's creditors and preferred stockholders, but did not leave a cent for the common stockholders. So my $2,500 went down the drain.

*ADVICE: Never buy shares in a company for which you are working if it is earning over 100 percent return on equity. In our free enterprise system that high rate of return will not last. Capital will pour into that industry from other sources, and ultimately the rate of return even in the best of companies will decline to 15 to 20 percent. You will almost certainly take a loss on the investment that you made when the rate of return was too high.*

# Stock Market

During the 1920s, when everyone was making easy money in the stock market, I had almost no capital, but I do recall going to a broker and giving him an order for one share each of twenty stocks. If he hadn't been my cousin, he would have told me where I could go. In 1927, thinking that everyone had gone crazy and that prices were far too high, I sold out.

After the 1929 crash, however, I began to study all the statistics that I could get on many of the leading companies listed on the New York Stock Exchange. By early 1931, as a result of making dozens of charts showing the past earnings records, prices, net worth, net working capital, and cash position of many leading companies, I decided the time had come to buy. But what could I use for money?

I showed all my charts to a friend who was an insurance broker in Providence. He was very impressed with the details I had developed in analyzing each situation, and made a deal with me. If I would take out a substantial amount of life insurance he would guarantee a $100,000 bank loan for me to purchase a diversified list of stocks.

I took out $500,000 worth of life insurance and borrowed $100,000 with his guarantee at a local bank. But when England went off the gold standard in September 1931, I lost my courage, sold everything off, and took a substantial bath—but not as bad as if I had hung on.

*ADVICE: In an extreme bear market such as occurred after the 1929 collapse, it is almost impossible to pick the bottom. In those days it was possible to borrow on very high margin, so it was especially risky for me to have attempted to make a success of this program at that time. Unfortunately, my experience in 1931 did not teach me a lesson. I was to make many more mistakes in the stock market.*

# American Associates

In the summer of 1932 I heard about a closed-end investment trust called American Associates which had been operated out of Nashville, Tennessee, and was in complete liquidation. All of their saleable securities had been liquidated at a loss of approximately $3,000,000. All that was left was an assortment of "cats and dogs"—all selling below a dollar a share, if indeed they were saleable at all. They had a possible market value of $25,000 but an original cost of over $3,000,000. I persuaded the owners of the controlling interest to sell their shares to me instead of liquidating the company and losing the possible tax benefits that might be available by keeping the corporation alive.

I ultimately bought over 90 percent of the stock for approximately $25,000 and then, as the market recovered after 1932 and even the "cats and dogs" in the portfolio began to have real value, I borrowed against that portfolio to buy other securities. By the summer of 1936 the portfolio had a book value of over $2,000,000 after deducting all indebtedness.

The market collapse in September 1937 was fatal. I had made the mistake of selling all my good listed stocks when I thought prices were too high and switching to unlisted securities of good companies with lower multiples but which had limited marketability. It became impossible to sell those shares in the bear market. American Associates went belly up. I had lost over $2,000,000 of potential profit in a couple of months—some stock market expert!

*"That stock of yours must be listed <u>somewhere</u>. Have you looked in the obituary column?"*

*ADVICE: Don't borrow heavily against unlisted securities with limited marketability. If you have to sell fast in a bear market to pay off debts you'll take an awful bath.*

Here is a fascinating sequel to the American Associates story. In October 1937, I set up a trust for the benefit of my children, using my 90 percent ownership of American Associates as the only contribution. Since the company was bankrupt, I never filed a gift tax return with the IRS. Believe it or not, an agent came to see me a couple of months ago—forty-two years later—and said, "Mr. Little, you didn't file a gift tax return in 1937 when you set up the October trust which is now worth several million dollars. How come?" I replied, "The statute of limitations has expired." To my amazement he stated, "That statute does not apply in cases of failure to file a gift tax return."

If I should lose this case I would be subject to 252 percent back interest. I guess I've lived too long.

*ADVICE: If you ever donate worthless securities that might have some come-*

*back potential, to anyone, be sure you file a gift tax return. Then at least you'll have the protection of the statute of limitations.*

# Oil Drilling in Texas

In 1936 an oil operator from Texas hired a socially prominent Boston investment banker to raise capital in New England to drill oil wells. His proposal sounded fantastic. He raised over $20,000,000 in New England, including $250,000 from American Associates.

The proposal was a simple one. For every $50,000 that we would put up the operator would drill a well. If he did not develop a producing well for us with our money he would drill wells with his own money until he did develop one with sufficient production to meet our requirements. Those of us who participated had a leading Boston law firm prepare the contracts that were to state the definition of a producing well—that is, the minimum number of barrels per day of production that would be required for us to accept the well.

This program seemed too good to be true. The operator, who had been successful in finding oil and getting good production for his own oil company, now was putting his total resources of several million dollars back of our commitments. How could we lose?

What happened, of course, was that those who got into the project early enough got their producing wells and came out all right provided they did not reinvest in more wells. Those of us who were latecomers were in effect putting up the money to guarantee the oil operator's commitment to deliver a producing well to others. At the time none of us was sufficiently familiar with oil well drilling operations to know that the industry figured on drilling eight dry holes for every producing well. Our hero ultimately went broke.

At one stage of the operation this company actually borrowed money from a large insurance company. When the whistle blew and it looked as though that company was going to fail, the Reconstruction Finance Corporation somehow or other bailed out the corporate investor with federal funds.

*ADVICE: Whenever an investment opportunity from Texas gets all the way up to New England after having been offered to the smart money in Texas, St. Louis, Chicago, Philadelphia, and New York, BEWARE! If the project had been any good the New England investor would never have had the opportunity even to see it.*

*Our driller was just the forerunner of the infamous Home-Stake Production Co. promoters who recently bilked movie stars and prominent business people out of millions with a similar Ponzi-like scheme.*

# *Herrick Berg*

In late 1936, when I was president of Franklin Rayon Corporation, the synthetic yarn dyer and processor that was the predecessor of Textron, I inherited $200,000. In January 1937 Charlie Guild, a roommate and classmate at Harvard, told me that Walter Herrick, the senior partner of Herrick Berg, wished to become a limited partner; therefore it would be possible for me to take his place as a 20 percent general partner in Herrick Berg with an investment of $200,000.

Because I had had great difficulty in raising capital for our small company ever since starting it as Special Yarns Corporation in 1923, I felt that there was an opportunity for an investment banking firm like Herrick Berg, which had never been an underwriter, to start a department to handle the raising of capital for smaller companies that had shown excellent growth in earnings. Small companies were having great difficulty in raising capital for expansion. Since I was to head this particular department and it would require a minimum amount of my time to line up a couple of ventures of this sort, I decided that I could take on this responsibility and still run Franklin Rayon.

Shortly after I joined Herrick Berg an investment banking company in St. Louis, Francis Bros., got in touch with us about joining them in financing Hussman-Ligonier, a Missouri company run by Ben MacMillan, a son-in-law of Sewell Avery of Montgomery Ward fame. MacMillan's company had been extremely successful in building up a profitable business manufacturing equipment for chain stores to display all sorts of products requiring refrigeration and cooling. Unfortunately the company's common stockholders had preemptive rights, so when Francis Bros. and Herrick Berg worked out the underwriting agreement it was going to be necessary to give their shareholders three weeks to decide whether or not they would subscribe to their proportionate number of shares.

The public offering was set for the day after Labor Day in 1937, but by midsummer of that year Guild and my other partners were getting worried about the market and they tried to persuade me to cancel our commitment. I was unwilling to do so since I felt that it would end our chances of ever developing an important underwriting position. I then got permission to go ahead with the transaction, provided I guaranteed my partners against loss.

Unfortunately I did not get a tax lawyer to set up the guarantee arrangement properly, so that if the transaction proved to be unsuccessful and I lost money on the guarantee I could deduct that business loss against my very high earned income from the firm that year.

The offering price was $22 per share and the underwriters were to pay $20 per share for any stock left over that the company shareholders failed to take down. Unfortunately, the day after Labor Day was the start of another stock market disaster. It fell out of bed.

The Hussman shareholders took up only 10 percent of the stock, leaving Francis Bros. and Herrick Berg each with 45 percent of the stock at $20 per share. When the unsubscribed shares were picked up by Herrick Berg, my capital account was charged under my verbal guarantee arrangement. I could not afford to run the risk of carrying these shares in my account so one month after the closing I made a deal with the directors of Hussman-Ligonier as individuals to buy my shares for $10 each. At the bottom of the market in 1938 the stock sold as low as $5. Since I had told my partners that I would guarantee them against loss on this transaction I deducted the entire amount against my very high ordinary income that year, feeling that it was a proper business expense. To my horror, however, the Internal Revenue Service claimed that I had taken a short-term capital loss and not a business expense, with the result that I lost my entire $200,000 capital and had to liquidate the Herrick Berg partnership completely in 1938, abandon my exciting underwriting venture in New York, and return to Franklin Rayon in the boondocks.

*ADVICE # 1: All investment bankers now realize that the risks are too great in underwriting an issue where the common stockholders have preemptive rights. It is therefore imperative that any company wishing to raise capital get the shareholders to give up preemptive rights. Otherwise the company will find it impossible to sell stock.*

*ADVICE # 2: Have a tax lawyer prepare a legal document that will stand up as a true guarantee, so that in a similar situation a tax deduction can be taken against ordinary income instead of having to be taken as an unusable capital loss.*

Although losing my entire liquid capital was a disaster for me at the time, that particularly dark cloud had two silver linings. First, my short experience as an underwriter gave me a tremendous advantage in the future in dealing with the investment banking firms that underwrote the many public offerings that I was later to be involved with. Second, I was so burned up by the arbitrary way that the IRS had treated me in the business expense case that I decided to learn something about the tax laws. If the government could take advantage of a technicality in the law perhaps I could do the same to them in return. Every technicality that I have ever taken advantage of since then has been completely legal—no cheating, no iffy cases. What the IRS gained by treating me unfairly in 1937 has cost them many, many millions of dollars since.

# *Industrial Rayon*

In 1937 our business was excellent at Franklin Rayon Corporation. One of our principal yarn suppliers was Industrial Rayon of Cleveland. I knew from experience that when our business picked up it was just a matter of months before the business and earnings of the rayon suppliers would improve and their profits would be excellent.

With this background, I bought ten thousand shares of Industrial Rayon at $50 per share on margin when I was certain that their earnings would be very high that year. Everything went very well with the stock. When it reached $65 and business began to slow down at Franklin Rayon I decided to protect my position in Industrial Rayon by putting in a stop-loss order at $60. Unfortunately there was an unusually bad shakeout in the market shortly thereafter.

In a severe market break a stop-loss order becomes a market order when its price is reached, so my large block of stock was added on the specialist's book to the sell orders at $60 he already had. Meanwhile there were not sufficient buy orders to cover this enormous increase in the sell position. The New York Stock Exchange stopped trading in Industrial Rayon until one of the governors came around to the post to try to solve the problem. Without contacting my broker to see whether I wished to withdraw my sell order, the governor got in touch with Industrial Rayon to see if the company would like to put in a bid to clean up the market. Industrial Rayon told the governor that the company would pay $40 per share for all of their stock that was offered for sale.

The governor instructed the specialist to execute the orders, and my potential profit of $150,000 went down the drain. I lost $100,-000. The amazing thing was that when the market opened the next day the price was up over $60; I had been taken.

*ADVICE: Don't ever think that a stop-loss order is a guarantee against loss. I doubt if there has ever been so extreme a case on the New York Stock Exchange. My stop-loss order at $60 was executed at $40—two-thirds of the stated price.*

# Eagle Lock Company

Back in 1937, a small-time security dealer who over several years had accumulated a substantial position in the common stock of the Eagle Lock Company of Terryville, Connecticut, came to see me about this situation. Eagle Lock was a fine old Connecticut company that had been started back in the 1830s to make padlocks. For many years it was the leading lock-maker in the country, but more efficient producers had cut in on its sales.

The plant was a multistoried, red-brick building right in the center of town. Its workers all lived nearby and they were skilled craftsmen. The president of the company at that time was an ultraconservative New Englander. He didn't believe in telling his stockholders anything about sales and earnings. The books were never audited by outside public accountants. My broker friend was utterly frustrated. He couldn't find out whether Eagle Lock was making or losing money. A large part of his firm's capital was tied up in this one investment. He couldn't afford to buy control and no one would buy his stock, so he was really locked in (pardon the pun).

The year before, at the annual meeting that practically no one attended, the president had finally let my friend make a copy of the company's balance sheet as indicated in pencil on a sheet of paper.

No annual report had ever been mailed to the stockholders. A stockholder had to come to the meeting in person to ask questions and even then couldn't get satisfactory answers. Since this was early in the days of the Securities and Exchange Commission, Eagle Lock was too small to be on that agency's hit list. Since my friend had run out of money and no longer made a market in the shares, most stockholders were eager to sell at any price.

When I saw Eagle Lock's balance sheet, I was intrigued. Eagle Lock was loaded with cash. The receivables and inventory were very low because the company had lost so much market share. The depreciated plant account was just about zero—no substantial fixed asset investments had been made in years. There were no bank loans, no long-term debt, and only about $50,000 in total current liabilities. If they had been making money there would have been some federal income tax accrual. By dividing cash by total outstanding shares I discovered to my amazement that the market price of the stock was less than the cash per share in the bank.

This was similar to a situation I had seen in 1932 with the shares of many big corporations far beyond my reach, but here was one I could buy. How could I go wrong? My former boss Eliot Farley and my investment group bought enough shares in the market and from the broker to take over control at the annual meeting in early 1938. Since Eliot and I had been general partners in Herrick Berg in 1937 and were now liquidating that investment banking firm, he agreed to move his family to Terryville and become president of Eagle Lock. We persuaded half a dozen leading businessmen in Connecticut to join us on the board to assist us in rehabilitating that fine old company: the president of International Silver, the president of a Hartford bank, and four other top executives of prominent local companies. My principal job at that time was, of course, running Franklin Rayon in Providence.

The first thing we did was to bring in our friends at Rath and Strong (an industrial engineering firm) to tell us what had to be done in the factory to bring our manufacturing costs in line with competition like Sargent, Segal, and Corbin. After a couple of months Rath and Strong made a devastating report to the board. They said Eagle Lock was a museum piece. It was the only lock company left in the United States whose workers still used the ancient "file and fit" method of assembling locks one by one by hand. Everyone else had long since switched to precision castings so that they could eliminate "file and fit" and use assembly-line methods to put locks together. The engineering study indicated that we would have to double production with half the number of workers in order to increase sales and reduce costs sufficiently to earn at least 10 percent pretax on sales. In addition, although Eagle still had a fine name in the trade for quality, all of the lines needed to be redesigned—a huge engineering job.

Eliot did a fantastic job in reorganizing the place but he had a problem with the local board members. None of them owned stock and their principal objective was to maintain employment in the town as long as possible. Many of the "file and fit" old-timers had to be laid off and replaced with women who had the manual dexterity to keep up with the assembly lines.

Another problem: our beautiful surplus cash position was disappearing fast. New machinery purchases, heavy design and engineering expenses, rapidly increasing sales requiring bigger receivables and inventories, and continuing operating losses were a cash drain, just like water running through a sieve. I was really worried. The board members living nearby couldn't stand the local criticism of Eagle's laying off inefficient workers. They wanted us to borrow heavily from the Hartford bank, modernize the plants, redesign the product line, increase sales, and ultimately break even without drastically increasing efficiency by assigning proper workloads and laying off unproductive workers. That wasn't the way I had planned it—I had hoped to make Eagle the lowest-cost producer of well-designed locks in the country. It would have created a hell of a stink in the state if we had fired all our prominent local directors and gone our own way.

I finally solved our confrontation with the board by selling Eagle Lock to Bowser, the Chicago manufacturer of filling-station pumps, and taking back a lot of long-term paper. My mistake at Eagle Lock taught me two lessons.

*ADVICE #1: Don't put prominent local people on the board of an acquisition that needs drastic reorganization. Their primary loyalty will be to the community and your employees, not to the stockholders.*

*ADVICE #2: When you buy a company loaded with cash that has to be completely reorganized and expanded, don't count on that cash lasting very long. Just doubling sales will use up most of it in increased receivables and inventories. Fixed-asset investment and reorganization expenses will use up the rest. Whenever you make a long-term forecast of sales and earnings it is vitally important that you project estimated balance sheet positions for at least every quarter of the period involved.*

# Cattle Ranch

Some years ago, it seemed to be the thing for businessmen to own cattle. I made the mistake of trying this investment by leasing forty thousand acres in the sandhill section of Nebraska near Whitman. I purchased four thousand head of Hereford cattle so we could utilize the land on the 10-to-1 basis that was customary in that part of Nebraska where it was impossible to do conventional farming because of the shallow nature of the soil.

All of the topsoil, which was only a few inches thick, rested on top of sand with the result that if that surface layer of soil were plowed the whole country would turn into one great sand dune. As a matter of fact, there were many instances where small areas of the surface soil were punctured, creating what were called blow-outs. These areas would enlarge very rapidly as the wind moved the topsoil, and soon there would be created what would be an absolutely perfect bunker for a golf course. There were no rivers in that particular area but there were many shallow ponds around the edges of which it was possible to grow hay for feed. The ranches in the sandhill country of Nebraska were therefore operated with drilled wells for water and fenced-in areas around the ponds where each year's hay was harvested, stacked, and then in winter pitched over the fences to supplement the meager grass that the cattle could feed on in normal times.

This venture was quite exciting to me since I had spent many years on a cattle ranch in California as a boy. When we visited the ranch in Nebraska we stayed in a tiny hotel along the railroad tracks at Hyannis. Every time a train passed by at night the hotel shook so badly and there was so much noise that you were certain that the locomotive was coming right through your bedroom.

Since my operation of the ranch was strictly an absentee owner-

ship situation, I hired a professional organization in Omaha by the name of Bryon Reed to manage it. They handled the operation of many ranches and farms owned by easterners and did an excellent job. I was much impressed with their efficiency, but I must say that raising cattle is not a profitable operation in most years for an absentee owner.

I bought my large herd at what turned out to be the absolute top of the market and I found that my neighbors who had equally large tracts of land were particularly pleased with the profits they were making that year. I remember being surprised at the reaction that I received when I asked some of them how many head of cattle they owned. There was an absolutely stony silence. Apparently, being on a cash basis for income taxes, the last thing that any of them who owned big spreads wanted the IRS to find out was how many head of cattle they carried over each year in inventory.

After enjoying this wonderful investment in cattle for a couple of years I finally decided that financially it made no sense for businessmen in the East to own and operate large spreads in Nebraska. The year I sold out proved to be the absolute low in the market so that in my experience in the cattle business I made two records. First, I got in at the top and then I sold out at the very bottom. That record is hard to duplicate.

*ADVICE: If you are a business executive in a growth company forget about cattle, oil wells, and other tax-saving investments. Put your capital in your own company and leave it there. If you and your associates do a good job you'll be far better off in the long run than if you had diverted time and money to a venture in which you would be an absentee owner.*

# *Wakefield Bowling Alleys*

Fifteen years ago bowling alleys were being built all over the country using the automatic pin-setting machines built by AMC and Brunswick. Although this new automatic equipment was very expensive to install compared to the old-fashioned lanes, it had far lower operating costs since it did not require pinboys.

The total investment on a 24-lane unit including land, building, lanes, and pin-setting equipment ran to about $800,000. I realized that this type of operation might be overdone in large cities and that ultimately the profits would be reduced below what the original investors anticipated. However, I lived in Narragansett, a small community in southern Rhode Island; the area, including Wakefield, has a total population of only about twenty-five thousand.

Three local businessmen of high character whom I knew came to me with the idea of building an alley in Wakefield which would be a first-class operation. A restaurant would be included in the new building that they were going to put up. One of the three businessmen was a contractor who agreed to build at cost, another was a restaurant owner who agreed to run the restaurant without loading it with salaries, and the third was an independent businessman who was just contributing capital. All of them agreed that they would alternate the management of the operation on a sixteen-hour-a-day basis without charging salaries since they had income from their regular businesses. These men were all popular in the community, all were well known, and I felt that here was an opportunity to finance one fine bowling alley in this area. I was certain that when the facilities were completed no one else would try to start a bowling alley anywhere within fifteen or twenty miles. It looked as though here was a chance to prove that a bowling alley could be successfully operated without the threat of the competition that bowling alleys in large cities have with their multiple alleys located relatively close to each other.

As a result of my enthusiasm to help build a facility of this sort

where I lived, I persuaded Business Development Company of Rhode Island, whose purpose was to finance small businesses in the state, to put up $100,000 subordinated to the banks and the equipment manufacturers to provide the working capital needed to assure the success of the operation.

When the lanes were completed, opened up, and promoted locally they were very heavily used. It looked as though the operation would be a huge success. Everybody who went there was impressed with the new automatic pin-setting units since they had bowled previously only on lanes where the pins had to be set up individually by hand. Here was a beautiful new installation with a restaurant where they could go with their friends and with their business leagues and really enjoy modern bowling techniques.

The initial success ran into trouble after a couple of years. The operators had been taking in $280,000–$300,000 a year from the people in the community during that period. Unfortunately this was just too much money for the people in this area to continue spending on that kind of amusement. We were pulling more money out of the community than it could really afford. The Business Development Company's loan has never been paid.

*ADVICE: Before you build a facility for the entertainment of people in a small community be sure, through some type of survey, that they can afford such a luxury.*

# Great Harbour Cay

For many years I had been spending some time in the winter in Nassau in the Bahamas and for the past few years have had a place to stay at Lyford Cay Club on the northwest corner of the island of New Providence on which Nassau is located. This is a beautiful spot with an excellent golf course, beautiful beaches, and an unusually fine membership. In the past I would often fly down to Nassau on Friday morning, play three rounds of golf Friday, Saturday, and Sunday and fly home Sunday in time for another four days of work.

I was particularly interested in fine golf courses and heard about the new development at Great Harbour Cay, the largest of the Berry Islands, located about sixty miles north of Nassau and halfway to Freeport. Apparently the partner of Mr. Grove who had been involved in the Grand Bahamas Development had had a falling-out with him. Grove bought out his partner at a substantial profit. With this money Grove's former partner bought Great Harbour Cay from the Bahamian government, put in a marina and an attractive central clubhouse, and built an excellent golf course. Then began a high-pressure lot sales program.

The company that was developing the area had a plane in which they flew prospects free from Nassau to the island and back. I had been flown over several times by friends in their own jet and we had enjoyed playing the course very much. One day, however, I made the mistake of taking the group over on the developer's plane. To my amazement one of their top salesmen turned out to be a man who had worked for me in Textron in the Menswear Division when we were promoting the Textron label merchandise to leading retail stores.

Because of this meeting I was put under considerable pressure to buy a lot, although I already had an attractive place to stay at Lyford Cay Club. It got so that every time I went to play golf at Great Harbour Cay I got a terrific sales pitch from my former employee.

Then I made the mistake of walking the beach and picking out a beautiful piece of land, something less than an acre, with a magnificent ocean view.

I had a session with the top people in the development who assured me that there would be tremendous building activity shortly on the lots that had been sold and that they were going to raise the price of lots 20 percent every January 1 in the future and encouraged me to buy my lot at once in order to participate in this fantastic future potential.

Apparently they were selling many lots to wealthy English investors who wanted to get capital out of England and could transfer funds into the Bahamas without exchange control problems and later resell to American investors in order to convert sterling to dollars. There was quite a lot of activity therefore in lot sales but practically no building. There were two houses that had been constructed, one of which was said to belong to Jack Nicklaus and the other to Brigitte Bardot. I am sure that neither of them ever paid a cent for these homes. This was just a promotional ploy to get others to build on the island.

I finally weakened and, wanting to help my former employee, bought something less than an acre for about $50,000. I am sure you will have no trouble guessing what happened. It wasn't long before the whole operation was in financial trouble, new owners came in unsuccessfully, and now the whole project is in a painful reorganization.

*ADVICE: Never buy land on an isolated island expecting somebody in the future to bail you out at a handsome profit.*

# *Tom Drake*

The other day when my secretary was on vacation I made the mistake of answering my own phone. The conversation went something like this: "Good morning, Mr. Little. This is Tom Drake. I am a very close friend of Phil Singleton (a director of Amtel, of which I was chairman). Phil has asked me to get in touch with you and tell you about a problem that my wife and I have. I am just finishing up a course at Columbia University where my wife is helping to pay my tuition by operating a stationery supply business at the college. I have been admitted to the Yale Medical School and have gotten a very fine scholarship which will pay for 80 percent of the cost of my first year. In order to take advantage of this, we must immediately sell our entire inventory of supplies at our shop at Columbia University, and Phil Singleton has suggested that I get in touch with you, a good friend of his, to see whether you could help me out." At that point, I said, "If Phil Singleton is such a good friend of yours, why do you come to me? Why doesn't he solve your problem?" To which he answered, "Phil has really been wonderful to me. He has bought everything in that inventory except 35 gross of felt point pens. Phil told me that you were a very generous man, and have helped many students with scholarships. He thought that you might join him in cleaning out the balance of my inventory." I said, "Are you with Phil now?" He said, "No. I was with him earlier today and everything is arranged to get the money I need except for the 35 gross of felt point pens which I would certainly appreciate your taking off my hands if it were possible to do so." I said, "What in the world would I do with five thousand felt point pens?" He said, "Well, you're chairman of the board of a large company, Amtel, aren't you? Well, the company could use these." I replied, "That would be impossible. It would take a couple of years for us to use that many pens." I then said, "If Phil Singleton really wants me to help you out, perhaps I could buy the pens and give them as a present to the shop at the Science

Museum in Boston where I am a trustee." Drake said that by doing that I could get a tax deduction and that if I told him to go ahead, he would enter the order and have it shipped that day (Friday).

I must admit that I was a little upset that my friend Phil Singleton had suggested that I help out Tom Drake; but I finally authorized Drake to ship the five thousand felt point pens to the Science Museum in Boston and bill them to me. Tom Drake gave me his phone number in Providence: 723-2500. The following Monday there was an Amtel board meeting. When Phil Singleton showed up I said, "Phil, I had a call Friday from your friend Tom Drake who asked me to buy five thousand felt point pens that you suggested he call me about." Phil said, "I don't know any Tom Drake." So apparently I had been taken. If my secretary had not been on vacation Drake would never have gotten through to me. However, at the board meeting when I told the story everyone had a good laugh. Evidently this is a standard way of getting unsuspecting people, like myself, to buy huge quantities of supplies that they don't need, based entirely on some hard-luck story. We got in touch with the Better Business Bureau but they could not find Tom Drake. When we called 723-2500 the operator said they were certainly not in the office supply business—their company sold bricks.

My secretary then advised the Science Museum not to accept the shipment and to be sure it was returned to the company. The next day my secretary had a call from the company that had made the shipment wondering why it had been returned. When she explained that a fraud had been committed and so the museum had been notified not to accept the shipment, the president of the small supply company told her that "Tom Drake" had come to his office Friday right after talking to me. He claimed he was a great personal friend of mine and mentioned half a dozen important names and asked that the company pay his commission. The result of this whole transaction is that I did not get stuck after all, but the company shipping the merchandise had paid the commission to "Tom Drake" before they had received payment of some $1,600 for the shipment. I am convinced that there is no such person as "Tom Drake." I am telling this story hoping that it may keep the reader from getting hornswoggled by this type of fraudulent sales plan.

*ADVICE: Don't answer your own phone when your secretary is on vacation.*

# Pre-Textron Days

# Special Yarns Corporation

Since the Lustron Company appeared to have no future, in view of the competition from the well-financed Celanese Company, the shareholders decided that it should be liquidated gradually over the next few years. So in 1923, when we came up with a new idea to start an operation in New England to do dyeing and processing of synthetic yarns for the New England textile industry, the Lustron Company shareholders wanted no part of it. They had become completely disillusioned with their investment in the artificial silk business as it was called in those days.

As a result, Harry Mork, who was a chemical engineer, Eliot Farley, the founder of Lustron Company, and myself started the Special Yarns Corporation to do dyeing and processing of synthetic yarns for the New England textile industry while I was running out and liquidating the poor old Lustron Company.

Harry, as a chemist, was to run the dye house. Eliot Farley had moved to New York and had an excellent job as head of a big coal company, so he could not be active at the South Boston plant. He agreed, however, to endorse the new company's $10,000 loan at the First National Bank of Boston to provide the capital necessary to start this wonderful new venture. We split the stock three ways and off we went into the wild blue yonder! I, as president, was to be in charge of sales, manufacturing, bookkeeping, and sweeping the floor. We took over a tiny building next door to Lustron and began originally to process and sell Lustron twisted with cotton and worsted for use as resist striping material in woolen fabrics.

In that first year, 1923, our sales were $75,000 and we made a $3,600 profit. We soon began to get substantial orders for dyed and processed Viscose and Celanese yarns, all of which at that time had to carry the artificial silk label so that the customers would know that it was not real silk. Within a couple of years our sales volume increased to over $1 million of dyed and specially packaged undyed yarns for use primarily for stripes and checks, rather than entire fabrics, by the huge cotton mills in New England. Formerly, they had to purchase these yarns either in New Jersey or Philadelphia from the dyers and processors of real silk yarns.

In a short time it was obvious that we were performing a vital service to a local industry and that we did not have sufficient capital to handle this rapid increase in business. To solve that problem we made a unique factoring arrangement with William Iselin and Company in New York. They agreed to guarantee our receivables, and advance up to 90 percent of our sales upon receipt of invoice in view of the fine credit of the New England textile mills to whom we were selling. Even that financing was insufficient so Iselin went further and advanced a high percentage of our raw material cost of Viscose and Celanese yarns. They advanced the money for us to pay for our incoming shipments, which arrived in hundred kilogram cases (220 pounds). Because synthetic fibers had been invented in Europe, the metric system was adopted for the shipping units as soon as these products were introduced into the United States, so in a way the United States went on the metric system very early so far as synthetic yarns were concerned.

The arrangement with Iselin gave us the money as soon as invoices were received, and since the yarn producers' terms were net thirty days with no discount, we were able to pick up a lot of cash by pledging our raw material inventory in case form to Iselin against their advances. As soon as we opened a case of yarn and put it in process we had to send a check to Iselin to pay for it.

This was a unique arrangement since we were getting advances on our inventories and also on our receivables. You might say we were burning the candle at both ends. As a result, we very quickly doubled our sales, but factoring and interest charges to Iselin used up all of our operating profits. Although we were doing a relatively large business on a tiny capitalization, we were not building up net worth. Since we started with 100 percent debt financing and not one cent of equity money, we were getting nowhere fast. Iselin, however, considered us to be a very fine account and was most disappointed when we gave them up over twenty-five years later.

In 1925 we heard about a young man by the name of Kenneth Lindsey, whose father had been born in Fall River and had picked up some very important patents to make on textile looms complete cartridge belts and knapsacks for government use so that the pouches and carrying portion of the knapsack were woven on the loom. (Formerly, flat woven fabrics had been produced and then each pocket or container had been sewn by hand or by machine

onto the belts and knapsacks.) This was such a tremendous labor savings and such a high quality product that Mr. Lindsey, Sr., had started plants in England, Japan, Germany, and the United States to make products for those governments. He had made his first fortune during the Boer War, and although he lost his German plant in World War I, his remaining plants were particularly successful at that time so that he had accumulated tremendous wealth.

Therefore, in 1925 he told his son that he would be a very wealthy man someday and should learn how to invest money before his father's death and this wealth came into his control. He gave $500,000 to Ken and instructed him to put $100,000 into each of five different small companies, to go on the board of directors of each, and learn how business operated. He told Ken that he was certain the money would all be lost, but that it would be a great experience for him and would teach him how to manage all the money he would inherit someday. Here was our pigeon—I made a beeline for this guy.

Through Eliot Farley I contacted Ken Lindsey and ultimately persuaded him to put $100,000 into Special Yarns for 20 percent of the common stock. Ken Lindsey, along with the three of us who had founded the company, then became one of our principal shareholders. Although this seems like a very small injection of capital, it gave us a breather and enabled us to cut back to some extent on the heavy Iselin factoring charges. From then on we earned a profit every year for the next thirteen years.

Now that we were fairly well established in New England, we saw an opportunity to do the same thing in the South, and in 1926 in cooperation with Jimmy James we formed the Carolina Dyeing and Winding Company in Mount Holly, North Carolina (affectionately known in the trade as "Carolina Dining and Wining") to do dyeing and processing primarily of cotton yarns for the southern textile mills. The plant was built and leased to us by the American Textile Company next door who were large manufacturers of cotton mercerized yarns for distribution throughout the country. They needed a dye house so that they could supply their customers with dyed yarns as well as those in natural form. As a result of their wide sales representation and the efforts of Jimmy James, we got that operation into production in short order and were soon developing several million dollars' worth of sales a year.

Unfortunately, this venture was unsuccessful. Unlike their northern competition, the southern textile mills tended to integrate and equip to dye and process their own yarns.

*ADVICE: Don't start a service business in an industry where the customers themselves can provide the service you perform, unless you have patent protection.*

## 1928 MERGER—FRANKLIN RAYON CORPORATION

The Franklin Process Company, with headquarters in Providence, Rhode Island, had obtained control of the patents for the dyeing of cotton yarn in wound package form instead of by previously used methods. The process was so much more efficient than either skein or chain dyeing that Franklin Process was successful in supplying the New England textile industry with their dyed cotton yarns and soon expanded. Because of their great success in Providence it was very easy for them to raise the money from their shareholders to start subsidiary operations in Chattanooga, Tennessee, and Greenville, South Carolina, as well as a branch plant in Philadelphia, Pennsylvania.

The genius behind this operation was Gene Graves, who had gotten control of the patents and had raised the original capital. He had been wise enough to pick really competent managers for all his plants, and Walter Traver, who was the president of the company, had done a fantastic job in converting this untried new basic idea into a highly profitable large-volume commercial operation.

In 1926, about the time we were starting an operation in North Carolina, Franklin Process got control of the patents for package dyeing synthetic yarns in wound form instead of in skeins. Although this new method of dyeing promised substantial savings over skein dyeing, there were far more technical problems to be solved than dyeing cotton in packaged form.

The Franklin Rayon Dyeing Company was financed by stockholders of the Franklin Process Company, but Franklin itself ended up with 85 percent of the equity. Since Franklin Rayon Dyeing had lost money for the last two years they approached us in 1928 with the idea of merging their operations with Special Yarns Corporation to form a new company to be called Franklin Rayon Corporation. Walter Traver was to be president and I was executive vice president and general manager. Now this idea appealed to us because it would greatly increase our volume and beef up our finances. We felt sure we could straighten out their technical problems and bring the Providence plant around to a profitable basis.

The merger was set up so that the Franklin Rayon Dyeing common stockholders would receive the same number of common shares as our stockholders. It was a fifty-fifty deal. On the other hand, we were in a leased plant in South Boston and they owned their own building at 86 Crary Street in Providence so they had more net worth than we did. Second preferred stock was issued to both shareholder groups in direct relation to the net worth of the two companies at the time of the merger. In addition, Gene Graves recommended that we raise $500,000 of new capital through the sale of a first preferred stock of which he was to sell half and we had to raise the other $250,000. Because of Graves's success with all his other ventures it took him less than one day to raise his quarter of a million. Of course we had to raise $250,000 or lose control of the company.

Eliot Farley, our families, and friends put up $200,000 but we were still $50,000 short. I went to a good friend of mine in Boston who was an investment banker and showed him the prospectus that we had prepared. I asked him whether he could raise the rest of the money necessary to close the deal. Bear in mind that this was in 1928, when it was possible to sell anything to the public—the stock market was booming, practically any new venture had no difficulty in raising money—but after studying my figures, my friend said, "Roy, I am sorry. I can't help you on this one. It looks to me too much like two drunks trying to help each other home."

In order to get that final $50,000 we did something that I strongly urge others never to do. But we had to. We raised that $50,000 of preferred stock from a young man who was familiar with the textile business, and whose family was quite wealthy; we gave him a job for which he really was not qualified—treasurer of the new company.

Franklin Rayon Corporation was the name of the new company formed when Special Yarns and Franklin Rayon Dyeing were merged. As a result of this transaction Special Yarns Corporation really was the predecessor for what later became Textron. In 1930 we built an addition at the Crary Street plant in Providence and moved out of our leased space in South Boston to consolidate all of our dyeing and processing in one location. Our business expanded and we made money in 1930 and 1931, but then in the bottom of the 1932 Depression things really got tough. Our yarn-processing volume was greatly reduced, and the special 5 percent rebate that we received from Viscose, Celanese, and DuPont as distributors of their yarns decreased substantially. We did survive 1932, making $52,000. We discovered that in severe recessions one can eliminate all bank debt as we did and get into very liquid condition since inventories and receivables shrink so drastically.

That same year, when we got by with a very small profit but in good liquid condition, the Franklin Process Company still made excellent profits. They couldn't understand why we weren't able to do the same. I began to realize that there was quite a conflict of interest between the two companies. For example, although we did no cotton yarn dyeing we felt that we should handle all of the spun rayons since they were synthetics. On the other hand, the Franklin Process Company insisted that those yarns, which were becoming a major factor in the trade, should be dyed in their plant. Feeling that we might someday come to an impasse, my family investment company, American Associates, picked up quite a large amount of Franklin Process Company stock, which at the time was selling for approximately their cash in the bank—like many other companies at the bottom of the market in 1932.

Then in 1936, our conflicts came to a head and Franklin Process insisted that we employ Barrington Associates to make a study of our management, perhaps hoping they would make a recommendation that I be fired and somebody else be brought in to manage Franklin Rayon Corporation. Fortunately Barrington Associates pointed out to them that our situation was quite different from theirs, and that in analyzing our competitors in synthetics they felt we were doing a reasonably competent job and that the Franklin Process Company should leave me alone to run the operation without their interference.

Realizing that we did not have a particularly happy relationship any longer, I made a deal with Franklin Process by which we swapped my Franklin Process stock, which I had bought at a very low price in 1932 but which was worth much more in 1936, for Franklin Process Company's 85 percent interest in Franklin Rayon. (Franklin Rayon's name was later changed to Atlantic Rayon Corporation.) We could then go into competition with them on spun rayons and some other products that had been in conflict before. Because of the many hectic changes that had occurred during those years, Bill Brown, who was the sales manager for rayon yarn at DuPont, suggested that I should have named the company "Frantic Rayon." We resisted that temptation.

When talking to a group of businessmen some years later about the early days of Special Yarns and Franklin Rayon, I said: "I guess I just had a natural flair for business. During the first five years we almost broke even. The company was saved from bankruptcy in 1928 by merging with a relatively wealthy firm. They had $10,000 in actual cash in the bank. Under my management, however, this condition of affluence was short-lived. Hardly a year had passed before our loans were being called by some of the finest banks in the country."

Unfortunately, it has been impossible to find any annual reports of Special Yarns Corporation or Franklin Rayon Corporation prior to 1936. As a result, the story to date has been derived primarily from my personal recollection. Fortunately, Textron has in its files all the annual reports from 1936 on, and it is going to be interesting to quote directly from those reports to show how cyclical the textile business was in those days and what a low profit margin we obtained even in relatively good years.

# Franklin Rayon, 1936

By 1936 our business had improved materially and we were not only doing dyeing of synthetic yarns but we were doing a multitude of special processing of yarns, packaging them in many different forms for the New England textile industry, which was by this time a substantial user of rayon, Celanese, and other synthetics. There had been many small weaving mills started in New England that wished to use synthetic yarns but were unable to finance their purchases direct from the big producers who would not extend terms over thirty days. Because we were receiving a special 5 percent discount as a distributor, which no mills in the country received no matter how large they were, we were in a position to give sixty to ninety day terms to these smaller mills on their synthetic yarn requirements, and since we carried substantial stocks of the principal sizes in standard case form at our Providence plant, we could also give them prompt delivery. This service helped us build up volume in addition to dyeing and processing yarn.

The 1936 report starts off as follows:

Early in 1936 the directors temporarily discontinued all dividends in order to use earnings for completing our package-dyeing expansion program. Shortly after the contracts had been placed for this equipment Congress adopted the Undistributed Net Earnings Tax, making it advisable to change policy and arrange through new financing to pay expansion commitments.

The proposed undistributed net earnings tax of 1936 was an attempt on the part of Congress to force corporations to pay out substantially all of their earnings or face a heavy penalty tax. I recall appearing as a witness before the House Ways and Means Committee that year as a representative of the National Association of Manufacturers to try to show the committee that such a tax would be disastrous for small companies like Franklin Rayon Corporation. I tried to convince them that this would greatly limit the growth of small businesses in the future since there was no way that such a company could use its earnings for expansion when it had to pay them all out in dividends. The law became effective for a few years but was later abandoned as being completely impractical. Now going back to the quotations from the annual report: "$496,-000 net after commissions but before deduction of other expenses was realized through an underwriting agreement with Distributors Group, Inc. and the latter still holds an option until January 29, 1938 on 10,000 common shares at $10 each."

To show the unusually bad effect that the Undistributed Net Earnings Tax had on Franklin Rayon Corporation, we paid out $138,273.60 in dividends from earnings of only $185,360.37. As you will see from later reports, this money going out of the business created a crisis in future years when the banks called our loans. Going back to the annual report, it said: "As usual our business showed relatively rapid turnover and low percentage profit on sales. Customers totaled 644 in number. Dollar volume increased 25% over the preceding year and the ratio of net profit to sales was up from 2.93% in 1935 to 3.4%."

Sales that year were $5,500,000 and because of the new common stock financing, current assets were $1,400,000, and current liabilities $400,000, showing a 3⅓-to-1 ratio. Total net worth was $1,761,-000, a large portion of which had been provided through injections of capital rather than retained earnings.

For example, Ken Lindsey purchased $100,000 of common stock in 1925, the Franklin Rayon Dyeing Company had approximately $250,000 of net worth left at the time of the merger; $500,000 of preferred stock was sold when Special Yarns and Franklin Rayon Dyeing were merged and the half million dollar offering of common stock in 1936 brought the total of capital put in the company up to $1,350,000. Therefore, after dividends were paid out the increase in net worth from retained earnings was only $411,000.

The report continues, "Outlook for future is mixed. An unusually prolonged rayon shortage beginning last August may continue until early 1938." Like all businesses big and small, when there are shortages of raw material, overexpansion occurs; and very often disaster lies ahead. Franklin Rayon was no exception. We put too much capital into plant expansion and, as you will see later, this caused very serious problems in the future. A particularly interesting point about operations in those days was that the company paid only 17.4 percent of its earnings in federal income taxes.

In 1936 we were obviously quite enthusiastic about the following years' prospects since we had predicted that there would be rayon yarn shortages until 1938. Whenever there were shortages of raw materials we were certain to have profitable operations since we had very large allocations of synthetic yarns from the major producers. Now let's see what happened.

# *Franklin Rayon, 1937*

Here's what the 1937 stockholders report said when written in February 5, 1938:

Net earnings of the company for the year ended December 31, 1937 were $107,807.09. These earnings were the lowest on record for the last seven years with the exception of 1932; the seven year average earnings approximating $154,000. This result was caused by the sudden change in business volume during the last quarter of the year. The poundage sold dropped from 2,368,000 pounds in the first quarter to less than 1,000,000 pounds and it became necessary to lay off 165 workers and to put the remaining 360 employees on a part-time basis for nearly three months with an average of approximately one day per week pay. Nothing approaching these conditions had been experienced by the company before, even during the worst of 1932.

Those of you who were in business in the 1930s will recall that there was a severe collapse in the stock market starting the day after Labor Day in 1937. In addition, since textiles have always traditionally been the forerunner in business recession as well as business recoveries, the fourth quarter results of Franklin Rayon bode ill for 1938. The 1937 report went on to say:

On January 21, 1938 rayon prices were drastically cut by the manufacturers and we decided to charge earned surplus (not 1937 operations) $86,420.21 to reflect this potential in future loss which if realized will be charged against 1938 operations. The current price of 54¢ per pound for both 150 denier viscose and acetate rayon compares with 1932 lows of 55¢ for Viscose and 90¢ for Acetate. [Remember Lustron Company had sold 150 denier acetate for $7.75 per pound in 1919.]

Further showing the intensity of the business recession, the report went on to say: "In an endeavor to readjust to the new business conditions with which we are now faced, overhead and operating expenses have recently been reduced over $100,000 annually."

That year sales dropped from $5,400,000 in 1936 to $4,800,000, and our current ratio was 2-to-1 compared to 3½-to-1 the prior year. Because one of its preferred stock issues was called that year, net worth dropped to $1,538,000.

# Atlantic Rayon Corporation, 1938

In 1938, the directors changed the name from Franklin Rayon Corporation to Atlantic Rayon Corporation since we had severed our connection with the Franklin Process Company.

Nineteen thirty-eight was a disaster. On sales of $5,821,271.90, the loss was $72,028.76—the first loss that the company had ever sustained since it was started in 1923. As usual, we used a lot of alibis in the annual report to show how this happened: Loss on Inventory $100,000, Bad Debts $60,933.69, Claims and Allowances to Customers $31,343.70, Hurricane Losses $10,000, Total: $202,277.39.

In the face of this horrible showing, what did we do? Did we pull in our horns? Well, hardly! We persuaded the directors to authorize an expansion of the throwing department involving the expenditure of $250,000 over the next eighteen months subject to satisfactory arrangements for financing. The report says:

The expansion of the throwing department is a natural development of our policy to equip our plants to serve the dyeing and throwing requirements of the New England textile trade. Our present throwing department representing less than 1% of the throwing spindles in the country, has operated profitably in every quarter except one for the last four years and is too small to take care of even the minimum requirements of our present customers.

As you can see from this program, I was always the perpetual optimist.

# *Atlantic Rayon Corporation, 1939*

In 1939's preliminary report, which followed the prior custom of being printed on one sheet of paper folded in half so as to have four printed pages, this statement is made: "This report on the financial condition of our company and the results of its operations is being furnished to stockholders in advance of a more comprehensive annual report which is under preparation for subsequent distribution." It was dated February 9, 1940, and one thing that is noteworthy throughout all these annual reports is that the entire certificate of auditors never took up over seven lines and never had any footnotes.

On February 21, 1940, Atlantic Rayon Corporation for some reason, which I cannot recall, suddenly produced a most elaborate twenty-page annual report, which had not only information about the company but also interesting statistical information about the whole synthetic fiber industry, much of which will be of interest to the reader. The report starts off by announcing that the number of shareholders had increased from 190 in 1935 to 736 in 1939. Net earnings for the year were $79,462.98 on sales of $7,468,015 or a volume increase of 28.3 percent over the previous year. Cash and accounts receivables exceeded the total current liabilities by $163,-537.22. Two thousand shares of $2.50 cumulative prior preference stock was sold for $94,000.

One thousand shares of the same preferred stock was issued to the Ames Textile Company for factory space on the Merrimac River in Lowell, Massachusetts, a large portion of which was to be used for our new throwing plant. Since many other miscellaneous trades like braiders, knitters, and narrow fabric manufacturers were also extensive users of synthetics, we saw an opportunity to start a plant to do twisting of synthetic yarn—a process known in the trade as throwing. This operation required the use of special

machinery where the spindles ran at high speed and put many twists per inch into the yarn to obtain special effects in crepes and other specialty fabrics.

We did not have sufficient room in Providence for the expansion of these operations so the abandoned textile mills in Lowell were just ideal for our needs. We went to one of the Providence banks and convinced them that this was a great opportunity to expand our business in New England for the benefit of local customers. We borrowed money to put the necessary machinery into one of the Lowell buildings to equip it as an efficient synthetic yarn throwing plant.

Regarding the Lowell plant, the report stated:

The Lowell property consists of 250,000 sq. ft. of floor space, a well-equipped boiler plant, a 1500 KVA of developed water wheel and generator producing capacity. The Corporation acquired permanent water rights in the Merrimac River thereby assuring an adequate supply of low-cost electric energy. The completion of the Lowell plant will quadruple the Corporation's throwing capacity and increase it to 10% of the New England textile industries rayon throwing requirements. The acquisition of the Lowell Plant provided the corporation with the opportunity to increase substantially gross sales without correspondingly increasing selling, administrative, and general cost.

Being unable to resist an optimistic note, the report ended: "The Management feels confident that the Corporation is in a splendid position to take full advantage of any opportunities that may be presented, and if business volume continues throughout the year at current rate, satisfactory results should be obtained." It took me many, many years before I learned to stop making predictions in annual reports. Things never happen the way you would expect them to, especially in the textile business.

Just as we got the Lowell operation in production we ran into one of the textile industry's cycles. With business bad in 1938 and 1939, a Rhode Island bank called our loans, and it looked as though everything that we had accomplished in the past sixteen years was going down the drain. It appeared we would have to liquidate the company to pay off the bank. Fortunately, a small New York bank that had been having difficulty getting new accounts in New England and was anxious to expand outside of New York came to the rescue and bailed out the local bank. This gave us a breather and within a few months the textile business was on the upswing again.

One important chart in the 1939 report is the only outstanding record of profits and dividends of the company for the ten-year period 1930-1939. It showed, for example, the following information:

### Ten-Year Record of Earnings and Their Distribution

| Date | Net Profits | Dividends Declared |
|---|---|---|
| 1930 | $    42,420.94 | $  None |
| 1931 | 164,334.04 | 78,750.00 |
| 1932 | 51,574.47 | 26,215.00 |
| 1933 | 284,985.18 | 108,648.75 |
| 1934 | 161,675.09 | 65,450.00 |
| 1935 | 126,510.87 | 31,323.25 |
| 1936 | 185,360.37 | 141,009.32 |
| 1937 | 107,807.09 | 116,011.09 |
| 1938 | Loss    (72,028.76) | 5,471.43 |
| 1939 | 131,600.45 | 6,002.68 |
| TOTAL | $1,184,239.76 | $578,883.42 |

It is amazing to discover that in spite of our constant shortage of capital, we paid out nearly 50 percent of our earnings in dividends during that ten-year period. As a result, earned surplus at the end of 1939 was only $505,766.56. These figures are particularly significant since we paid out possibly $200,000 more in dividends than we should have because of the undistributed net earnings tax in 1936 and 1937. If this tax had not been in effect and the $200,000 had been retained in the business, the bank would not have called our loan and nearly put us into bankruptcy, because it was just about the $200,000 margin that would have made the difference from the bank's point of view in our liquidity.

The 1939 annual report continued with this information under the title of "Rayon Industry":

The nation's first successful rayon plant was established in 1910. In 1911 this plant produced 365,000 pounds of yarn, an additional 1,700,000 were imported, and 2,115,000 pounds were consumed. In 1919 the consumption was 9,291,000 pounds and in early 1920 an all-time high price of $6 per pound for 150 denier was reached. Thereafter consumer usage increased at a phenomenal rate through the joint incentives of better quality and lower cost, with the result that 1939 demand, including staple fiber, was 462,000,000 pounds, with 150 denier price of 53¢ per pound.

It is interesting to note that no one in the United States made 150-denier filament rayon in 1976. This fiber has been replaced by acetate, nylon, polyester, and other fibers made from petrochemicals. The report also stated:

Acetate is the fastest growing filament yarn. Its usage has increased in fifteen years from 1,620,000 pounds to 100,250,000 pounds. Today, nylon stands where acetate did in 1925 with relatively high prices and small production. If technical and manufacturing improvements permit prices to reduce rapidly, nylon's future may surpass acetate's record.

Here is another interesting statistic—textile fiber consumption in 1939 compared with the same fibers in 1976:

|  | 1939 (Pounds) | 1976 (Pounds) |
|---|---|---|
| Cotton | 3,626,700,000 | 3,413,900,000 |
| Wool | 396,500,000 | 121,600,000 |
| Real silk | 50,700,000 | 2,500,000 |
| All synthetic fibers | 562,250,000 | 8,006,600,000 |

Another chart in the report shows that using the low price of 1932 as a base, rayon prices had actually gone down slightly by 1939, whereas cotton had doubled and wool and silk had tripled in price. To indicate how capital intensive the synthetic yarn industry is, the 1939 report stated:

One dollar of capital is needed to make one pound of yarn per year. With an average selling price of 54¢ per pound it would require nearly two years of steady operation for the total sales dollars to equal the capital investment. Approximately $500,000,000 of new capital would be needed to duplicate the country's present manufacturing facilities.

From this information you can see that for an investor in those days to put money into rayon yarn production a 40 percent pretax return on sales was necessary to make 10 percent after tax on total investment. This is why there were never more than sixteen domestic producers of synthetic yarns in the United States. Only large companies with substantial capital and extensive research could afford to enter that industry.

# My Career as a Flying Salesman

The first time I ever flew was in 1928, when Carlie Francis and I were making a business trip in the South to call on customers and had to get in a hurry from Chattanooga, Tennessee, to Atlanta, Georgia. We chartered an old World War I Challenger training plane with an open cockpit and a local pilot to take us on this trip. About halfway from Chattanooga to Atlanta we ran into a thunderstorm; we had to fly around it and soon became lost. In addition, we were running out of gas, so the pilot made a forced landing in a little town in North Georgia called Ellijay. This was quite an experience. We landed in a cornfield about a quarter of a mile out of town and started into town to pick up some gas. Meanwhile, absolutely everybody in that tiny village came running out to take a look at the plane. They said that none of them had ever seen a plane on the ground before; they had only watched a few planes pass overhead, and this was a thrilling experience for them to see one firsthand. Since Carlie Francis was tall and blond, they assumed he was Charles Lindbergh who had made his famous New York-Paris nonstop flight the year before. They hoped that Lindbergh had made a special trip to Ellijay to greet them. They were terribly disappointed when they found that none of us were famous. We ultimately got back in the air and completed our trip to Atlanta. In spite of this problem I became fascinated with the idea of flying, and decided that I ought to learn to be a pilot myself. In

1930, at the Providence airport, which was then located in a field halfway to Fall River, I took my training in a Kittyhawk plane—a biplane that could cruise at about eighty miles an hour, was very stable, and could take off and land in a short space. That was important because the original field was very short itself, and with a normal southwest wind one had to come in over the telephone wires and power lines to land. After about ten hours of instruction, the pilot one day stepped out of the forward cockpit and told me to take it around for my first solo. That was quite a thrill. The plane and I both survived that first experience. I then began to do quite a bit of flying in a club plane that was owned by several of us in Providence and one day I had to fly on business up to Elmira, New York. It was in the middle of winter, and since this was an open cockpit plane, I had a fur-lined flying suit, a helmet, and goggles. Before reaching Elmira the weather began getting bad and there was considerable snow on the ground. After locating the Binghamton airport some miles short of Elmira, I decided to cut my trip short and land there. Taking one quick fly by at low altitude over the field and noticing that the grass was sticking up through the snow I assumed that there was just a couple of inches of snow on the ground and came in at normal landing speed. However, they apparently hadn't bothered to cut the hay on the strip that fall. Landing in about eighteen inches of snow, the plane flipped over on its back. Having been told that the inverted engine in this plane tended to catch fire if it tipped over, without figuring on the force of gravity, I unfastened my seatbelt and dropped headfirst into the snow, getting away from the plane as fast as possible in case it caught fire.

Later on, in 1931, I picked up a secondhand Stearman Biplane for $2,500 with a J6-7 Curtiss-Wright engine, the same engine that Lindbergh had used in 1927 when he flew the Spirit of St. Louis to Paris. This was an excellent ship, very stable, with a cruising speed of about 105 miles per hour. I began to use it extensively on business trips to the South to call on our yarn customers at the big mills in North Carolina, South Carolina, and Georgia. By landing in the field, which this plane could do, beside the mill office, I discovered that the mill owners got such a kick out of having a salesman arrive in a light airplane that I was able to walk by all the other salesmen and accomplish twice as much business as anyone else. On one of these trips I got caught in bad weather and made a forced landing at Fort Benning, Georgia, which was really off limits for nonmilitary planes, but because of the emergency I was allowed to spend the night. The following Saturday morning, three of the army pilots asked me to tag along with them since they were going on leave to Atlanta, and as the weather was bad they thought they could help me reach that destination. We all took off in formation, and to my amazement they began disappearing into low-flying clouds so that they were invisible. This was the first time I had ever been in a jam like that. Fortunately, after a few seconds our four planes came out into the open, but then they disappeared into a cloud again. After about an hour of this hair-raising experience, we reached Atlanta. My ultimate destination was Charlotte, North Carolina. Checking the weather and finding that the ceiling was adequate, I decided that the simplest thing to do was to follow the Southern Railroad tracks from Atlanta to Charlotte without realizing that partway there the railroad rose to a considerably higher altitude than either Atlanta or Charlotte. This flight really got hairy. I was down to about one hundred feet over the tracks, flying sort of crab-fashion so I could see where I was going. Suddenly, a few hundred yards ahead the tracks disappeared into a narrow cut in the hill with no visibility above the sides of the cut. I had to make a sudden decision. I turned sharp left, flew back to the little town of Cornelia, Georgia, made a difficult downhill landing right near the town, tied down the ship, went in town, and found somebody to put me up for the night. The next morning was bright and clear and a young kid in town got permission from his parents to take a ride with me up to Charlotte. We climbed aboard, took off, and I dropped him off in Charlotte—giving him a terrific thrill since this was his first plane ride. In those days there was practically no sophisticated aircraft directional systems. The only thing at the time were radio stations at airports, which sent out a signal in a conical form so that when one was approaching a major airport that had this equipment it went – · · , a long and two shorts when to right; · –, a short and long if to the left; and a – ·, a long and a short if in the funnel headed for the airport. The result was that you swung back and forth into the funnel correcting your course from the beeps as you heard them. Obviously this was not the most efficient way to get to one place from another. For night flights between major cities, they had erected beacon lights at ten-mile intervals, so that if the weather was reasonably good you could always see the next light flashing ten miles ahead and not get lost. There were no omni stations in those days, nor any other sophisticated instrumentation. As a matter of fact, when one was going on a flight of over an hour or so, particularly over strange territory, one took a road map and a ruler and drew a line from point-to-point and then put a crossmark on that line to show where one should be every five minutes. The result of this was that all flying was so-called contact and one would look for the roads, railroads, rivers, and towns shown on the road map to identify whether you were on course. It was necessary before starting to determine your compass course for the line that you had drawn on the map so that theoretically if everything went well, you would identify your intermediate spots and end up at your destination. One day we planned to fly from Providence to Detroit to attend one of the famous air meets that they had in those days where they had races with souped-up planes that did at best a couple of hundred miles an hour. We arrived in Buffalo and refueled, but could not get any kind of map, not even a road map, for the rest of the trip. Going into the waiting room in the airport, I took a good look at the map they had on the wall showing Lake Erie, Lake St. Clair, Lake Huron, and the location of Detroit. The weather was good, so off we went. After flying over Toronto and Canada for an hour or so, I saw a lake ahead and decided that it was Lake Erie. Knowing that a river runs from Lake Huron into Lake St. Clair and that the Detroit River runs from Lake St. Clair by Detroit into Lake Erie, my course obviously had to be north. Thinking that Detroit was north, I flew along this big lake for about a half an hour and then realized that something was wrong. I landed in a farmer's field and asked him where I was, and he said "This is Lake Huron and you're one hundred miles north of Detroit." So having made a bad mistake, I took off, flew south, and landed at the old Detroit Municipal Airport right in the center of town, and as a result of my mistake missed a few of the air races. Another plan that came in handy when flying to Charlotte from Newark was to gas up at Newark and take off with the Eastern Airlines plane, which would stop in Philadelphia, Washington, and ultimately Charlotte. So instead of doing my own navigating, I would fly alongside these tri-plane monsters which also did 105 miles per hour. When they would land on the way I would refuel until they took off again, then fly alongside of them a few hundred yards away, wave to the pilot and the passengers, do the same thing again in Washington, and finally arrive very comfortably at Charlotte without having done any navigating myself. Finally, one day when Carlie Francis and I were

going to make this trip, we started from Boston to fly to Newark to catch Eastern's plane the next morning to Charlotte. Unfortunately, the weather got bad and since I had a professional pilot flying the plane and Carlie and I were in the front cockpit, I asked him to try to get into New Haven. This was impossible—it was fogged in. We then flew out across the sound and headed for Newark. When we were over Long Island, the radio from Newark announced it was now zero zero, so the pilot decided to make a forced landing. We landed downwind after letting out a flare to see where we were going, crashed through a fence, and wrecked the poor old Stearman. Nobody was hurt, but 1939 was the end of my career as a flying salesman.

*ADVICE: If you have just learned to fly, don't make any cross-country trips without adequate instruction and proper equipment. Never risk a trip in bad weather—it could be your last trip.*

# *Atlantic Rayon Corporation, 1940*

With all our expansion of dyeing and throwing capacity and our optimism and enthusiasm for the future, what happened in 1940? Sales were approximately $7,500,000 and we lost $19,000. What a business! Here we had struggled successfully for many years with-out a loss through 1937 and then in 1938 and 1940 after all our ex-pansion and optimism we lost money. It certainly looked as though there must be some better way of making a return on stockholders' equity than in the yarn processing business. That year's report stated:

The greatest contributing factor to the company's unsatisfactory results for the year was the low level of prices for throwing during its last nine months. Processing charges which the company obtained during and after the second quarter averaged 36% below those for similar services in the first quarter.

Since we had increased our plant capacity to service the New England textile companies' thrown yarn requirements, we made the false assumption that prices for the services would hold up even though increased capacity meant that we had to take business away from competitors, and we foolishly assumed that this extra competition would not create price cutting. Obviously, if one wants to expand one's position in an industry it is far safer to buy a competitor's business and not increase overall capacity. It took me many years to learn that simple lesson. At the end of December 1940, after eighteen years in business, we had built up the net worth of the company to only $1,765,000. No wonder we were get-ting discouraged.

# *Atlantic Rayon Corporation, 1941*

The year 1941 started peacefully, but on December 7 war was de-clared and from then on it was a whole new ball game. With most synthetic fibers being subject to priority requirements for govern-ment use, sales that year of $8,200,000 were the highest in the com-pany's history and earnings were $150,000. All bank loans were paid off and the mortgage debt on the Lowell plant was cleaned up ahead of time so that with close to 2-to-1 current ratio and no long-term debt, and common stock equity of $1,900,000, the company for the first time in its history—and next to the last time in all of its future existence—had no long- or short-term debt outstanding.

It was absolutely essential for us at that time to find some high priority government work to go into since Viscose, Celanese, and DuPont had withdrawn our distributor's discount of 5 percent which in the past had been a high percentage of our earnings. It was the suggestion of DuPont representatives, who told us that the government's requirements for parachutes were being increased from sixty thousand in 1941 to one million in 1942 that gave us the idea of going into this new business by starting Atlantic Parachute. It is doubtful whether the company would have survived if we had not made this important decision since the government's requirements for our other services would not have been sufficient for us to have gotten the allocations of synthetic yarns to keep our facilities going. In addition, as you have seen, the highly cyclical nature of the textile business and its relatively low margin of profit even in good times had convinced us that we must find some better way of making a fair return on our stockholders' equity capital.

The 1941 annual report carried an interesting item that will explain to the women of the country who were alive at the time why they suddenly had such lousy stockings: "The elimination of silk as a raw material for use in the manufacture of full-fashioned hosiery and the current diversion of nylon for defense purposes requires the substitution of rayon—at least temporarily—in this important field."

Older women will recall, rayon stockings were terrible, and may have been the real reason why women started going without stockings at all. Another interesting paragraph in that report stated: "The company faces under war conditions a particularly difficult personnel problem. Of its 948 employees on January 31, 1942, approximately 40% were male. With only 18 of its 90 key men over 45 years of age turnover to the Armed Forces is going to be unusually high. To date 36 former employees are already in active service."

There is a very significant statistic here. With 948 employees producing $8,200,000 in sales, or only $8,650 of sales per employee, no wonder the textile business was a lousy investment.

In 1976, Textron, with no textile operations, had sales of $41,049 per employee compared with $35,452 per employee in the Lowenstein Company exclusively in textiles. Another interesting point in the 1941 annual report was that federal income taxes of $59,000 on $220,000 of pretax profits were only 27 percent. This would be the last time that any such low average tax rate would be applied to the company's earnings unless it had a tax loss carry forward.*

# Atlantic Rayon Corporation, 1942

On March 31, 1943, when the stockholders received their report for the prior year, all it said was:

There is submitted herewith a statement of profit and loss for the year ending December 31, 1942 and balance sheet as of the same date certified by Messrs. Charles Rittenhouse & Co. It is expected that a notice of a special stockholders meeting and the necessary proxy material will be sent to all stockholders in the latter part of April. Royal Little, President.

For the first time I can recall, I made no comment about the year's operations and no predictions. Apparently I was rushing around the country trying to line up parachute and other defense business to keep our facilities operating.

Sales were $11,862,000 with pretax profits of $690,000 and after-tax profits of only $250,000. The excess profits tax came into effect that year and, since we had no substantial base earnings in the past to reduce the effects of the excess profits tax, we were hit with an average tax of 64 percent compared with 27 percent the prior year.

For the first time since we had public shareholders, our current ratio was terrible—only 1.45-to-1, with current assets of $2,824,000

---

* Under the tax laws, a company that has been profitable can collect taxes paid in the past if it loses money in the future—called tax loss carry back. After that credit is used up, continued losses can be offset against future earnings for up to seven years before federal taxes are payable—called tax loss carry forward.

against current liabilities of $1,945,000 and total net worth of only $2,080,000, meaning that half of our net worth was tied up in fixed assets and investment in the Atlantic Parachute Company.

Incidentally, the parachute company apparently filed a separate tax return and was losing money since our $200,000 investment in it showed a net worth value of only $75,000 at the end of 1942.

# Atlantic Parachute

As a result of DuPont's suggestion that we get into parachute production, I went out to Wright Field and met with the civilian purchasing agent explaining that we wanted to assist the war effort by making nylon parachutes. He sent me to see Mr. A and Mr. Z, who were the two civilian employees in charge of the Research and Development section, stating that before we could bid on a contract we must qualify by submitting a chute to A and Z for their approval. Once that approval had been received, we would qualify as a bidder.

The problem was that A and Z told us that they could not give us the specifications to make a chute until we had qualified as a bidder. This preposterous position by the civilian employees of Wright Field made me wonder whether the true purpose of this maneuver was to protect the existing suppliers, namely Irvin, Switlick, Pioneer, and a couple of others, who were well established as contractors. As a result of this runaround, I realized that we were never going to get into the parachute business by going directly to the Air Force.

We therefore went to Cheney Brothers in South Manchester, Connecticut, who owned Pioneer Parachute Company, and who were having difficulty in getting sufficient help to fill their orders because of the heavy commitments they had made to the Air Force. We proposed setting up a new company, to be called Atlantic Parachute Corporation, in one of our empty textile buildings in Lowell. We would put up all the capital, would own 60 percent of the common stock, and would give Cheney Brothers 40 percent of the shares in return for subcontracting parachute production with us and training our key people in their methods of manufacture. This plan worked out very well, as we were soon presenting chutes to A and Z for tests which they had to approve, so we started getting business directly from the Air Force.

As a result of our work making chutes and discussing problems with Air Force officers, we found that there were quite a few injuries to paratroopers and pilots because of the extreme oscillation, which caused them to hit the ground at a much higher rate of speed than the straight fall of sixteen feet per second. We did a tremendous amount of development work trying to produce a chute that would eliminate this oscillation, but every time we came up with a new model that was different from the Air Force specifications, A and Z advised us that the chute failed—that it wouldn't open—but they never let us watch the test when it was made.

Later on we found that the Air Force had a one-man cotton tent that weighed seventeen pounds, so we developed a two-man nylon tent that weighed only five pounds and presented samples to A and Z, pointing out that the Air Force obviously must be interested in reducing weight and that our nylon-coated fabric was strong and light, and would better suit their requirements. As a result of numerous alleged tests, we were again advised that our tent was unsatisfactory.

We then developed a very simple pilot chute that eliminated the complicated metal umbrellalike device that was used to open the pilot chute, which pulls out the main chute. We applied for a patent on this device, which was merely a solid ring of flexible stainless steel wire that could be folded over and put into the pack very conveniently but that would spring out and open up the pilot as soon as the ripcord was pulled. This was a big improvement over the device the Air Force had used for years, but again A and Z claimed it wouldn't work.

One day in a discussion of this situation with another civilian employee, he said, "Mr. Little, if you want to get that product adopted by the Air Force, the way you have to do it is to take the patent out in the name of A and Z, not in your name, and then it will be adopted very fast." I said, "Why in the world is that necessary?" He replied, "Under the regulations, civilian employees of the armed services are permitted to collect royalties on the civilian use of any product that they patent which is used by the Services. Of course, they get no royalties on government use. As a result of this arrangement the manufacturer who works out a deal with A and Z can pay them royalties and have the advantage of advertising their civilian product 'As used by the Air Force.' "

Well, this startling information made me realize that something was definitely wrong at Wright Field. Most suppliers had wondered why the Air Force was not using many of the improved products that were being offered to them by various manufacturers. I discussed the situation with DuPont, Playtex, and many other suppliers, all of whom were complaining about the lack of better products for the Air Force.

I then got a bright idea and went to the Patent Office. To my amazement I found that A and Z had forty-six patents taken out in their names for practically every product used by the Air Force. The following is a list of the products patented in their names:

1. Self-locking snap hook
2. Flying suit
3. Inflatable flexible boat
4. Separable fastener (listed with Hookless Fastener Company)
5. Helmet
6. Face mask
7. Flexible inflated device
8. Pneumatic airplane seat
9. Face mask
10. Pneumatic cushion
11. Oxygen distributor
12. Aerial trailer
13. Aerial trailer
14. Life saving apparatus
15. Aerial trailer
16. Safety belt
17. Aerial trailer
18. Life preserver
19. Parachute harness
20. Safety belt
21. Quick release connector
22. Retainer for D-rings for parachute harness
23. Aerodynamic release drag for tow target
24. Release coupling for parachute
25. Aerial tow target
26. Adjustable parachute harness
27. Extensible aerial delivery container
28. Parachute pack container

29. Respiratory apparatus
30. Non-freezing mouthpiece
31. Variable form parachute pack
32. Aerial delivery apparatus
33. Flying boot
34. Multiple weight aerial delivery container launching ring
35. Aerial delivery gun container
36. Controlled parachute canopy
37. Aerial delivery container
38. Stabilizing retractor for bombs
39. Automatic release aerial delivery container
40. Parachute canopy
41. Life raft
42. Life raft
43. Pneumatic mattress
44. Airplane troop launching means
45. Parachute
46. Fabric

No wonder new ideas were rejected at Wright Field! Could this be the reason A and Z delayed the use of electric flying suits for nearly a year, because they had patented a furlined flying suit and boot?

We got together with all of the manufacturers who had been complaining. We discussed the situation with the commanding general at Wright Field. Making no progress, we decided to go over the heads of everybody, directly to Bob Lovett, who was Secretary of the Air Force. Fortunately a classmate of mine, George Brownell, was his deputy, so I got an appointment. No one else would go with me because they were all afraid they would lose business with the Air Force if word got back to the civilian employees that they had participated.

I made a presentation to Bob Lovett, showing him all the patents in the names of A and Z. He said that they would quickly take care of the situation. When I told him that I was worried that we might lose business in the future he said, "Don't worry, Mr. Little. You will be protected. You have done us a great service in making this disclosure."

I left feeling that we had really done a great public service, but what happened was that Textron never received another order from the Air Force, so we were faced with a complete shutdown of all our facilities as soon as our backlog of orders ran out.

I learned later from sources at Wright Field that our record showed that we were "uncooperative" and that no future business was to be given to us. This action on my part cost the company at least $10,000,000 in lost profits.

*ADVICE: The Defense Department should discontinue its policy of permitting civilian employees to receive royalties on civilian usage of government articles patented by them. An impossible conflict of interests is bound to occur. Product improvement will be delayed. Even if A and Z had actually been the real inventors of the forty-six patents in their names, and I have no proof that they were not, it certainly was not in the public interest for them, or any other civilian employee who had the power of approval of competing products, to be receiving royalties of any kind.*

*For example, what is the civilian employee who has a patent on a bulky flying suit on which he is collecting nongovernment usage royalties going to do when a manufacturer of a far less bulky electrically heated flying suit (which will at least fit in the cockpit of a small fighter plane) submits his product to the patent owner for approval? Stall! What do you think?*

## PARACHUTE JUMP

In 1942, after we had manufactured many nylon parachutes for the Air Force, I decided that I should test one of our products by making a parachute jump. I had met John McCloy, Secretary of the Army, during a visit he made that summer to Narragansett, Rhode Island. He gave me a letter to the commanding general at Fort Benning near Columbus, Georgia, authorizing the general to permit me to make a jump in one of my chutes.

When I showed up at Fort Benning I received a cool reception, to say the least, from the commanding general. He explained that no army officer was permitted to enter the paratrooper school if he was over forty-two years old. Since I was then forty-six, the general was quite upset that John McCloy had given me permission to make a jump. I had assumed that I would fly into Fort Benning, put on some army fatigues, go out and make a jump, and go home.

The general made it clear to me that if I were to make a jump it would be necessary for me to go into one of the training groups of infantry officers who wished to become paratroopers and complete a full two-week course. This was certainly more than I had bargained for.

A two-week course involved getting up early every morning and running in squad formation for two miles with army officers half my age. It also involved climbing a rope to a forty-foot ceiling. It involved making some thirteen drops in a parachute from the tower with its automatic release, which gave one experience in landing but without the impact of the parachute opening. There were many other strenuous operations such as jumping off a sixteen-foot wall to the ground, which would also approximate the landing speed that one would have in a normal parachute jump.

One of the most interesting things that happened at Fort Benning occurred when our group was taken up a ladder to the top of a fifty-foot tower, where we watched some other officers in another group finishing up their program. Each man stood at the edge of the tower, where there was a narrow opening in the railing, and hooked his static line onto a cable that ran diagonally down to a pile of hay at the end of the one-hundred-yard slide.

What happened was that after hooking onto the static line one was supposed to jump out into space and at the end of the static line, which was some fifteen feet in length, your fall was suddenly arrested and you slid very fast down the cable into the hay at the bottom. There were hundreds of soldiers watching at the bottom of the tower to see how the officers made out. Just before our turn came the instructor at the top was having real difficulty with two young officers who were so frightened of height that they gripped the railing and refused to go over to hook up their static lines and jump when ordered to do so.

The officer in charge cajoled, pleaded, and ordered with absolutely no effect. These two young men were obviously acrophobiac and therefore appeared not to be qualified for becoming paratroopers. Apparently when they signed up, they did not realize that they were acrophobiacs, or they would not have have transferred to this service. Finally I went over to the officer and said, "Maybe these two kids will respond to your pleadings if they see an old geezer like me jump off the tower and slide safely down to the ground." He thought that that was a great idea, so he asked the two officers to watch while I took off. This really put me on the spot, so I walked to the edge of the platform, hooked up my static line, dove off into space, was yanked to a stop at the end of the static line, and slid one hundred yards down into a pile of hay with no problem. I then walked back to the foot of the tower and shouted up to the two officers whose hands were still frozen on the railing, "You ought to try it. It's great fun."

It was all to no avail, and I remember the officer in charge telling me later that he thought he should court-martial these two men for not following his instructions. I believe I talked him out of that approach by explaining to him that there are certain people who have acrophobia and that the thing he ought to do instead of court-martialing them was just to send them back to their infantry regiments where their feet would be solidly on the ground.

Finally, at the end of two grueling weeks, which had really gotten me into pretty good physical shape, sixteen of us who had never jumped before were taken up in a plane (I believe it was a DC-3) with no door and told to hook our static lines on to a cable running overhead the length of the plane. The jumpmaster said to me, "Mr. Little, would you like to stand in the door and be the first one out so that you can see where you are going?" I replied, "Hell, no. Put me on the end of the line so I'll get pushed out the door and won't see where I'm going." We all hooked up. The plane came over the field, which fortunately was sandy and easy to land on, at about one thousand feet. The next thing I knew, the sixteen of us were out in the air with parachutes open. To my amazement, the feeling of floating free in the air under a parachute was so exhilarating that everyone started to sing and holler as we drifted down to earth. That is an experience that I'll never forget—making the first jump with a bunch of young infantry officers who were anxious to transfer into the paratroopers. Oh, I almost forgot to say that the parachute I was wearing had been made in our Lowell plant. It opened perfectly, so I was completely satisfied that Atlantic Parachute was doing an excellent job for the Air Force.

*ADVICE: If you're manufacturing some product for the services, it really isn't necessary to test it personally. It probably wouldn't be as much fun as I had at Fort Benning, anyway.*

## JUNGLE HAMMOCKS

When the Air Force cut off our business because of the A and Z episode, we tried to fill in for a while with some other government work during the period when we were gradually converting over to Textron label products in our sewing plants. The war in the Pacific created demand for a new product. The Army found that the regular army tent in which soldiers slept on the ground was not suitable for use in a lot of the heavily forested areas in which they had to operate. There were all kinds of insects, scorpions, snakes, and bugs that created a demand for what the quartermaster corps called a "Jungle Hammock."

We were so desperate for something to do in our Lowell plant that we agreed to design a jungle hammock that could be swung between two trees and that basically would have a canvas hammock for the soldiers to lie in with a waterproof, tentlike nylon-coated fabric slung over the hammock. These two articles were to be held together by nylon netting around all four sides of the hammock and would have, of course, a zippered entrance for the soldier to get into the device. The result was that this product could be slung above the ground between two trees with thirty inches of headroom between the hammock and its top.

As a result of our research and development work on this product, the quartermaster corps drew the specifications exactly according to our design, so that when the first order for 100,000 of these hammocks was put out to bid we were the only bidder since no one else knew how to put them together or had lined up the sources of material necessary to complete the job. The pressure for production was so great on this item that the quartermaster corps asked us to run multiple shifts; the hammocks were needed immediately for use in the South Pacific.

At that time Eliot Farley, who had originally backed our Special Yarns Corporation and who was chairman of the board of Textron, took on the job as manager of Atlantic Parachute in Lowell and had the direct responsibility for producing these hammocks. He did a fantastic job in getting the organization geared up to do this complicated work, which required, in some cases, different types of sewing machines than parachutes. He gave pep talks to the people on both shifts, and we really increased the production.

But we weren't satisfying the quartermaster corps with our deliveries. The problem was that the quartermaster corps put one of their inspectors in our plant in Lowell and he didn't work with quite the same enthusiasm as the rest of us. He allowed hundreds of our completed hammocks to lie piled up in a corner of the plant and took his own good time in checking them for quality while the quartermaster corps was blaming Eliot Farley and me for slow deliveries.

What we should have done was to go to the Philadelphia quartermaster headquarters and ask them to put on more inspectors. But Eliot Farley made the slight mistake of offering to pay supper money to the inspector provided he'd come in after supper and get some more hammocks shipped. We got immediate results. He wrote a memo to his superiors in Philadelphia saying that Atlantic Parachute had attempted to bribe him and that we should be dealt with accordingly.

The situation was so serious that both Eliot Farley and I took the sleeper to Philadelphia that night and appeared before the quartermaster general and a group of his officers to face charges. We explained to them that all we had attempted to do was to persuade their inspector to get off his butt and clear hundreds of hammocks that we had completed, and had only suggested paying his supper money if he would cooperate. The general and his associates all burst into laughter and the whole matter was settled by them putting another inspector on the job so that we could expedite delivery of the hammocks so desperately needed by the services.

*ADVICE: If you ever have a problem of this sort, you should go right over the head of the inspector to the officers in charge and lay the cards on the table rather than attempting to solve it the way we did. If the product is needed badly enough by the services to justify additional inspectors, you can be sure that you'll get them.*

# *Textron Before Diversification*

# Textron, 1943

$N$ineteen forty-three was a year of drastic change and important decisions for the future of the company. Because we had built up such a large sewing plant facility both in Lowell and in Manchester, New Hampshire, it was necessary to keep these operations running fully. We were not getting any new orders for parachutes from the Air Force as explained earlier, so we decided to make some civilian products in these plants.

We picked the name Textron to connote "textile products made from synthetics." A wholly-owned subsidiary, Textron, Inc., was incorporated April 27, 1943, to be the vehicle used to start this operation. The company's total sales in 1943 were $23,800,000 with a pretax profit of $1,732,000 and an aftertax profit of $513,000 after taxes of $1,219,000 representing 70 percent of our pretax earnings.

Our future plans to build up a large consumer product operation under the Textron name required us to get control of synthetic fabric weaving mills, otherwise, with the shortages of materials not subject to government allocation, we would have been unable to have kept our large sewing plant operations going.

The June 19, 1944, report to shareholders said:

During the past year the manufacturing operations of the corporation have been expanded and integrated to include the production of consumer textile goods made from synthetic materials. In connection with this program the property of Suncook Mills was acquired to provide future weaving facilities for high grade synthetic cloths and an immediate source of woven rayon fabrics for manufacture in the sewing plants of the corporation into consumer products. These consumer products consist principally of shower curtains and draperies; lining materials; men's pajamas, shirts, and shorts; women's woven lingerie and housecoats, made in various styles, colors, and patterns. These products are nationally advertised at suggested retail prices and are being distributed to the country's leading retail stores under the TEXTRON name.

*A typical Textron product advertisement.*

We were fully convinced that our new concept of complete integration was the future potential for the company, and that we should rid ourselves of operations that did not tie into that program. We hoped ultimately to have spinning mills, weaving mills, piece dyeing, and printing plants to prepare the fabrics for our huge sewing operation that would enable us ultimately to become one of the leading producers of high quality textile products of all types under our Textron label.

With the most unsatisfactory results that we had had since starting the company in 1923 in the highly cyclical textile business, we were certain that the closer we got to the consumer with a forceful advertising campaign and high quality merchandise, the easier it would be to eliminate or soften the cycles that occurred in the textile business because of its highly fragmented nature which resulted in building excess inventories at all stages during boom time and the overliquidation of inventories at all stages in recession periods. We felt that through creating consumer demand for our brand name merchandise we would persuade the public to go to the leading department stores in the country and demand Textron label merchandise, thereby eliminating the cycles of the past.

When we acquired Suncook, I had been tremendously impressed with the thoroughness of the accounting done for them by Stewart, Watts and Bollong. As a result, we shifted auditors at the end of 1943 and they have carried on ever since, later becoming part of Arthur Young and Company.

The purchase of Suncook and financing the $12 million increase in sales from the prior year had put an extraordinarily heavy load on our balance sheet. Even though our common stock equity had increased to $2,115,000, we were turning our capital over almost nine times a year and our current assets were $5,700,000 with current liabilities of $4,300,000, showing a very poor 1.3-to-1 ratio. Although we had no substantial long-term debt it was important for us to lighten up and sell off some of our operations. The report for 1943 said:

The corporation has operated a yarn dyeing and throwing plant in Providence, R.I. for many years in connection with its activities as an important yarn distributor for leading rayon manufacturers. As distributors' discounts have recently been discontinued and in our opinion will not be reestablished post-war, the directors have decided to sell the dyeing business as it has no direct relation to our integrated Textron operations, and to move the throwing equipment to a more favorable operating location.

This meant, in effect, that Textron was going to abandon the entire business for which the company was founded in 1923, and really move into completely integrated brand name consumer textile products. This daring new concept, never attempted before on such a scale by anyone in the industry, showed our continuing disenchantment with our former business and our desperate search for a way to earn an adequate return on capital after the war. This was a momentous decision.

During 1943 the 40 percent interest that Cheney Brothers held in Atlantic Parachute was purchased and consolidated with the parent company. Two significant notes to the financial statement indicate why our new plans for complete integration were being rushed: "During 1943 certain government contracts were terminated prior to completion at the request of the United States Government. There have been additional terminations of contracts occurring in 1944 of a presently undetermined amount."

As a result of these cancellations, with no further parachute business from the Air Force, we were forced to move quickly to keep our large sewing plants running. Otherwise, we might have been faced with a complete liquidation of Textron, because we were selling all of our original synthetic yarn dyeing and processing business. We put together a strong organization of stylists and merchandisers for all the different product lines we planned to produce and sell.

Since it was necessary to have showrooms in New York so that store buyers could inspect merchandise in a convenient place, we bought the old Tiffany Building on Fifth Avenue near the Empire State Building. To remodel it for our specialized requirements meant changing a lot of the partitioning. When we went to the Building Department in New York City, they insisted that in addition to the modest expense that we would have had to prepare the building for our occupancy we should spend an extra million dollars, which we had no need for, to get their permission to proceed. Their requirement covered rebuilding stairwells and making elevator improvements. When we pointed out that Tiffany had occupied the property for over forty years without any such expenditure, they stated that a change of ownership gave them the opportunity to require major alterations even though minor partitioning was all we needed.

*ADVICE: Never buy an old building in a big city without getting permission from the building inspectors, in advance of the purchase, for the changes you need to make. If you use that approach and the inspectors make unreasonable demands, you can still walk away and not be subject to a potential shakedown.*

*Since we were unwilling to pay off somebody to get relief, my mistake at the Tiffany Building cost the company $1,000,000.*

The following is from the *New York Times* in 1977:

### MOON SECT BUYS BUILDING

A Fifth Avenue building that formerly housed garment-industry show-rooms has been purchased for a reported $2.4 million by a publishing operation associated with the Unification Church of America, headed by the Rev. Sun Myung Moon.

A spokesman for News World Communications Inc. which filed state incorporation papers last October to produce a daily newspaper and radio and television programs, said a deal was closed Monday for the purchase of the seven-story building at 401 Fifth Avenue at 37th Street.

The spokesman, Nancy Belot, said the property was to be used for office space for the staff of News World in New York.

With the Moonies in our old building this is a case of "From the sublime to the ridiculous."

# *Textron, 1944*

Sales for 1944 were $26,255,000, with earnings of $614,000. The tax rate was approximately 75 percent due to excess profits taxes. At year-end, the company's balance sheet was unusually strong, with current assets of $5,676,000 and current liabilities of $1,925,000—a current ratio of 2.9-to-1.

A most important thing happened in September 1944. We sold $2,000,000 worth of 5 percent 15-year debentures, convertible at $20 per share, and callable at 102½ in whole or in part at any time. In addition, there were detachable warrants to purchase forty common shares with each $1,000 debenture. Prior to October 1, 1945, the warrant price was $12.50; this advanced to $15 in 1946 and $17.50 in 1947. The underwriters for this offering were Blair and Co. and Maxwell, Marshall and Co., who were intrigued with our long-range plan of developing a completely integrated textile operation from raw material through to finished Textron label products for sale through leading department stores to the general public.

It would have been completely impossible for Textron to have raised any capital through a public offering at this time if we had just been synthetic yarn processors. There is no question that the Textron label idea and its glamorous consumer advertising had made this financing possible. The combination of convertibility and detachable warrants soon got christened the "Christmas Tree Issue" on Wall Street. It had been a long time since anyone had put out such an intriguing offering.

In addition to normal commission on the offering, the underwriters received a bonus of warrants to purchase 20,000 shares at a favorable price. Since our total common stock issue at the end of 1943 was only 221,620 shares, there was enormous dilution in this offering as the total new stock that could be issued through conversion, warrants, and bonuses was 200,000 shares. On the other hand, since our common stock equity at the end of 1943 was only $2,115,000, and we doubled our capital and raised enough money to continue our program, we felt the dilution was worthwhile.

As previously voted by the directors, on June 30, 1944, the entire Providence yarn dyeing division was sold to Harold Wilcox and a group of the Providence division's employees for $463,888.80. Harold had been with the Franklin Rayon Dyeing Corporation at the time of our merger and was a superb salesman. What little success we had had in making a small profit in the synthetic yarn dyeing and processing operations was due largely to him and the rest of the key people who participated in the purchase of that division.

At the same time, Suncook's Flightex Division was sold for $1,-062,000 to a group including Val Dietz, who was manager of that division. As president of the operation when it was sold, he had been responsible for its past success.

The footnotes to Textron's annual report for that year, dated March 23, 1945, contained this statement:

The company made an offer to the stockholders of Manville Jenckes Corporation to purchase their outstanding shares of preferred and common stock on the basis of $55 and $11 a share respectively. The offer has been accepted as of March 17, 1945, with stockholders owning in excess of 90% of the outstanding shares of both classes. This percentage represented the required minimum in accordance with the offer. In connection with this offer, the company has made arrangements to finance the purchase involving approximately $5,571,000 by a bank loan of $4,550,000 and an unsecured loan of $500,000 from other sources.

This acquisition had been arranged originally for some $5,071,-000 with everything all set to go when a competitive bid made us increase the price by $500,000. Unfortunately, the banks would not increase their loan and rather than lose the acquisition the Textron board agreed to borrow $500,000 from my family's investment company, American Associates, without my voting on the matter. Because of this possible conflict of interest and several other transactions between Textron and various charity trusts and foundations, a derivative stockholders' suit was filed against me and the directors (which will be discussed later).

By the end of 1944, the company's net worth had increased to $3,000,000. Rapid progress was being made in expanding the company's completely integrated consumer product program under the Textron label. Because of the enormous war demand for textile products, there was an acute shortage of textile fabrics available. Textron was fast developing into a fine source of supply for a wide range of consumer items under its label. To supply this demand and broaden its scope, it became necessary for us to buy several other textile mills.

# *Textron, 1945*

Nineteen forty-five was a most unusual year. Our sales increased from $26,255,000 in 1944 to $46,853,000, due in part to acquisitions which had been made that year. On the other hand, our pre-tax profit of $2,017,000 was reduced by income taxes of $1,713,000—an average rate of 85 percent. From the remaining $304,000 aftertax profit the auditors deducted "earnings of subsidiaries prior to date of acquisition by parent, $451,252.02." Believe it or not, the final result was a loss of $147,338.45. This certainly must be one of the most outstanding examples of the mysteries of the accounting profession.

Nineteen forty-five was a year of great activity, although no one would have known it from the thirteen-line annual report. At least I'd stopped making predictions!

The acquisition of Manville Jenckes Corporation was completed March 16, 1945, and Lonsdale Company was acquired October 31, 1945. In addition, on December 31, 1945, we acquired 45 percent of the shares of the Nashua Manufacturing Company. The balance of the shares were subsequently purchased at $100 per share for a total purchase price of approximately $10,000,000. These purchases were financed primarily with bank loans, which were subsequently paid off through these public financings: $5,000,000 face amount of 4½ percent convertible debentures were issued as of April 1, 1945, and the original $2,000,000 issue of the previous year was called in June 1945 with the result that most of it was converted into common stock. Then, in October 1945, a $5,000,000 issue of 5 percent preferred stock convertible on a share-for-share basis into common stock was sold and the April convertible debenture issue was called. And again the bulk of it was converted into common stock.

As a result, in just a thirteen-month period, the net worth of the company increased from $3,000,000 to $14,726,000, largely through the conversion of $7,000,000 worth of debentures into equity plus the addition of $5,000,000 worth of preferred for a total of $12,000,000 of added capital. Part of this new financing was used to retire a small preferred stock issue. If it had not been for the remarkable interest created by our complete integration program for the manufacture and sale of Textron label merchandise none of these public offerings could possibly have been sold. (The Nashua acquisition and its subsequent problems will be covered later.)

Another significant event in 1945 was the creation of the Sixty Trust (also covered more fully later), the retirement pension plan for all the company's salaried employees. This plan was adopted when the directors cancelled an insurance company plan that yielded only 2½ percent on our investments.

That year approximately $215,000 was paid into the trust, which was to be administered by an individual trustee instead of by an institution. The directors also instituted a self-administered profit sharing plan, later called the Market Square Trust, for the benefit of all salaried employees with an initial contribution of $450,000.

Thereafter annual contributions equal to 5 percent of the net profits before taxes were to be made.

## NASHUA MANUFACTURING COMPANY

Nashua Manufacturing Company, one of New England's oldest
textile companies, which occupied some 3 million square feet of
space in Nashua, New Hampshire and, in addition, had a cotton
fabric mill in Cordova, Alabama, was the largest producer of blankets in the country. It also produced sheets and the famous Indian
Head fabric, which was a brand name that originated back in the
1820s and was extremely well known to all of the women in the
country.

Nashua was publicly owned and its stock was selling for about its
working capital per share. We offered to buy all shares at approximately 80 percent of book value for a total cost of $10,500,000, and
took control in December 1945. Nashua's past sales and earnings
had been most erratic:

| Year | Sales (in thousands) | Profits (aftertax) (in thousands) | Total Assets (in thousands) |
|------|------|------|------|
| 1920 | $25,883 | $ 1,311 | $28,272 |
| 1921 | 12,670 | (317) | 25,936 |
| 1922 | 8,205 | (1,457) | 20,263 |
| 1923 | 17,262 | 1,692 | 24,640 |
| 1924 | 16,112 | (716) | 23,664 |
| 1925 | 16,062 | (155) | 23,449 |
| 1926 | 14,338 | (178) | 20,155 |
| 1927 | 17,999 | 1,209 | 22,845 |
| 1928 | 17,625 | 437 | 21,482 |
| 1929 | 16,070 | 553 | 21,730 |
| 1930 | 11,202 | (1,642) | 18,445 |
| 1931 | 9,364 | (1,760) | 16,145 |
| 1932 | 6,829 | (835) | 14,126 |
| 1933 | 8,891 | 268 | 16,695 |
| 1934 | 10,786 | 150 | 17,066 |
| 1935 | 11,013 | (1,330) | 14,652 |
| 1936 | 11,479 | (21) | 13,081 |
| 1937 | 14,435 | 553 | 13,269 |
| 1938 | 8,376 | (243) | — |
| 1939 | 11,319 | (6) | 13,957 |
| 1940 | 12,440 | (247) | 14,767 |

| Year | Sales (in thousands) | Profits (aftertax) (in thousands) | Total Assets (in thousands) |
|------|------|------|------|
| 1941 | 22,070 | 1,354 | — |
| 1942 | 32,659 | 1,360 | — |
| 1943 | 36,175 | 894 | 17,375 |
| 1944 | 33,618 | 652 | 17,890 |
| 1945 | 32,344 | 673 | 16,831 |

Nashua, however, was making substantial pretax profits when we bought it, because of the shortage of merchandise available to consumers after the war. Looking ahead, however, we knew that we must modernize these plants and get the productivity of the workers up to that in southern mills. Since Nashua was supplying merchandise to a national market, the ultimate consumer did not care whether the goods were made in New England or in the South. It was, therefore, essential that the mills be competitive. Our policy had been to use the firm of Rath and Strong, who were outstanding engineers, in determining the work assignments that could be achieved in any type of textile operation. We had them make a study, which took a whole year at the Nashua plant, to tell us what had to be done to make these plants competitive with modern southern mills. Their study recommended that we put approximately $1 million into new equipment so that any obsolete machinery could be replaced.

Their report stated that to make Nashua efficient, approximately 1,500 mill workers would have to be dropped from the payroll to achieve comparable cost to mills in the South making similar products. This program meant eliminating over 35 percent of the entire work force in Nashua. We realized that it would be extremely difficult to sell any such drastic reorganization to the workers.

We therefore went to the head of the textile union, Emil Rieve, in New York City with representatives of Rath and Strong. Rieve brought in his time-study expert and agreed that if we would spend a million dollars on the required new machinery and if his time-study expert agreed with Rath and Strong's work assignments that the union would cooperate with us in attempting to achieve this end result. We convinced Rieve that over 4,000 textile workers in Nashua would ultimately lose their jobs in that high-cost New England plant unless it was modernized and efficient. It would be better to help us save 2,500 jobs than to lose everything.

We spent our $1 million on new machinery, but Rieve was unable to persuade the workers in the plant to adopt the new work schedules. At the end of the next year little had been accomplished. We announced therefore that we were closing the mill and abandoning all operations except the Indian Head dyeing and finishing at Nashua.

*ADVICE: Don't count on union leaders to be able to sell such a drastic work reassignment. It just cannot be done.*

Although the whole Nashua episode turned out to be a dark cloud over Textron because of the resulting Tobey hearings, there was a silver lining. Jim Robison, who started with Nashua as a salesman, became sales manager after we took over, then executive vice president of Textron, and in 1953 headed up the Indian Head spin-off. Jim was the best thing we acquired at Nashua.

# *Textron, 1946*

A stockholders' derivative suit was brought against all of the directors, certain charity trusts, and American Associates, resulting from Textron's financial dealings with those entities. (This action will be discussed later under the heading of "Pomerantz.")

When the 1946 annual report was written, we really thought we'd made the big time. Our sales were twenty-one times greater than 1936. Our consolidated aftertax return on common equity was over 45 percent—excess profit taxes were eliminated that year. Very few other companies, regardless of industry, could approach that performance. There certainly was nothing wrong with the textile business the way we ran it! We'd solved the problem of return on capital—now let everybody else in the industry follow our lead and eliminate once and for all the dreadful cycles we had all suffered. Every mill should become completely integrated and deal directly with the ultimate consumer. It was a beautiful dream!

Hadn't we made $8,385,000 on sales of $113,000,000? Our net working capital was over $18,000,000. We operated 13,600 looms and 543,700 spindles in 7,000,000 sq. ft. of floor space with 16,000 employees. One red flag warning that we completely ignored, however, was that our sales per worker that year were only $7,500—a highly labor intensive situation.

In May 1946, Textron Southern was formed to acquire twelve textile plants in North and South Carolina formerly owned by the Gossett Mills and Chadwick Hoskins. In view of Textron's very heavy indebtedness, it was not possible at that time to acquire this entire operation as a division of Textron. Textron Southern was set up with Textron putting up $2,000,000 for the Class B stock, $6,000,000 from the banks, and $4,000,000 from a group of institutional investors for the controlling Class A shares:

| | |
|---|---|
| Rhode Island Charities Trust | $2,000,000 |
| A prominent Providence businessman | 1,000,000 |
| MIT Trust | 500,000 |
| Rayon Foundation Trust | 500,000 |

The report written on April 13, 1947, states:

The bank loans, incurred to purchase the Nashua stock and to purchase the properties acquired by Textron Southern, together with borrowing for current purposes, reached a peak of $17,272,000 on September 1, 1946. These borrowings were reduced to $7,000,000 by the year end and currently stand at $3,500,000.

The amazing thing in retrospect is that these bank borrowings for acquisitions carried an interest rate of only 3½ percent. Another paragraph from the report says:

During 1947, vigorous promotion of our many brand name consumer products will be continued. It is anticipated that the advantages of complete integration will be particularly noticeable this year as non-integrated competition in many lines will be squeezed by higher finished cloth prices and increasing resistance to rising prices and low quality. We will continue to improve the quality of our brand name products without increasing prices whenever possible.

To indicate how dedicated we were to this new concept and how confident we were of its long-range success, the annual report under "TEXTRON—An Outline of Its Progress" states:

Plans made during the war for the peacetime organization of Textron were based on building an integrated operation for the manufacture and sale of brand named consumer products. Integration, or more specifically 'vertical' integration in the case of Textron, combines under one management operations which are usually performed by independent companies such as spinning, weaving, finishing, designing, sewing, and merchandising. It was decided in 1944 when the trade name TEXTRON was adopted to concentrate on quality products, distinctively styled, in medium price range to be sold directly to selected department stores and other retail outlets throughout the country. With the aid of advertising designed to familiarize the public with Textron's brand name and products in a nationwide sales organization, Textron's products found ready acceptance.

Doesn't this sound like a terrific idea? Integrated production had been successful in the past only in sheets, blankets, and women's lingerie. Textron was going to make it work for all kinds of high-style merchandise for men and women's wear, sheets and blankets, piece goods, shower curtains, and any other product that our mills and sewing plants could produce. This whole concept created much interest in the market. Many old-timers in the textile business predicted complete failure, but we in the company were sure that we had created something completely novel, revolutionary, and highly successful for the stockholders.

As a result of the acute shortages of consumer products after the war, all of the principal stores in the country were clamoring to buy our products. We never made any so-called private label merchandise for the chains since our theory was that by spending at least $1 million a year advertising in magazines, on the radio, and at the retail level we would create such an enormous consumer demand that when the shortages were over and business returned to normal our loyal Textron customers would insist that the stores carry our merchandise. We were so certain of the success of this operation that we not only had our sales offices in the old Tiffany Building, but we also moved our principal offices out of Providence.

During 1946 the directors put into effect an option plan to purchase the company's common stock at $25 per share with a total number of 67,500 options outstanding as of the end of the year. Contributions to the Sixty Trust, the salaried employees pension fund, were $522,203 that year, and the Market Square Trust received $316,731. All things considered, 1946 had really been a phenomenal year. After contingency reserves and before including Textron Southern, parent company earnings were $6,475,000 or $6.16 per share. This was a 38 percent return after taxes on net worth. Not bad for an industry that normally had trouble averaging better than a 5 percent return!

That year's dividend of fifty cents was low because of the capital needs to finance our burgeoning business. The market price of the shares, which were then traded on the New York Stock Exchange, was substantially over book.

## POMERANTZ

On January 8, 1946, several charity trusts, American Associates, the directors, and I were sued by Lillian Berger of Boston who owned fifty shares of Textron common stock. Her husband was a derivative suit lawyer in Boston who persuaded Abe Pomerantz to bring the action. As you probably know, Abe is the dean of derivative suit lawyers and has caused directors and officers of large corporations to reimburse companies for possibly as much as $100 million during his career. He works on a contingency fee basis and usually receives 20 to 30 percent of any settlement or judgment.

The plaintiff, Lillian Berger, alleged among other things that:

(a) At all such times the other directors and officers of Textron were, and they still are, subservient to the wishes and directions of defendant Little without regard to the best interests of Textron.

(b) In and before 1937 defendant Little conceived a plan of enriching himself and the other directors and officers of Textron by diverting Textron's funds to their personal advantage.

(c) It was part of defendant Little's plan to establish various charitable trusts; to bestow upon them the assets of Textron; to create a public belief that the gifts made by such trusts were made through his generosity and bounty; and thus to acquire, at Textron's expense, a reputation as a public benefactor.

(d) It was further part of defendant Little's plan to obtain complete control of the properties of the trusts to be established and to use them to his personal advantage.

(e) The individual defendants who were or became directors or officers of Textron or trustees of the trusts established by defendant Little knew of this plan, conspired with defendant Little to consummate it, and participated in its consummation.

(f) At all times since the Little Family Trust was established defendant Little, as its trustee, did and he still does own a substantial majority of

*"Innocent until proven guilty, Your Honor."*

the capital stock of defendant American Associates, Inc., a Delaware corporation.

Sure sounds as though I was the worst crook in the country. Bear in mind, however, that in a suit of this type the plaintiff can make the most outrageous charges without being subject to libel action.

Because of the many mill acquisitions that Textron made when it was short of capital, the banks would not lend us money to purchase fixed assets when we needed fabrics for our integrated operations. We were always able to borrow money to finance working capital items, but we were forced to find investment groups that would purchase the fixed assets and lease them. It was obvious, under the tax laws of the time, that we could make the most favorable arrangements in those days by having educational institutions and foundations, which were tax-exempt, borrow money to buy the plants and net lease them to Textron. During these years it had become common practice for many of the leading retail store chains of the country to raise capital by selling their land and buildings to universities and other tax-exempt institutions and then leasing the properties back on a net rental basis for a long period of time. The tax-exempt institutions could borrow 100 percent of the purchase price on the credit of the leasees. This practice was later stopped by a change in the tax law of 1954. However, since this was a perfectly legal transaction in 1946, there was no reason why Textron could not raise capital in this same method, by having the tax-exempt institutions buy the fixed assets and lease them to Textron when mills were acquired.

One transaction of this type not included in Pomerantz's suit involved the purchase of a tricot knitting plant by Noble and Greenough School (the one I had attended before going to Harvard). Textron leased the plant for five years with renewal options at a rent that would pay off the school's indebtedness. They would have any residual values in case we ultimately abandoned the property. A similar arrangement was made with the Rayon Foundation to purchase the plants of the Lonsdale Mills. Textron financed the working capital and the foundation borrowed the purchase price of fixed assets against a net net lease.*

One other transaction occurred when Textron entered into a contract to purchase the Manville Jenckes Mill for a fixed dollar amount. Textron had the bank financing lined up and everything set to go, when the sellers suddenly advised that competition had raised the price by half a million dollars. There was no way that Textron could persuade the banks to put up the extra money. In this case, the only place that we could find the money fast was from American Associates, which was the Little family's personal holding company with several hundred outside stockholders.

Textron and American Associates had separate boards of directors, so I refrained from voting in both cases. Lawyers advised that because it had outside stockholders, American Associates should get something more than just 6 percent interest on the half million subordinated loan. The plan approved was to have Textron agree that some small percentage of Manville Jenckes's production should be sold to American Associates, which had an export department, at the full price under the price control in effect at the time by the Office of Price Administration (OPA). The interesting thing was that this transaction cost the Textron stockholders nothing, since American Associates could resell the fabric for export under a markup permitted for exporters, which was not permitted to the mills like Manville. In other words, if Manville Jenckes had

* The term "net, net lease" may sound redundant but it is commonly used in real estate to mean a lease in which the tenant pays absolutely all costs such as real estate taxes, insurance, maintenance and repair, and so forth.

sold the fabric for export, they could not have received a higher price than American Associates paid. The lawyers felt that since Textron was not penalized profit-wise in any way on this transaction, it fell within the requirements of Rhode Island state laws on conflict of interest. If American Associates had not made the loan, Textron would have lost Manville Jenckes to another bidder. Unfortunately, there was not time to have the shareholders of both companies approve the transaction at special meetings. If we had been more foresighted, we could have minimized the chance of a minority stockholder suit by having had all these various transactions approved subsequently by Textron shareholders. However, we neglected to do so, and so gave Abe Pomerantz the opportunity to bring the action. He must have thought that he had caught one of the worst crooks in the country when he brought the action in a New York County Court.

There were fourteen separate causes of action involved in this case. If Textron's credit during that period had been stronger, it could have financed the purchase of fixed assets as well as working capital. The only way that the company could acquire so much textile fabric production in such a short time with so little financial risk was to have the tax-exempt institutions buy the plants and lease them to Textron. Since the company was in the 95 percent excess profit tax bracket in those years, the cost of these transactions to the stockholders was minimal and the trusts being tax-exempt paid no taxes on the rents received.

Because of the frequency of actions of this sort, normally called "nuisance suits," in New York, the state legislature had passed a law whereby the defendant could require the plaintiff to post a bond of $100,000 to cover the defendant's cost in case the plaintiff lost the suit. We had this requirement made by our New York lawyers. Meanwhile, I was not to go to New York; otherwise I could be served with a summons.

As a result of the bond requirement, Pomerantz moved the action to the federal court in New York, hoping that court would not follow the procedure required by the state legislature. The federal judge, however, did require a bond and Pomerantz, discovering that there was no such law in Rhode Island, moved the case to the federal court in Providence.

We then proceeded to go again through endless examination before trial.

The trial was held in Judge Hartigan's court and went on for many days. Each separate trust, American Associates, and each director had to have different lawyers. It was obvious that this whole action was going to be a lawyer's delight. There were as many as ten different law firms involved before we got through with the case. All corporations have provisions that protect directors and management against the cost of defending themselves in cases of this sort, provided they win the case; or, and this is most important, provided there is a court-approved settlement. In other words, if the management and directors fight these derivative suits all the way through to the finish and lose, they not only have to pay the damages, but the company cannot reimburse them for their expenses involved in the suit. This is why there are so many court-approved settlements.

After the suit dragged on for years, Pomerantz, realizing that he didn't have a bunch of crooks stealing money from the company, suggested a fantastically attractive settlement. He proposed that the way to solve this whole problem was for Textron to issue some of its common stock for all the assets of American Associates so as to eliminate any possible conflict of interest in the future. This actually appeared to be the best of all possible worlds for all concerned. Textron would receive more asset value than the market value of its shares to be issued. None of the foundations, directors, or officers would be involved in the settlement in any way. Therefore, the company would be permitted to pay all the management's and directors' legal fees.

Judge Hartigan approved it as a reasonable settlement, but he insisted that both companies be required to call special meetings and vote on the plan.

The stockholders' meetings were held and the settlement was overwhelmingly approved. When we came back to court, to everyone's amazement, Judge Hartigan read a statement into the record that he had made some technical mistake and was sorry that he put us to all this trouble. He disallowed the settlement. Everybody was confounded by this decision, except me. I am convinced to this day that it was the textile union that persuaded Judge Hartigan to make this fantastic reversal of decision in the case.

Next thing we knew, Judge Hartigan was appointed to the appellate court in Boston and we had to start all over again with Judge Leahy who took his place in the federal court in Providence. This meant all new depositions before trial, and months of preparation for the case. After the entire transaction was started all over again, Pomerantz suggested another settlement. This time, after Pomerantz had spent seven years on the case, he approached the various trusts and American Associates and suggested that if they would pay a total of $300,000 to Textron, he would recommend a settlement to the court. He asked nothing whatsoever from me or any of the directors. He admitted to me later that this had been one of the most frustrating cases he had ever been involved in. Then, believe it or not, just when we were going to propose the settlement, Judge Leahy became deathly ill and was in the hospital, unable to preside at court. If he were to die we would have had to go through this whole procedure completely for a third time. Finally one of Edwards and Angell's lawyers went to Boston, saw the chief justice of the appellate court, Judge MacGruder, and persuaded him that he, MacGruder, should come to Providence, get the settlement papers, take them to the hospital and persuade the sick judge to sign them on March 30, 1953. As a result, after these seven years of wasted effort on everybody's part, we could all go back to work.

Who won this case? The stockholders of Textron? Well, hardly! The $300,000 settlement and more had gone to the lawyers. Pomerantz and other lawyers who had joined his action received about $100,000; probably the lowest fee per hour that this brilliant lawyer had ever received in his highly successful career. Textron had to pay out more than the balance to reimburse the legal expenses of officers and directors. My own bills alone were $164,000. In addition, the lost production time of all of us at Textron undoubtedly cost the company millions of dollars.

Actually, I was probably the only winner. I now listen more carefully when lawyers tell me there is a possible conflict of interest in any situation. Also, I became an admirer of Abe's and have frequently persuaded him to work the other side of the street with me. His advice and services have been of great value on several occasions. I even retained him to represent me in the present Amtel suit.

*ADVICE: If it becomes tempting to have dealings between companies in which you are interested in both sides, avoid it if you possibly can. If it is a matter of great importance to all concerned, be sure to have ratification of any transaction—preferably prior to the completion of the transaction—by the stockholders of both companies. Otherwise, you may be subjected to this kind of minority stockholder suit.*

I am now convinced that if all the complicated transactions that took place in these fourteen causes of action had been approved in advance by Textron shareholders, Abe Pomerantz would never have brought the suit.

During the Pomerantz case I asked my lawyers at Cravath, Swain and Moore to give me their idea of the perfect client. Their reply was short and to the point: "Rich, scared, and guilty."

# Textron, 1947

The year 1947 showed continuing progress with sales of $124,776,-000 and net profit of $6,317,000. The common dividend was increased from fifty cents to one dollar per share, and during the year we withdrew a proposed public offering of $7,500,000 worth of preferred stock issue because of poor market conditions.

At the end of 1947, the company's working capital was over $18,-567,000 with a better than 2-to-1 ratio. In addition, there was very little long-term debt and the outlook for the future appeared to be excellent. We were all more convinced than ever that our program for completely integrated production of Textron label merchandise would be a winner. Return on net worth before contingency reserve was 36 percent. For the first time since 1923 we discontinued factoring our accounts receivable with William Iselin and Company.

## PUERTO RICO

In 1947, the Puerto Rican government started a program called "Operation Bootstrap" with Ted Moscoso head of the Puerto Rican Industrial Development Company. We thought this might be a good opportunity for us to get the Puerto Rican government to finance a new plant to make cotton print cloth in Puerto Rico, to supply our converting department with the material needed to expand piece goods sales of dyed and printed fabrics to the retail trade.

Since there was no duty on shipping either raw cotton into Puerto Rico or the fabrics back into the states, and since Puerto

Rico had a ten-year income tax exemption on profits made on the island, this idea seemed most logical and attractive.

In 1947, greige goods prices for eighty square print cloth were as high as 36¢ per yard which made it most attractive to produce these fabrics. It would be possible therefore to pay the entire cost of the proposed mill in a few years. We figured that the new mill could be built and equipped with new machinery by the Puerto Rican government for $4,000,000 and leased to us over a long-term period at a most attractive rent. We in turn agreed to put up $1,-000,000 as working capital. Based on the fabric prices available at the time, we could have paid the rent readily and made at least a 100 percent return annually on our million dollar equity.

Before going ahead with the project, we decided to study the operations in other countries of Latin American background to see how the efficiency of the workers compared to that of our low-cost southern mills in similar product lines. We visited a mill in Cuba, which was highly profitable, owned by an American named Hedges. We went to Medellin, Colombia, where we inspected five large textile plants, all of which were efficiently run, and earning close to 100 percent after taxes annually on their equity due to war created shortages and protective tariffs on fabric at the time. In addition, we had the opportunity of inspecting many textile plants in Mexico, and again found highly successful operations.

As a result of these investigations, and our confidence that the price structures on print cloth fabrics would hold for some time in the future, the building was constructed in Ponce, Puerto Rico, machinery ordered and put in place, and a small group of supervisors sent to get this mill started. Unfortunately, it was 1949 before we produced a yard of fabric and by that time the price of eighty-square print cloth had dropped from 36¢ to 16¢ a yard. At that price even our most efficient southern plants couldn't earn money.

After several years, we were able to get excellent efficiency in the Puerto Rican plant, but because the fabric had to be shipped back to the United States to be dyed and finished, and since Textron had abandoned its whole garment and piece goods manufacturing and distributing operation, the Puerto Rican venture was disposed of at a loss of over a million dollars. I understand that today it is operated by BVD, which has taken out the looms and put in knitting machines, and is making jockey shorts and other knitted consumer products under their label for distribution throughout the United States.

*ADVICE: In the textile business, it is dangerous to count on high profits continuing in any phase of this business. Invariably, capital pours into the production of any product that is unusually profitable, and within a couple of years there is overproduction and no longer high profit.*

*A good recent example of this situation was the double knit craze, which has cost hundreds of millions of dollars in losses to the yarn producers, the yarn processors, and the knitters—all of whom overexpanded that business.*

*ADDITIONAL ADVICE: A ten-year tax holiday is worthless if you don't make money.*

# *Textron, 1948*

Textron's 1948 results showed a substantial reduction in sales to $98,847,000 with an aftertax profit of $7,106,000. There were 1,132,631 shares outstanding, with earnings of $5.77. Working capital increased $3,800,000 to $22,359,000, and all bank debts were paid off by year-end. Additions to property, plant, and equipment amounted to $5,587,000 and the number of employees was reduced from 15,700 to 10,300, largely as a result of disposing of high-cost New England mills. As a result of these changes, the average sales per employee increased from $7,500 to $9,600, showing the benefit of getting away from some of the labor-intensive operations in spinning and weaving textile fabrics.

It is interesting that no reference was made in this report to the Tobey Senate Investigation Hearings, which will be covered in this book shortly. A somber note appeared in this report issued March 21, 1949: "Demand for TEXTRON brand name products was strong until early November when sales at retail stores throughout the nation dropped below their anticipated volume. Thereafter, the orders from our customers were disappointingly low." Alas, the time had come to head for the storm cellar!

Another paragraph in the March 21, 1949, report stated: "During 1948 the Textron Pension Trust acquired all the outstanding capital stock of the Cleveland Pneumatic Tool Company. At the year-end the trust was actuarily funded so that no contribution by the company was required in 1948." As a matter of fact, no future contributions were made until 1977 for salaried employees pension benefits by the parent company itself. It had continued to remain overfunded through 1976. The Sixty Trust, which operates the fund, will be discussed later.

## TOBEY HEARINGS

When we announced the closing of the Nashua Mills in 1948, we made the mistake of publicizing the union's failure to complete their part of the bargain. Our charges hit the press, with the union receiving very bad publicity. Senator Charles E. Tobey of New Hampshire was going to be up for reelection in 1950. Tobey had been unable to get the support of the Republicans. Wesley Powell was the party's choice, so Tobey was going to have to run as an Independent. Tobey, therefore, really needed help. The Textile Workers Union of America was very smart politically, and they realized Tobey was in trouble.

As a result, they persuaded Tobey to have a Senate investigation of why Textron was closing down the Nashua Mills. Tobey got the Senate Committee on Interstate and Foreign Commerce to appoint a subcommittee with himself and Senator Brian McMahon (the latter never showed up) as members. He appointed his son Charles W. Tobey, Jr., as special counsel for the subcommittee and a cousin as clerk of the subcommittee.

As soon as the union had persuaded Tobey to take over this venture, they required us to check off an extra dollar per month from our Nashua employees as additional union dues.

For the benefit of anyone who has not been the subject of a Senate investigative committee, let me summarize the lack of rights involved. The person being investigated is absolutely on his own; he cannot cross-examine witnesses or have a lawyer testify for him. All accusations made by any member of the committee, including its counsel and any witnesses, are privileged and not subject to libel. The most fantastic charges can be made that, since the hearings are open to the press, then find their way into the headlines of the newspapers.

The hearings were originally slated to be held in Nashua in a very small courtroom, but the union persuaded Tobey to transfer them to the high school auditorium so that they could pack each

session with Nashua workers who would obviously be pro-Tobey and anti-Little.

The result was that when we were asked to explain why we decided to shut down the Nashua plant, we went into great detail about the Rath and Strong report and the failure of the union to live up to its part of the agreement. When I announced how many cards per man, how many spindles per operator, and how many looms per operator it would be necessary to run to meet southern competition, the boos from the audience were absolutely deafening.

Tobey was quite an orator, and he took advantage of this first session to really play on the emotions of the workers in the audience. He had whipped up such enmity against me and the company that I was hanged in effigy on the main street in Nashua that night. The next day was even worse. Tobey again so played on the emotions of the audience that if he had said, "What Little is doing is an outrage—you should take him out right now and hang him," the crowd in that room would have rushed to the stage, hauled me down, and hanged me. This sounds like an overstatement, but it actually could have happened.

After the third day, as a result of pressure from the governor and the New Hampshire Development Commission, Tobey was asked to move the hearings out of New Hampshire. Because of the wide publicity on the hearings, half a dozen large companies that were currently negotiating to build plants in New Hampshire took the position that if this was the way the chief executive of a company

*"Congratulate me. I faced defeat like a man."*

operating in New Hampshire was treated, they wanted no part of it.

The hearings were moved to the federal court in Boston, far enough away from Nashua that none of the workers attended, and only a couple of union lawyers and the press sat in for the next couple of months. It was very interesting that Tobey, during these sessions in Boston, permitted the two union lawyers to go into the judge's chambers with him and give him a whole list of questions to ask. He would then come out with this schedule of questions all written out on a long sheet of paper.

After leaving Nashua, the hearings abandoned any further discussion about the Nashua closing and concentrated on a group of foundations which had been set up years before for the United Fund of Providence, the School of Design in Providence that trained textile executives, Massachusetts Institute of Technology in Cambridge, and the Noble and Greenough School.

In the case of these charitable trusts, they were operated by independent trustees, tax-free on all income provided the income was paid out to or set aside for the benefit of the ultimate beneficiaries. When originally organized with very little capital there was the opportunity of building up through various types of investments substantial capital in these foundations for later distribution.

Tobey attacked this whole procedure and claimed that we had taken advantage of a technicality in the tax law permitting investments in these trusts that benefited Textron. The way the hearings operated gave Tobey an enormous advantage in gaining wide publicity, which of course anyone running for office welcomes. It was also extremely difficult to stop an investigation of this sort so long as the local newspapers gave Tobey front page coverage. He loved it! The textile union's research director, Solomon Barkin, had for some years prior to the Tobey hearings given speeches and written articles about how charitable foundations should be taxed, so it was Tobey who gave the union the opportunity to follow up on the campaign they had been launching to try to have foundations taxed. Hence the reason for including the examination of foundations and charity trusts which I had set up.

During the hearings in Boston, Senator Tobey and I, and others involved in the hearings, stayed at the Parker House. After almost every session, as we left the hearing room, Tobey would put his arm around me as we walked down the hallway and say, "Mr. Little, everything is going to turn out all right for you. You're doing a fine job." What a character!

Then, one evening after the hearings had gone on for some days, Tobey asked me to come to his room with Hugh Gregg, who was later mayor of Nashua, to talk things over. He showed us an article (I believe it was an editorial in the *Manchester Union Leader*) accusing Tobey of hurting New Hampshire by continuing the hearings. Since Tobey was up for reelection and the Manchester paper had a wide following, he was sensitive to this adverse publicity. He got very emotional and tears actually came to his eyes as he presented us with a copy of the newspaper. He said, "I really need some good publicity up in New Hampshire. Could either of you think of anything that will help me?" Well, I thought of something real fast. I knew that Senator Tobey was a sponsor of the Crotched Mountain Center that took care of crippled children. This was a wonderful organization and an excellent charity, so I suggested, "Senator, why don't you take credit for setting up a foundation for the benefit of the Center? One of its principal purposes will be the industrial rehabilitation of Nashua with the Crotched Mountain Center as the ultimate beneficiary." I said, "If you will do this, Senator, I'll get the Textron directors to sell our entire three million square feet of floor space, including approximately one million square feet in the relatively modern Jackson Mill, to the foundation for five hundred thousand dollars with a down payment of only a hundred thousand dollars and the balance of four hundred thousand dollars to be paid over the next five years as properties are sold off or leased." Tobey thought this was a wonderful idea. Hugh Gregg agreed to raise $100,000 from businessmen in the town to launch this great project. In effect Tobey was creating a foundation exactly like those that I had started. So I waited to see what would happen.

The next day at the close of the morning session, Tobey announced: "As a result of meeting with Mr. Little and the business people of Nashua, I have created a wonderful new foundation for the benefit of Crotched Mountain Center." We recessed for lunch. The afternoon papers immediately picked this up and wrote, in effect: "Tobey is blasting Little every day because he set up foundations for charities. Now Tobey is doing identically the same thing himself. What's the difference?"

The technique Tobey used in the hearings was very interesting. He would wait until about quarter of twelve every day and then make some absurd charge against me. When I stood up to answer he would say, "Sit down, Mr. Little. You can answer that after lunch." As a result the afternoon papers carried big headlines, but when the correct answer was given it would appear on the last page the next day.

He did the same thing in the afternoon at quarter of four, since the hearings ran from 10:00 to 12:00 and 2:00 to 4:00. Again Tobey stole the headlines in the Boston and Providence papers the next morning.

*ADVICE: If it becomes necessary to abandon a plant that is beyond the hope of saving because of high costs, whatever you do, don't blame the union. They are politically too powerful to take any such adverse publicity without retaliation. My stupidity in blaming the Textile Workers Union for the closing of Nashua Mills cost the stockholders of Textron millions of dollars.*

Excerpts from the Tobey hearings are typical of the methods the senator used to arouse the passion of our employees and later to browbeat the trustees of the foundations being investigated:

*Wednesday, September 22, 1948 at Nashua, N.H.*

SENATOR TOBEY: Mr. Little, I assume you have a prepared statement?

MR. LITTLE: New England must go back to work. Many of our factories are no longer competitive with those in other parts of the country. Our workers are no longer the most efficient and productive. In other areas, men and women, eager to improve their living conditions, are producing more units per hour than we do. So long as others work harder than we do, we shall continue to lose our industries. New England today stands at the crossroads. One way leads slowly and rather painfully downhill to industrial stagnation. The other road is tough and rough, and requires action, hard work, and more pioneering spirit.

From now on, the housewives of the nation are going to set the prices we receive for our products and services. Even New England housewives will not buy sheets and blankets made in Nashua, N.H., if they can purchase products of equal quality made elsewhere at lower cost.

The textile industry is New England's outstanding example of lost jobs. In 1923 there were 209,000 persons employed in cotton textiles in this area, compared with 74,226 in 1936.

We purchased, in May 1946, the Gossett Mills, with 11 low-cost rayon and cotton units in North and South Carolina. Thereafter, we were able to make detailed cost comparisons between the North and South, and to measure accurately the productivity of the workers in both areas. We soon found that while take-home pay of northern workers was 10 percent more than in the South, our Carolina employees produced from 25 percent to 100 percent more yards and pounds per hour than many of our people in the North. For example, we found that efficient southern mills were producing wide muslin sheeting at the rate of 9.62 pounds per man-hour against Nashua's rate of 5.37.

I would like to read into the record a clipping from the papers today which is very significant:

> Nashua is closing down because it cannot meet the competition of the Dan River mills and other low-cost southern mills. Today the Dan River mills announced that they are going back to a 6-day operation and that they are considering increasing the production of sheetings.

*Thursday, September 23, 1948*

The subcommittee met, pursuant to recess, at 10:10 A.M., in the auditorium of the Nashua High School, Nashua, N.H., Senator Charles W. Tobey, Chairman of the subcommittee, presiding.

TESTIMONY OF EMIL RIEVE, GENERAL PRESIDENT, TEXTILE WORKERS UNION OF AMERICA (CIO), ACCOMPANIED BY ISADORE KATZ, GENERAL COUNSEL, AND SOLOMON BARKIN, RESEARCH DIRECTOR.

MR. RIEVE: In the last few months the management of Textron, Inc. has destroyed the jobs of nearly 7,000 textile workers. It has now threatened to destroy 3,500 more jobs. This is important enough in itself, but the Textron case goes much further. It represents a philosophy which threatens millions of jobs, because it threatens the whole country.

You have heard Mr. Little tell you about his company. He has told you, in effect, that he is simply an ambitious capitalist trying to get along in the world.

In the last few days Mr. Little has talked a good deal about "high cost" mills. He has talked about wages and work loads in the North compared to those in the South. He is obviously trying to put the blame for his actions on the New England workers and on New England itself.

One result was that by July 1947, employment in the Nashua mills had dropped from over 5,000 to a little over 4,000.

But Mr. Little was not satisfied. In July 1947 he offered what he called the new Nashua plan. . . . Mr. Little offered this proposition to Nashua: He must have lower wages, higher work loads, and reduced taxes. He must be free to fire workers without regard to seniority. He must, by these and other means, save at least $2,000,000 a year in labor costs.

He said if he got these things, he would continue to employ about 2,500 workers in Nashua, and would spend 1.2 million dollars on modernization. He would help bring new industries to occupy space in the mills. But if he did not get what he wanted, he would liquidate.

Mr. Little called this an epoch-making agreement. He said he had received such fine cooperation from the union that he would go right ahead with his plans to improve the mill and keep it running. This was one of many such assurances by Textron officials. . . . Now Mr. Little announces that the plan has failed. . . . Mr. Little is supposed to be a manufacturer—but on the record, he is an undertaker. He buys mills in order to bury them.

[Applause.]

SENATOR TOBEY: The Chair would state if you were down in the United States Senate and in the galleries "Manifestations of applause are not in order. You are the guests of the Senate. Please conduct yourselves accordingly."

But there is a distinction between the Senate and this room today. I would be awfully sorry, friends, if we didn't have a spirit in these meetings, no matter who was testifying, Mr. Little or Mr. Rieve or anybody else, like unto our New England town meetings that we like so much and appreciate so much, which are the great bulwark of democracy.

So I wouldn't divorce that from the hearts and minds of the people here assembled, whoever they favored if they manifested applause and approval and the good humor in our souls.

MR. RIEVE: I would suggest that a hearing can be conducted in secret,

*"Well, then, wouldn't it be
a good idea for me to buy some stock in the C.I.O.?"*

like the Un-American Activities Committee is doing, because many of
these men may not freely want to testify in public. By the way, I feel that
that is a job for the Un-American Activities Committee because I think
that Mr. Little through his manipulation is doing more of undermining
private enterprise than all the Communists in this country could do in a
lifetime.

[Applause.]

MR. RIEVE: I do not claim to have proved that Mr. Little is a criminal;
but I do say his company is a racket—possibly a legal racket, but a racket
just the same.

It seems to me that these are the questions before you. First, have the
operations of Textron been legal?

Second, if such operations are legal, can we afford to have them
continue?

Third, what type of legislation is needed to prevent them?

Personally, I think that many of Mr. Little's manipulations have been outside the law. But I do not consider this is the most important point.

It is my hope that your committee will agree that America can no longer afford robber barons, legal or not, whose financial manipulations endanger the livelihood of thousands of workers.

I hope you will agree that such manipulations threaten our whole national economy.

And I hope you will be able to devise a remedy to check them in the future.

The Textile Workers Union of America stands ready to help you in every possible way.

This man has been a blight upon Nashua. Let him make restitution and depart in peace.

[Applause.]

MR. TOBEY: Mr. Rieve, is it probably true that New England is not producing as many units per hour as the worker in the South?

MR. RIEVE: I say that mill per mill, machine per machine, lay-out for lay-out, New England is producing on par with any mill anywhere in the country. [Applause.]

COMMENT: *As a result of the animosity created by Rieve's statement and Senator Tobey's method of running the hearings, I was booed when I spoke and Rieve was applauded.*

As a result of Rieve's charges, New England newspapers had a field day with their headlines.

*The Evening Bulletin,* Providence, R.I. headlines for Thursday, September 23, 1948:

# "Rieve Calls Little Cash Manipulator, Not Manufacturer"
## "TWUA President Urges U.S. To Look Into 'Deals' "

*The Boston Daily Globe.* Thursday, September 23, 1948 (evening).

## "Union Head Rejects 'Offer'— Flays Textron Mill Official"

Was Rieve or Little correct about production in New England mills compared to that of southern mills?

Data supplied recently by the American Textile Manufacturers Institute, Inc. indicate that in February 1923 there were 19,001,661 cotton system spindles in place in New England compared with 16,274,772 in place in the cotton-growing states. In November 1976 there were only 280,000 spindles in place in New England compared with 17,699,000 in the cotton-growing states.

*Tuesday, October 26, 1948*

The subcommittee met, pursuant to call, at 10:10 A.M., in courtroom No. 3, Federal Building, Boston, Mass., Senator Charles W. Tobey, chairman of the subcommittee, presiding.

SENATOR TOBEY: This morning we shall take up a particular phase of the Textron situation, namely, the matter of charitable trusts. Therefore, we now turn to the subject of charitable trusts and your and Textron's participation therein, and I now ask counsel to take over the examination.

Mr. Tobey, Jr., counsel for the committee.

MR. TOBEY: Would you please state the names of all so-called charitable trusts or charitable foundations with which Textron Incorporated, Textron, Inc., Textron Southern, or any of their subsidiaries or affiliates have done business.

MR. LITTLE: The Rhode Island Charities Trust; MIT Trust, Rayon Foundation Trust, Lansing Foundation Trust, the Selbon Trust . . . The Textron Pension Trust is called the Sixty Trust. Those are the trusts with which the company or various subsidiaries have had dealings.

[*COMMENT: Solomon Barkin, the research director for the Textile Workers Union, had been publicly advocating that Congress should revoke the tax exemptions from all foundations and charity trusts. It was basically because of his recommendations that the hearings about the Nashua closings were expanded to cover the activities of tax-exempt foundations that had dealings with Textron.*]

MR. TOBEY: Do you wish to have it understood, from what you have said, that the net result of these various sales to trusts and leases back has been that Textron and its affiliates have been required to pay a greater amount of taxes to the Federal Government than it otherwise would have had to pay?

MR. LITTLE: Actually in the transactions in which Textron has sold property to charity trusts, the reason that was done was to provide working capital with which to increase the volume of business; by providing that extra working capital and increasing the volume of business, we increased our profits and increased our taxes.

. . .

MR. LITTLE: Mr. Rieve has also submitted a document entitled "The Misuse of Trust Funds," which is replete with false statements. He admits

that he does not know what the activities of the trust have been. He simply makes flat, unsupported statements to the effect that the trusts have been used as a means of siphoning off the profits of operating companies.

All of the transactions of these trusts have been completely investigated by the Bureau of Internal Revenue and no claims for taxes have been levied against them.

Mr. Rieve has attempted to cast doubt on the legality of the investments made by these charitable trusts. These trusts operate in complete compliance with all applicable laws.

*Thursday, October 28, 1948*
TESTIMONY OF BAYARD EWING, PROVIDENCE, R.I., RAYON FOUNDATION TRUST, ACCOMPANIED BY THOMAS BLACK, ESQ., OF GREENOUGH, LYMAN & CROSS, PROVIDENCE, R.I.

[*COMMENT: After many hours of questioning the trustees of various foundations, the following quotations from the report are of interest.*]

SENATOR TOBEY: Your intention was to avoid taxes.

MR. EWING: My intention was to benefit the Rayon Foundation.

SENATOR TOBEY: But comes along this fantastic arrangement of these so-called charitable trusts, which I don't think will stand the test of careful analysis by fair men. You say we are doing this for two reasons, first to get risk capital and then to benefit somebody, which happens after Mr. Little passes away.

Now about this situation: You have saved a large sum of money in your operations in the Rayon Trust here by avoiding taxation—put it that way—and you haven't had to pay the taxes which everybody else in this room, if they are doing business as individuals, would have to pay to the Federal Government. Every time you avoid those taxes, what do you do? You put that tax burden on 130,000,000 people in this country proportionately, and you are doing it under the guise of creating risk capital *pro bono publico* and, if you please, a charity trust that won't take effect in its entirety in any substantial amount until Mr. Little dies, and I hope that will be many years off. In the meanwhile the whole enterprise may cave in if things go wrong in this country. There won't be any charities trust. But meanwhile you have had your tax avoidance that is the big *desideratum.*

That is what is going on. I am going to carry back to the Congress of the United States, I tell you now, from these hearings here a horrible example, exhibit A, of a devious scheme to avoid taxes and put the burden on little people in this country, and I am against it.

That is a speech sir.

MR. EWING: A very good one.

*The Providence Journal.* October 29, 1948. (Morning edition)

## "Tobey Calls Trusts of Type in Textron Case Tax Dodges"
### "Says He Will So Report to Congress; Bayard Ewing Defends Rayon Foundation as Bona Fide Setup Whose Good Is to Aid Research, Students"

*COMMENT: The Rayon Foundation is currently earning sufficient income to pay the Rhode Island School of Design substantial amounts annually. The Rhode Island Charity Trust, which I started with $500 in 1937 and which has been ably managed since 1945 by independent trustees, contributes nearly $1,000,000 yearly to the Community Fund.*

As a result of Senator Tobey's charges he continued to steal the headlines: *The Boston Herald.* November 9, 1948.

# "Probe Hears Textron Trusts Highly Speculative"

*The Boston Globe.* November 9, 1948. (Morning edition)

## "Textron Trustees' Power 'Amazes' Tobey at Probe"

*The Boston Globe.* November 9, 1948. (Evening edition)

## "Tobey Compares Textron Trusts to 'Shell Game' "

*The Boston Globe.* November 10, 1948. (Morning edition)

## "Tax System Seen Sapped by Textron"
### "Tobey Cites Use of 'Loophole' by Charitable Trusts"

*COMMENT: In a hearing of this type, all statements and testimony are privileged, so that they are free from any possible action for libel. Even though Senator Tobey knew from the testimony that the various trusts and foundations were completely independent of Textron, he repeatedly referred to them as Textron's trusts, with the result that the headlines in the newspapers repeatedly misinformed the public.*

*The Boston Herald.* November 10, 1948. (Late city edition)

# "Textron Trusts Said to Owe U.S. Big Sum"

*COMMENT: The Internal Revenue Service never made any assessment against the various trusts involved in the hearing, either before or after the hearing. As a result of the hearings, however, Congress changed the tax law in 1954 so that most of the income of charity trusts and foundations had to be paid out to beneficiaries each year or lose their tax exemption. The new law eliminated the old provision that gave such organizations tax exemptions if earnings were set aside for the benefit of but not paid out to charities. As a result of this legislation, no one in the future could start a trust or foundation with a nominal contribution and build up substantial capital to the ultimate benefit of charities. In addition, this new law required many other institutions of this sort all over the country to pay out millions of dollars that might otherwise have been temporarily retained. Senator Tobey therefore helped many charities throughout the country as a result of these hearings.*

*Monday, November 22, 1948*

SENATOR TOBEY: Mr. Little, this morning at the outset of the hearing, we had a slight discussion about your desire to make a statement in your own way.

MR. LITTLE: Senator Tobey, in view of misapprehension which exists in the minds of the public, and perhaps in your own mind, as to taxes and the facts relating to charitable trusts, I wish to make the following statement:

Any fair-minded person, after considering the whole story, will agree that Textron is not shifting the burden of taxation either to its competitors or to individual taxpayers.

I want these points understood:

None of the charitable trusts which has been mentioned here was created by Textron.

Likewise, none of these trusts is controlled or dominated in any way by Textron.

The statement has been made repeatedly in the press that these were Textron trusts. This is utterly false and misleading. Not only were these trusts not created or operated by Textron, but at the present time 76 percent of the trusts' entire assets is invested in securities and properties of companies other than Textron; and these trusts in the aggregate hold less than four-tenths of 1 percent of the outstanding capital stock of Textron.

*Tuesday, November 23, 1948*

MR. LITTLE: You asked that I should cooperate, that I should reconsider, that Textron should reemploy those people, and at your request we had meetings and we did agree to keep the Jackson sheeting mill open. But, sir, after the way that you whipped up the feeling of those people against me and against Textron I assure you that it is going to be an extremely difficult job for us to be successful in that operation.

Now, sir, as a result of the manner in which those hearings were held, your constituents in Nashua, N.H., were so disgusted that they requested that the hearings be moved out of Nashua, N.H. Then the hearings came to Boston.

Since these hearings have been held in Boston, you have repeatedly bullied witnesses, you have browbeaten witnesses, you have coerced and intimidated witnesses, and I charge, sir, that you are not carrying on these hearings in an American manner, and I now request you, sir, to make the apology which you stated you would make last night.

*Boston Evening Globe.* Tuesday, November 23, 1948.

# "Little Blasts Tobey Tactics"

## "Textron President Charges Senator Uses Un-American Methods, Asks Fair Play —U.S. Tax Chief Fails to Appear"

*COMMENT: Although the hearing continued through December 8, 1948, Little was never again permitted to testify after this headline appeared.*

In the 1950 Republican primaries Tobey ran as an Independent Republican against endorsed candidate Wesley Powell. The results: Tobey 39,203 (50.8 percent), and Powell 37,893 (49.2 percent), a total difference of 1,310 votes. In Nashua, Tobey received 1,595 (60 percent) votes to Powell's 1,067 (40 percent), a total difference of 528 votes.

In the final election that fall, Tobey beat his Democratic opponent and returned to the U.S. Senate for another six years.

At the time of the hearings we were certain that the Textile Workers Union had agreed to support Tobey in the 1950 primaries in return for his having run the hearings to embarrass Textron. During the period between the start of the hearings and the election, the union required Textron to substantially increase the regular checkoff of union dues from payrolls. As a result of this, we were later advised, the union turned over to the senator approximately $6,000, which had been collected through this device. In addition, since there was no penalty in New Hampshire in switching from voting Republican in the primary to voting Democratic in the final election, the union persuaded large numbers of Textron's textile employees in New Hampshire to vote for Tobey in the 1950 primary without jeopardizing their ability to vote in November of that year for anyone they wished to. There was no question that union activities enabled Tobey to beat the party's endorsed candidate, Powell, by 1,310 votes.

After the Tobey hearings were over, one of the two top union lawyers came to me and said, "Why in the world did you have to publicly blame the union for the Nashua closing? If you had gradually shut the operations down the way most other New England textile mills have been closed, there would never have been a Tobey hearing."

As a result of these hearings we had to compromise and continue to operate part of Nashua for several years at a cost to the stockholders of well over a million dollars. With the political power that the unions now have in this country, anyone making the mistake I made in Nashua is asking for real trouble.

In spite of the April 10, 1950, *Manchester Union Leader* attack on Tobey published just prior to the New Hampshire primaries (which is quoted below), the previously given figures on the primary election indicated that the union had greater influence on the voters than the New Hampshire newspaper.

## TOBEY AND TEXTRON

Junior Senator Tobey's utter disregard for New England's economic well-being, so glaringly demonstrated in his attacks on Textron, were patently prejudicial and punitive at the time of his rantings in Nashua against the company.

They become even more so now, in the face of figures in Textron's annual report, just issued. A net loss of $1,693,922 was shown for 1949, compared with a net profit of $6,936,723 the year before.

Tobey, who knows nothing about textile manufacturing or about the always delicate textile situation, didn't take, for purposes of his own, conditions into account. Times have been less prosperous. In textiles, there have been sharp price and volume readjustments. For Textron in particular, there were heavy mid-year inventory losses, and the necessity of making certain heavy plant expenses.

To men conversant with economics, Textron's loss of $1,693,922 comes as no surprise, although distressing it certainly is.

When Tobey first began to attack Textron, this newspaper made the point that he was sorely hurting all New England industry. The second point was made that New England textiles needed every encouragement if Southern competition were not to make even deeper inroads. In that connection, it is significant to note that, while Textron's Nashua blanket business lost more than a million dollars last year, Textron's yarn and gray goods mills in the South made $2,559,000.

Despite this loss in the North and gain in the South, Textron is making improvements in New England. Its rayon and nylon weaving and dyeing operations in Manchester, for example, are being modernized.

This is an example of returning Textron good for Tobey bad. The junior senator ought to be mightily embarrassed now that the losses have been made public, also Textron's efforts to keep New England plants in operation.

*ADVICE: If you're ever the subject of a congressional investigative committee, don't take it lying down. The members of the committee love all that free publicity. Find something to charge them with. If you steal their headlines, they'll drop you like a hotcake.*

# Textron, 1949

In March 1949 it was obvious that our whole program of complete integration for the manufacture and distribution of a wide variety of consumer products under the Textron label was going to be severely tested. Had we made a dreadful mistake in this whole concept or would we survive? Nineteen forty-nine was a bitter pill to swallow. All our hopes for stability in sales and earnings on the integrated brand name operation went up in smoke. Whereas our Textron and other brand name operations in 1946, 1947, and 1948 had produced over $50,000,000 in sales each year, those sales that we had counted on as being really solid and reliable dropped to $38,000,000 and all of us were certainly disillusioned. With $67,-896,000 in sales, we showed a $1,694,000 loss after taking advantage of a loss carry back, cashing some LIFO reserve,* and using part of the $3,000,000 reserve for contingencies.

In the first seven months of the year, the loss was $6,064,000. Contributing to our losses were the inefficiencies of the northern textile operations compared to the south. For example, Nashua Manufacturing lost $1,405,000 on sales of $9,600,000, whereas the low-cost Textron southern plants had sales of $26,000,000 and profits before taxes of $2,600,000.

One thing that we rediscovered as a result of having gone through the depression of 1932 and the recession of 1938 is that in periods of bad business, inventories and receivables shrink and well-run companies get much more liquid. For example, at the end

---

* An accounting procedure which permits corporations to reduce taxes and improve cash flow by valuing inventories on a last in, first out (LIFO) basis during inflationary periods such as we've had in this country for over forty years. The other method is first in, first out (FIFO), which works better in long periods of deflation. At present, TEXTRON's inventories are undervalued by $100,000,000 as a result of LIFO. If TEXTRON had always used FIFO accounting, more taxes would have been paid, but earnings would have been increased by over $50,000,000.

*"I'm sure you're all familiar with the concept of business cycles. Now, at this point in time we are in the lousy part of this particular cycle."*

of 1949, current assets were $31,642,000 and current liabilities only $5,937,000—in other words a ratio of better than 5-to-1. As a matter of fact, our cash assets of $8,460,000 exceeded our total current liabilities of about $6,000,000, but the results for the year were such a shock to us, particularly with our Textron label merchandise, that we had to do some long-range planning to again make a major decision as to how we could be sure in the future of making a fair return every year on the stockholders' capital.

That year's annual report carried this interesting statement: "For many years in the past the directors of the company had made awards in current earnings to a large number of key people as additional compensation. The directors have recently adopted an incentive compensation plan, based upon engineering studies, which will be directly related to the return which management makes on capital used in operations."

This was the first time that we put into effect a new type of incentive compensation based on return on assets rather than a year-end handout or bonus based on a percentage of profit. (This whole concept of incentive compensation will be covered later.)

With the disaster that occurred in the Textron label product operation, the company folded its tent in New York, abandoned the

Tiffany Building at a substantial loss, and quietly moved its headquarters back to Providence.

## SUNCOOK MILLS

In 1943, Textron purchased the Suncook Mills in Suncook, New Hampshire, as its first acquisition of production equipment to supply fabrics for its proposed garment operations. This was a very efficient synthetic fabric plant weaving staple fabrics for sale to the converting trade. It had good water power so that its costs were reasonable, and it had an excellent work force. Being near the Merrimack River, it had been customary for French Canadians looking for work in the States to come down the valley and work in textile mills at Suncook, Manchester, and Nashua. Suncook had originally been a cotton mill that had been converted to synthetic fabrics. The quality was excellent and the productivity of the employees was better than in most other New England plants. Because of the high proportion of French Canadians, all of the signs throughout the mill were bilingual. After Textron started its label merchandise operation for distribution to the retail trade, one of the largest divisions was women's lingerie. These garments used a special fabric called multifilament crepe, made with acetate warp and a moderately high twist rayon filling. In order to be completely integrated from synthetic yarns through to finished garments, we spent approximately $1.5 million at Suncook putting in all specially equipped wide looms to make this fabric for our women's underwear division. All of the other looms were moved out and the mill was operated 100 percent for our own consumption. This was an enormous change for the workers who adapted very well and were pleased to have all new machinery. The twisting of the yarns for the filling was done at Suncock's throwing plant and the warp yarns were supplied on beams by Celanese. Our women's underwear division did an excellent job in styling, making top quality Textron label merchandise with the proper number of stitches per inch and superior Suncook fabric.

Unfortunately, shortly thereafter a knitted fabric called "tricot," which was made from nylon, began to be used in the lingerie industry. To supply this material to our women's underwear division, we had to start tricot plants in Lowell, Massachusetts, in East Greenwich, Rhode Island, and in Willimantic, Connecticut. Over the next few years, the women of the country switched their lingerie preference to the knitted fabric. Therefore, our $1.5 million investment in the special looms at Suncook Mills to make the woven underwear fabric, which was no longer in demand, was a total loss. This was a great disappointment to us since we had spent a lot of money equipping this well-run plant with excellent workers to make a fabric that was greatly in demand at the time of the decision, but which three years later became practically obsolete for its particular market.

*ADVICE: Don't make a large investment to make a single specialty product, which may become obsolete. One of the reasons that Textron failed in its efforts to develop a completely integrated textile operation from raw material through to the finished garment was that, with our big plant investment, we were always committed to make fabrics that our garment operations no longer required. In other words, our competitors in the garment business had more flexibility and, of course, far less capital tied up in productive equipment. They were able to switch the design of garments to the fabrics most popular with the consumer, while we were stuck with production that was no longer in demand.*

## MANCHESTER WEAVING PLANT

Although we had found out through the purchase of the Gossett Mills in the Carolinas that it was possible to produce fabrics cheaper in the South than in New England, we tried desperately to prove that New England still could compete, by spending approximately $1 million to put new machinery in floor space that we owned at Manchester, New Hampshire, to make rayon lining fabrics. The reason we chose this particular construction to test our ability to meet southern competition was that it had the lowest labor component of any synthetic fabric. We could purchase warp yarn on beams and filling yarn on cones directly from the producers. By the use of Unifil winding attachments, it was possible to supply the filling yarn needed for the bobbin on the loom, eliminating the cost of a separate winding operation. As a result, this weaving was so automatic that we figured there might be a chance of proving that a completely modern plant in New England could meet southern competition.

We put 960 new Draper looms in Manchester equipped for this one type of material, which was needed in enormous yardage to supply the basic lining fabrics used in all types of men's and women's garments. Our production would supply less than 1 percent of the total market. This time, unlike at Suncook, we had not run the risk of equipping the plant to make a highly specialized fabric.

The Manchester mill was, of course, unionized, and in spite of the work assignment studies we had made indicating that with this new automatic equipment a weaver could run one hundred looms and a fixer could take care of many looms, we were unable to persuade the union workers to accept these engineered assignments. We therefore built a beautiful new, single-story, windowless plant in Williamston, South Carolina, and equipped it with about a thousand identical automatic looms to make exactly the same fabric we were weaving in Manchester. When the mill announced that we were ready to accept applications for jobs, we had over five thousand young people off the farms in the countryside apply to get work. This was twenty times more than was needed. We had no difficulty in getting people to work three full shifts, and even to operate the plant on Saturdays, if the demand for fabric was sufficient to warrant this overtime production. The same was not true in New England.

Within six months of starting up, the Williamston plant was running at a higher loom efficiency than New England. The weavers were tending one hundred looms each instead of forty-eight as in Manchester, wages and fringes were considerably lower, and power costs were half those in the North. It was a most successful operation.

In spite of taking some of the northern workers to see the Williamston plant—which was identical to theirs—we never could get them to try to meet the work assignments that were standard procedure in the southern mill.

Finally, after this sad experience, we gave up any further hope of operating textile mills in New England competitively with southern plants. Although power and labor costs were much lower in the South, the big differential was that the southern mill workers produced twice as much per man hour as those even in the most modern northern plants. The Manchester experiment cost the company over $1 million, but it certainly convinced our directors and stockholders that we must concentrate all our future operations in the South if we were to survive. So we increased the size of the Williamston plant by 50 percent and abandoned Manchester.

*ADVICE #1: All of the top people in the textile business with whom we discussed our Manchester venture told us that we were crazy—there was no way that a New England mill could produce at as low cost as a southern mill making identically the same fabric on the same type of equipment. I was stubborn however and had to see for myself whether the industry leaders were right. It usually doesn't pay to be butt-headed.*

*ADVICE #2: If you have two plants making identical products, one being a high cost unionized one and the other in a non-union low cost area, don't pour new capital into the high cost plant hoping to make it competitive. It can't be done. It would be just sending good money after bad.*

## HARTWELL PLANT

We started a completely new plant in Hartwell, Georgia, under very favorable conditions in a small southern community where there was very little other manufacturing. When we let it be known that we were going to hire three hundred people to run the plant, we were swamped with applicants, mostly young people, who came in by car off the farms to apply for jobs. With the mechanization of farms, the sons and daughters of the farmers in the area were no longer needed to operate the farms. As a result of our starting many plants in rural areas, these young people were able to live at home and, in effect, bring the family a cash crop from their work in the mills. The amazing thing is that in all the mills that we started from scratch in the South, the average age of the employees when we began was about twenty-three. On the other hand, the young people of New England were too smart to go to work in textile mills. They knew better than those of us who operated the plants that there was no future in New England textiles. The average age of our workers in the New England mills was over fifty-five years.

# Textron, 1950

In 1950, profits were $3,189,000 on sales of $87,546,000, but the significant statement was the following from the annual report:

In June the directors decided to discontinue the company's apparel and drapery divisions and to concentrate future expansion primarily on synthetic cloth production. As a result of operating and liquidating losses at these abandoned divisions there was a deficit of $798,000 during the first half of the year on $34,128,000 sales. With the elimination of this burden on the company's basically sound mill operations and with the increased activity and higher prices accompanying the Korean War, earnings before taxes amounted to $6,924,000 on $53,419,000 sales during the last six months.

The report continues:

The recent world shortages of natural fibers and record high prices for wool and cotton have given tremendous impetus in this country to the further development and expansion of the new synthetics. For example, in 1948 production of nylon and other new fibers amounted to 50 million pounds. Based upon announced plans for the expansion of nylon, Orlon, Chemstrand, Dynel, and Dacron, the annual production of these new fibers will be increased by 1953 to 400 million pounds.

It is Textron's intention to continue to expand its facilities to the knitting and weaving of these new synthetic materials. Locations have been selected and building plans completed for the erection of two new weaving mills and one tricot knitting unit which would raise the company's capacity on synthetics to 8,000 looms and 240 tricot knitting machines. Based on 144 hour production at present prices, such a program would increase the company's sales potential to $200,000,000 by 1953.

In order to finance this program it will be advisable to make a public offering of some type of security as soon as such an issue can be advantageously distributed.

What an optimist! We still thought investors would pour new capital into Textron in spite of our lousy record. Of course, no one

did. To show just how brash we were, the cover of that year's report was a picture of the universe with a piece of woven fabric connecting the moon to the earth with this caption: "Based on planned expansion, Textron will weave enough cloth each year to reach from the earth to the moon."

In other words, our Textron label plan turned out to be a complete flop that cost us millions of dollars, and here we go again on another brand new idea in our relentless search to try to find a way to make a fair return on the common stockholders' equity investment. This time it had better be good, or we might just decide to throw in the sponge and abandon the textile business entirely!

# *Textron, 1951*

Sales were $98,290,000 in 1951, with a net profit of $4,746,000—a 15 percent return on year-end common equity. A comparison of this report with prior years showed clearly that the company was swinging rapidly from highly labor intensive operations to more capital intensive businesses by eliminating sewing plants with high labor content and investing heavily in fixed assets requiring less labor and more capital. For example, 7,800 employees were now averaging $12,500 in sales per year compared with the low point in 1946 of only $7,500 per employee. The annual report said:

Our earnings and those of the industry reached a peak during the first quarter as a direct result of over-buying by ultimate consumers and by all segments of the textile trade following the outbreak of the Korean War. High prices overstimulated production. More yards of cotton and rayon fabrics were woven in this country during the first three months of the year than in any other similar period in the past. In all branches of the trade excessive inventories were purchased at peak prices.

Charts in the report showed drastic downward price trends in many basic fabrics from highs in the first quarter. The extreme example was 62-inch multifilament crepe, used in women's lingerie, which dropped from sixty cents per yard in January to forty cents in November.

With the complete failure of our integrated brand name operation, which had certainly cost the stockholders at least $10 million to liquidate, we were more determined than ever to push our expansion of low-cost fabric production in the most modern mills that we could build in the South to prove that we had finally discovered a way to make a fair return on common stockholders' equity. We purchased a synthetic weaving plant at Honea Path, South Carolina, which was under construction, and enlarged it from 360 to 600 looms in its existing floor space. Then, having run out of credit to build any more plants, as the 1951 reports says:

Textron currently has three new projects authorized by the Directors: at Elizabethton, Tennessee, a tricot knitting plant to process the new man-made synthetics such as nylon, orlon, and dacron into finished fabrics; in Monroe County, Mississippi, a long staple blend unit; at Meridian, Mississippi, a plant to make Indian Head work clothing fabrics. Through expansion programs of this type, the Directors hope to replace the sales volume lost through curtailment of operations in other areas. All three of these projects should provide the company with low cost modern facilities to supplement and diversify present lines.

How in the world could we finance this $20 million mill expansion if the machinery manufacturers and banks wouldn't carry us? Simple! We had discovered that the state of Mississippi would issue full faith and credit revenue bonds under their Balance Agriculture With Industry (BAWI) program to finance not only the buildings but also the land, machinery, and all the installation costs. Textron would provide the working capital for inventories and receivables and would enter into long-term net leases to cover the interest and amortization on the state-guaranteed bonds. Since Mississippi's credit was good, these bonds would carry extremely low rates. The huge new tricot operation to be built at Elizabethton, Tennessee, was to be financed through similar revenue bonds, although in that case without that state's guarantee.

To show the magnitude of this expansion program, the footnotes to the 1951 report say:

The Company has entered into long-term lease agreements covering mill properties and offices which provide for payment totalling $909,000 annually, plus in the case of certain leases, the cost of taxes, maintenance, and protection. The rental payments required during the terms of the leases subsequent to December 29, 1951 amount to $5,717,000.

This statement covered only the leases on existing properties before undertaking the new projects, but it gives an idea of how heavily involved Textron had become in lease financing rather than debt financing. In addition, total long-term debt would soon exceed $10 million. The auditors' notes continue:

Subsidiaries of the Company have also entered into long-term lease agreements with certain municipalities covering the rental of certain proposed mill properties and equipment. The construction of these properties will be financed by the sale of municipal securities, and the leases will not become effective until such financing is completed. On the effective dates of the leases, the subsidiaries will be required to pay amounts equivalent to the first year's rental, estimated at $1,140,000.

Since these were to be long-term leases, we were now talking about adding over $25 million of fixed rental cost to the company's long-term rental obligations. At just that time, the investment bankers were holding an annual meeting in Florida. They were particularly worried about the trend toward these huge municipally financed industrial operations since they feared if carried to excess Congress would ultimately eliminate the tax exemption of all municipal bonds.

One of the most fortunate things that ever happened to Textron was that the municipal bond community got together at that meeting in Miami and decided to boycott Mississippi's municipal bond offerings to finance our plants, even though the state's credit was good enough to justify their sale. I am now convinced, based on what has happened to the textile industry since then, that these leases would have been disastrous. Furthermore, when Textron later decided to get out of the textile business entirely, it probably would not have been able to do so with that rent load around its neck. Although at the time I was furious with the municipal bond dealers for their action, I must admit I am now very grateful to them for having prevented me from making a $25–$30 million mistake.

Another interesting statement in the annual report was:

In 1948 we sold to the Nashua, New Hampshire Foundation approximately 3,000,000 square feet of floor space, retaining by lease about one-third of this area for our own use. The Foundation has since done a magnificent job in attracting new industries to Nashua to occupy the available space. There are currently more workers employed in widely diversified industries in these buildings than Textron employed in Nashua prior to the sale to the Foundation. Largely responsible for these results was Lawrence C. Plowman, who has become general manager of our Industrial Building Department.

About that same time there was an editorial in the local Nashua paper which in effect said instead of having hanged Royal Little in effigy on the main street of Nashua during the Tobey hearings in

1948, the people should have erected a statue to him in the center of town since they now have some twenty diversified industries employing twice as many people as had ever been employed in Nashua.

# Textron, 1952

In the 1952 annual report, Textron's sales were reported as having been $98,745,000, and the company as having lost $6,423,000 before computing the benefit of a tax carry-back. This disaster was entirely my fault. In the early part of 1951, when fabric prices were high and customers were buying eighteen months ahead, most other textile mills were selling 1952 deliveries at extremely profitable prices. I was unwilling to do this because the OPA had announced that they were going to roll back prices on all future textile deliveries in spite of firm contracts. Since we had no idea how much prices might be rolled back, we made the disastrous decision not to accept future orders until we knew the prices. If we had followed the practice of other mills who had booked ahead for 1952 the Textron story might have been entirely different—we might have stayed in textiles.

The OPA never rolled back prices so we had to accept orders at a loss to keep our mills going in 1952. That one bad decision on my part cost the company at least $15 million. We certainly would have made close to $10 million pretax on fabric sales in 1952 had the orders been booked in 1951 when all other mills were selling ahead at high prices.

*ADVICE: Don't underestimate the political power of the important southern textile industry. The roll-back of textile prices by the OPA never occurred, and all of our important southern competitors made enormous profits, as shown in the figures given below, compared with Textron's loss.*

|  | Burlington | Lowenstein | Stevens | Textron |  |
|---|---|---|---|---|---|
| 1952 sales | $320,261,000 | $173,255,000 | $387,148,000 | $98,745,000 |  |
| Pretax Profit | 16,416,000 | 5,552,000 | 18,133,000 | (6,423,000) | Loss |
| % on Sales | 5.1% | 9.0% | 4.7% | (6.5%) | Loss |

By the end of 1951, I realized that I had made another dreadful mistake by not accepting future contracts at high prices. We finally decided that the prospect of achieving our profit goal in the textile business with a group of low-cost southern mills was hopeless. The textile business had proven to be extremely competitive and cyclical.

Most of the low-cost southern mills were family controlled. The last thing they wanted to do was pay out huge dividends to avoid punitive undistributed net earnings taxes. So they poured capital into more mills in boom years, thereby creating enormous overcapacity. An analysis that we made of the performance of the leading textile companies and of data that the government put out each year indicated that the average return on capital in the textile industry was lower than that of any other industry year after year, with 5 percent after taxes on equity being par for the course.

Finally, after having tried desperately in the past to make a success of (1) yarn processing, (2) parachute manufacturing, (3) the completely integrated Textron brand operation, and (4) low-cost southern mills, I decided that there must be some better medium than the textile business in which to use the stockholders' capital to their advantage. I recalled that back in the middle twenties Eliot Farley, who had endorsed the original $10,000 note to get Special Yarns started, had told me that he thought there was a great opportunity to put together a lot of completely unrelated businesses in one corporation and even suggested the name—Disassociated Industries.

Then I also remembered that in 1948 the company had lent $900,000 to its pension fund, the Sixty Trust, to enable it to buy the Cleveland Pneumatic Tool Company, which earned $1 million a year after taxes on a net worth of $3.7 million, if one disregarded the surplus cash in the company, or 27 percent on equity.

In 1948, our articles of association and charter were so limited that we could employ our capital only in the textile industry; therefore, when Textron wanted to purchase Cleveland Pneumatic Tool the lawyers would not permit it. By 1951, however, we knew that the Sixty Trust had made an extraordinary profit on that investment, so we were tempted to try unrelated diversification ourselves. We therefore decided to ask the shareholders at the annual meeting in 1952 to amend the articles of association so that Textron in the future could go into any type of business the directors felt advisable. Meanwhile it would be necessary for us to keep our textile operations going while we attempted to acquire some non-textile businesses to see whether, at last, we had found a formula that would produce a fair return on the stockholders' equity.

To prepare for our future plans for widely diversified operations, I became chairman and chief executive officer, and our annual report stated: "Robert L. Huffines, Jr., formerly president of Burlington Mills Corporation of New York (the sales company for Burlington Mills) has recently been elected president of the company and has been given responsibility of general management of all textile operations with complete charge of purchasing, manufacturing, and selling." With the treasurer, secretary, and all future acquisition managements reporting to me, this move freed up much of my time to investigate companies for sale.

Reading the 1952 report, I notice that I did not have the courage at that time to admit the horrendous error I had made in not selling production ahead at very profitable prices and explaining to the stockholders why every other major textile company made money that year except Textron. There is no comment in either the letter or the footnotes about why the stockholders were being asked to change the articles of association. In the past, I had told the shareholders that we had great prospects as a synthetic yarn processor. That was followed by a wonderful new success story for our Textron label merchandise. Finally, after failure in those two ventures, we predicted that the solution to all our problems was to make Textron the lowest-cost producer of synthetic fabrics in the country. After all those bombs, no wonder I was afraid to tell them on March 23, 1953, what I really hoped to accomplish through completely unrelated diversification in the future.

I would like to include a paragraph from that 1952 annual report:

It is with deep regret that we report the deaths during 1952 of three beloved and able men close to the affairs of the company, all of whom contributed much in service and advice to the development and expansion of Textron. Eliot Farley, former Chairman of the Board, was a co-founder of the business in 1923. Godfrey B. Simonds, whose sound judgment and enthusiasm will be greatly missed, was a member of the Executive Committee. Lawrence E. Green served as our tax counsel and was the original trustee of the Textron pension trust.

It would have given me tremendous satisfaction if Eliot Farley could have lived to see what finally happened to Textron. He was not only the one who arranged the original financing of Special Yarns Corporation, but he constantly put up capital when needed; and he came up with the original idea of "Disassociated Industries."

Godfrey Simonds also not only served Textron well, but he was one of the three trustees who succeeded me when I resigned in 1945 as trustee of the Rhode Island Charities Trust. He, along with the other trustees, built that tiny foundation, which I started in 1937 with a $500 contribution, into a multimillion dollar trust with contributions to the United Fund last year of nearly $1,000,000. Not a bad return on a $500 investment!

Larry Green was the original trustee of the Sixty Trust, Textron's pension trust for salaried employees. It was his courage and foresight in purchasing the Cleveland Pneumatic Tool Company in 1948 that earned so much money for the trust that Textron, the parent company, did not have to make a single contribution toward the pensions of most of its salaried employees from 1947 until 1977.

Back in early 1952, when I realized that we had made a disastrous mistake in not selling ahead, and that we would undoubtedly have trouble making money that year, I said something like this to Bill Mewhort, our treasurer: "Bill, this is going to be a tough year. I think from a liquidity point of view we should figure on cleaning up all our potential losses and getting the maximum tax loss carry back against past earnings in order to strengthen our balance sheet this year. We should get prepared for our future plans of operating in diversified businesses other than textiles. Please let me know what you think you can run up in the way of losses in order to accomplish this result." He came back a few weeks later and said, "Roy, I've gone over all of the properties that we should consider getting rid of and I believe that we can come up with at least a $6,000,000 loss before any tax recovery." To show how accurate his estimate was, we actually lost $6,423,000 before tax adjustment. The result of this decision, however, was that we ended up 1952 with $26,585,000 in current assets and only $6,452,000 in current liabilities, for a ratio of better than 4-to-1 and no short-term bank debts.

A look at the ten-year review published in the 1952 annual report will certainly convince any casual observer how cyclical the textile business had been and what a lousy job we in particular had done.

| Date | Sales | Pretax Profits |
|------|-------|----------------|
| 1943 | $ 23,743,000 | $ 1,748,000 |
| 1944 | 26,255,000 | 2,348,000 |
| 1945 | 46,853,000 | 2,017,000 |
| 1946 | 112,952,000 | 16,194,000 |
| 1947 | 124,776,000 | 14,904,000 |
| 1948 | 98,847,000 | 11,151,000 |
| 1949 | 67,896,000 | Loss (2,716,000) |
| 1950 | 87,547,000 | 6,129,000 |
| 1951 | 98,290,000 | 8,510,000 |
| 1952 | 98,745,000 | Loss (6,423,000) |

To indicate how badly Textron had done since it became a direct competitor of the large southern textile mills in the production of huge quantities of synthetic and other fabrics, listen to this. In 1951 Burlington had sales of $310,000,000 and earnings before taxes of $27,000,000 or 8.8 percent; Lowenstein, sales were $144,-500,000 with a profit of over $12,000,000 or 8.4 percent; Stevens with sales of $350,000,000 and profit before taxes of $44,000,000 had 12.5 percent profit on sales.

Since Textron also lost money in 1953, $881,000 on $71,000,000 sales, let's see what the others did that following year: Burlington, $360,000,000 sales and $23,000,000 profit or 6.3 percent; Lowenstein, $180,000,000 sales and $16,000,000 profit or 8.5 percent; and Stevens with $335,000,000 sales and $19,000,000 profit or 5.6 percent. Since I constantly kept track of the results of the competition, you can see why I was completely discouraged with our results by the time of our stockholders' meeting in 1952, when we got the stockholders to authorize investments in businesses other than textiles.

# Textron After Diversification

# Textron, 1953

Nineteen fifty-three was another unprofitable year. Sales were $71,017,000 with a net loss of $171,000 after a tax carry-back credit of $710,000. Again, comparing results with the leaders in the textile industry, we were not being effective. As part of our plan to gradually get out of textiles and become diversified in non-textile industries, we sold the Indian Head operations to a new corporation in which we let the management group of Jim Robison, Jim Flack, and John O'Sullivan buy a few shares before spinning off the balance of the stock to our shareholders on the basis of 1/10th of a share of Indian Head for each share of Textron. This was a tax-free dividend in 1953 in lieu of any cash dividend that year.

On September 30, 1953, we purchased the inventories, trade name, and business of F. Burkart Manufacturing Company, of St. Louis, Missouri, for $1,801,052, exclusive of certain assets which were thereafter disposed of without profit or loss. This was our first non-textile acquisition. Our basic concept of unrelated diversification at that time was to accomplish these objectives:

1. Eliminate the effect of business cycles on the parent company by having many divisions in unrelated fields.
2. Eliminate any Justice Department monopoly problems by avoiding acquisitions in related businesses.
3. Eliminate single industry's temptation to overexpand at the wrong time. Finance the growth of only those divisions which show the greatest return on capital at risk. Rather than overexpand any division, use surplus funds to buy another business.
4. Confine acquisitions to leading companies in relatively small industries. Never buy a small company in a $5 to $10 billion industry. One of my particular "No-No's"—never buy a company that manufactures a product with an electric wire attached—no radios, televisions, washing machines, driers, electric stoves, or refrigerators.
5. Having made a complete analysis of all major manufacturing companies' return on net worth and found that only about twenty-five in 1952 earned over 20 percent on common stock

*"I can't really tell you what business I'm in. I'm
almost frighteningly diversified."*

equity, I set that rate of return in 1953 as Textron's goal for the
future.

## BURKART MANUFACTURING COMPANY

With the change in our articles of association in 1952, Textron
could now acquire businesses in any field. We decided, because of
our long experience in manufacturing, to confine our acquisitions
to companies that were manufacturers—not retailers—service industries, or in natural resources. We also felt that it would be advisable not to buy any businesses that were in huge industries
doing $5 or $10 billion in sales, where the company we might purchase would be a tiny part of such an industry. It appeared to us
that if we could buy a leader in a relatively small industry we
would be far better off.

The first opportunity was brought to us by Gordon Scherck of Scherck, Richter and Company in St. Louis. The F. Burkart Manufacturing Company was operated by Harry Burkart, who was getting along in years. He and his family were the principal shareholders, although there was some public ownership in the over-the-counter market. Burkart began business in 1877, manufacturing saddle girths and horse blankets. Keeping pace with changes in transportation in the country, this division successfully made seating equipment for wagons and buggies and was one of the leading suppliers of batts and pads for automobile, train, and airplane seats.

By curious coincidence, this opportunity had been offered to Larry Green, who was chairman of the trustees of our company's pension trust—the Sixty Trust, because Larry's office was at 60 State Street, Boston. This opportunity was brought to him by Millar Brainard, a former officer of the First National Bank of Boston who had retired to become a business broker. Larry had turned this down as an inappropriate investment for the pension fund and had never disclosed the fact to Textron that such a company was available. We first talked with Harry Burkart at the end of 1952, and after a long period of negotiations, we finally arrived at a price for the fixed assets and the inventories that would be taken over, based on a joint audit at the time of closing.

In order to get a higher price for his shareholders, Burkart wanted to postpone the closing until September 30, 1953. Since Textron had lost money in 1952 and was now borrowing money again, we had to get approval from our banks, principally the First National Bank of Boston and Central Hanover in New York, since we owed them nearly $5 million.

I went to the First National and said to Roger Damon, "Roger, as you know, we now have approval from stockholders to diversify outside the textile business since we have not made an adequate return on capital. I hope that you are willing to help us in financing the acquisition of Burkart."

He replied, "Roy, I think your whole idea of unrelated diversification is crazy—there is no way that any one management can be bright enough to operate twenty or thirty different businesses in one corporation. I am certain that your plan is going to be a failure, but to help convince you that you are wrong, the First National Bank will assist in your acquisition of Burkart. Perhaps you'll learn a lesson from this one."

I then went to Jeff McNeill at Central Hanover Bank in New York and said, "Jeff, we have a chance to buy Burkart Manufacturing Company in St. Louis, which has an excellent earnings record. We can purchase the whole thing for less than three million dollars. It's really a good buy. We are paying less than eight times the aftertax earnings, but we need your approval under our present loan agreement to use your lines of credit for an acquisition. The First has agreed to go along."

"Roy, this whole idea of yours of unrelated diversification is unsound, impractical, and we certainly will not help you in the acquisition of Burkart or any other business that you might want to buy outside the textile business. The first thing you've got to do is convince us that you know how to run a textile business. After you have done that, perhaps we will consider financing some unrelated acquisitions."

Going back to the First National, I said, "Roger, Jeff won't go along. We're stymied. Can you help me persuade him to let us proceed with Burkart?"

"Roy," he said, "I still think your whole idea of unrelated diversification is crazy, but I will go to New York with you and see whether we can solve the problem."

As a result of a meeting in New York with both Jeff McNeill and Roger Damon, we finally were permitted to use our lines of credit to buy the inventories and receivables; in other words, only the working capital assets of Burkart. McNeill insisted that in return the banks must have a lien in the future on all our receivables from every source and that we must find someone else to buy the fixed assets and lease them to Textron so as not to use any of their lines in the purchase of fixed assets. He also insisted that any rental payments be contingent on earnings not fixed.

Although under today's laws it might not have been possible to do so, we finally arranged with the trustees of Textron's profit-sharing trust, called Market Square Trust, to buy the fixed assets and lease them to Textron for a period of ten and a quarter years (with rights of renewal) beginning October 1, 1953, at an annual rental of 20 percent of the first $1 million of the Burkart Division's annual net profit before provision for federal and state taxes on income plus 10 percent of the amount of any such profits in excess of $1 million.

After the acquisition was made as the first step in our diversification program, we paid a finder's fee of $100,000 to Scherck,

Richter and Company, since they were the ones who brought this opportunity to Textron.

Meanwhile, I had been in touch with Millar Brainard and explained to him that he had no claim for a commission in this case since he had discussed it only with the Sixty Trust and not with Textron. I also, to avoid another possible claim, had him write a letter to us stating that he recognized that Scherck, Richter and Company had the right to the finder's fee and that he and his group had no claim whatsoever in this case. Unfortunately, Millar Brainard died shortly after writing us and we were sued by the three other finders who had been involved with Brainard in trying to find a home for Burkart.

We had to defend the case in federal court in New York, and when the plaintiff presented their case to the judge and jury, the judge, without even hearing any of the evidence, threw the case out. It was appealed. The appellate court said the judge was in error—he should have heard our testimony before making his decision. Then we appeared before a new judge and a new jury.

We assumed we had an airtight case since we had paid the finder's fee to another broker. The group, including Millar Brainard's widow and son, claimed they were entitled to $300,000, to be split among the four parties involved.

This time it was a complete trial. We explained to the jury that Brainard had never contacted us and that, in fact, we had a letter from him acknowledging that Scherck, Richter and Company was the finder and that he had no claim against Textron.

When we were about to go into court the next day, the plaintiff's lawyer offered to settle the case, literally on the courthouse steps, for $75,000, which we turned down since we had an airtight case and we weren't about to pay anything.

However, when Millar Brainard's son was put on the stand he claimed that he happened to pick up an extra phone in Brainard's Marion home when I was talking with Millar, and he had heard me say, "Millar, don't you worry. We'll take care of you." At this point we entered as testimony the letter we'd received from Millar Brainard. The plaintiff's lawyer pointed out at the bottom of the letter; it said, "Dictated but not read," and the letter had been signed "Millar Brainard, by his secretary." We had tried to get Brainard's secretary to appear in court as a witness for us, but she refused to appear. The jury, which apparently didn't believe a word of my testimony, promptly came back and awarded $300,000 to the group who had nothing whatsoever to do with the transaction.

*ADVICE: When you have a large corporation involved in a jury case, don't count on the jury's being influenced by unimpeachable testimony. Be sure letters needed in court are signed by the principals—not their secretaries.*

Millar Brainard's widow sat through the whole trial in court dressed in black, and the jury believed the son's testimony not mine. But instead of settling the case, as we could have, on the courthouse steps for $75,000, we lost $300,000.

## INDIAN HEAD SPIN-OFF

The Textron 1952 annual report to stockholders dated March 23, 1953 reported:

In February 1953 the business and assets of the division making and selling Indian Head cotton cloth were sold on an installment basis to an inactive subsidiary, the name of which had been changed to Indian Head Mills, Inc. and substantially all of its stock was subsequently distributed on March 9 to Textron common stockholders in the ratio of one share of Indian Head stock of $1 per value for each ten shares of Textron common. Although this newly established organization begins operations with heavy indebtedness to Textron, its aggressive management inspires confidence and its operations should prove profitable. This transaction completes our withdrawal from the consumer products field.

The "aggressive management" was led by James E. Robison, who was executive vice president of Textron at the time of the spin-off and became Indian Head's president and chief executive officer. I tagged along as chairman of the board to keep an eye on these talented young men, hoping that Indian Head would ultimately pay Textron's $5 million loan.

Prior to the tax-free distribution of 119,654 shares to Textron stockholders, 6,500 shares of Indian Head were sold at $1 per share to Jim as a special incentive for him in this super-highly leveraged buy-out. He soon resold 4,500 of these shares at $1 each to other directors and an officer for the same incentive purpose and began to lay plans to enable many others in the company to share similarly in the fruits of the success he was determined would materialize.

The sale made a profit of $2,185,329, as those assets had a net value on Textron books of $2,987,439. The sales price was $5,172,-768, of which $414,432 was billed and paid for on open account; $3,000,000 was payable at the rate of $50,000 per month with interest at 4 percent during the ensuing five years; and the balance of $1,758,336 was payable without interest on February 7, 1958. Thus Indian Head's entire net worth was only $126,154 and its debt over $5,000,000.

For Indian Head's first seven-month fiscal period, sales were nearly $9,000,000 and profit only $336. Sales were about $11,000,-000 the next full fiscal year and profit after all interest and taxes was $185,729.

Twenty years later, Jim Robison retired as chief executive officer of Indian Head, Inc. A special publication for employees, "1953–1972—The Robison Years" summarized his career:

James Everett Robison was born on November 22, 1915 in the wheat-belt hamlet of Alfred, North Dakota. He spent most of his formative years in Mitchell, South Dakota. Entrepreneurial spirit is instinctive in him. At the age of 13 he began his own business in Mitchell—a hamburger and confectionary stand called The Breeze-In, and it is said that his thriving business even had a Dun & Bradstreet listing. Following high school, it was off to the University of Minnesota to earn his Bachelor's Degree in 1938 and then to the Harvard Business School, where he was a George F. Baker Scholar and earned his MBA degree in 1940.

At Harvard he met and was greatly influenced by Professor Malcolm P. McNair, a leading business philosopher who was later to serve for fifteen years on the Indian Head board of directors. Upon graduation, his first job was as a textile salesman for Nashua Manufacturing Company, an old New England firm with some very good products but which had been losing money regularly. He figured there would be some action in that situation.

In July 1942 Jim Robison took time out for another kind of action—war. He served in the Army Air Corps until May 1946, achieving the rank of Major. His military service earned him a chestful of medals, including the Distinguished Flying Cross and the Air Medal with Oak Leaf Clusters.

After the war, Jim Robison returned to Nashua as assistant sales manager. That is where he and I first met, because while Jim was at war Textron had acquired the company. Jim rose rapidly in our organization to become executive vice president of Textron. Soon thereafter, in our program to divest Textron of its consumer products operations, he came up with the idea of setting up the Indian Head operation as a separate company.

The small team of executives that Jim Robison put together were chosen for their entrepreneurial abilities. James M. Flack became the vice president for manufacturing, a responsibility he had held with Textron since 1946. He served as the chief for all personnel and industrial relations matters and was a superb labor negotiator. Charles O. Wood, who had long experience with Indian Head brand cotton fabrics and other domestic textiles which constituted the new company's initial product lines, became sales vice president. The fourth member of the team was John E. O'Sullivan, a young Textron budget specialist who had recently become Jim's executive assistant. He took on the treasurer and corporate secretary responsibilities.

Management participation in the fruits of success was a fundamental strategy for Indian Head and plans were laid out and authorized by the board and stockholders immediately after the spin-off.

To enable these men and a carefully chosen number of their subordinates to have a piece of the action, Jim proposed to the stockholders a package of incentive programs designed to achieve that objective. On March 10, 1953, a little more than a month after Indian Head went into business, the stockholders at a special meeting approved an incentive compensation and profit-sharing concept and also the sale for cash of 43,846 shares of common stock at $1 per share to executives and key employees. They agreed except in the case of death not to sell their shares under any conditions for five years except back to the company, and to do that at $1 per share if their employment should be terminated within three years. These shares were allocated 8,500 each to Mr. Flack and Mr. Wood; 1,106 shares to Mr. O'Sullivan; 21,500 to Jim Robison; and 4,240 shares to a few other key officers and employees.

The letter to Indian Head shareholders soliciting their proxies for this special meeting summarized the Indian Head situation:

Our difficult initial financial position . . . Indian Head owes Textron approximately $5,000,000 for the working assets purchased from Textron. The purchase contract requires (us) to make regular cash payments of

$600,000 each year until the debt is paid in full. In addition, about $300,-000 of the debt is carried on open account.

The letter wound up with this declaration:

Despite many apparent obstacles, your management is optimistic about the future success of our company. . . . It is essential that this group be held together by a sound incentive program that will serve the best interests of the stockholders. . . . We will strive to the very best of our abilities to meet this challenging opportunity. I hope and believe that time and events will prove us worthy of your continued confidence and support.

The stockholders voted overwhelmingly in favor of management's recommendations.

To the employees, Jim Robison issued a memo as soon as Indian Head operations started as an independent company. He said:

You are about to participate in the launching of a new business enterprise. . . . The future growth and expansion of our company will be limited only by the imagination, energy, initiative, and general competence of the management, supervisors, salesmen and workers. . . . I have no idea where we might end up five or ten years from now, but with your enthusiastic help and support I would defy anyone to place an outside limit now on where this business may go in the future.

The first real turning point in the fortunes of Indian Head came in 1955, with the first of more than fifty mergers and acquisitions. Indian Head merged with Naumkeag Steam Cotton Company, manufacturer of cotton bed sheets under the Pequot brand name. The tax-free merger, with a straight $25 preferred stock for Naum-

keag stockholders doubled Indian Head's sales and tripled its profits with no dilution of its common stock. Incidentally, the Naumkeag stockholders made out extremely well also. Their stock, which
had not been paying any dividends and was trading at about $10
per share, immediately started receiving $1.25 per share in divi-
dends and through the operation of a sinking fund, ultimately was
retired at $15 to $25 per share.

Jim Robison and his associates did a fantastic job with Indian
Head and, unlike me, they made relatively few mistakes. Over the
next few years, the company grew rapidly through carefully eval-
uated acquisitions in the textile industry, and strict attention to
sound business fundamentals. One of the most important of these
was expressed in the "Company Policy Statement," issued by Jim
Robison in 1953, soon after the company was started:

There is one basic policy to which there will never be an exception
made by anyone, anywhere, in any activity owned and operated by Indian Head. That policy is as follows:

Play it straight, whether in contact with the public, stockholders, customers, suppliers, employees, or any other individuals or groups. The only
right way to deal with people is forthrightly and honestly.

If any mistakes are made—admit them and correct them. Our commitments will be honored and Indian Head has the right to expect the
same performance from those people with whom it does business.

This is fundamental. We will not welsh, weasel, chisel, or cheat. We will
not be party to any untruths, half truths, or unfair distortions. Life is too
short. It is perfectly possible to make a decent living without any compromise with integrity.

As I look at the business scene in 1977, I see many companies
and top executives who have been seriously damaged by the revela-
tion of improper payments and other corporate misbehavior. Indian Head has never been embarrassed by any such improprieties.
Strict adherence to this simple concept of total integrity in all
dealings certainly can avoid a lot of agony and headaches.

Another business fundamental of Jim Robison's is outlined in
this quotation from his speech to the executive group at one of
their annual planning meetings:

Here I would like to reemphasize a basic concept of Indian Head's
management approach that we have talked about over the years. This has
to do with the order of management priorities which every executive in
Indian Head must keep in mind constantly.

Busy men never have time to do all of the things that need doing. Many have a tendency to get beguiled by the peripheral aspects of running a business. In Indian Head we have always said that the main priorities of executive attention are these, and *in this order:*

Number 1: Avoid catastrophe!!!

Number 2: Keep the show on the road. Meet or beat the current plan.

Number 3: Plan for future profit improvement.

Don't go off chasing rainbows with grandiose growth schemes until you are sure that you have been minding the store. DON'T START VAST PROJECTS WITH HALF VAST IDEAS!

The second big turning point for Indian Head came in 1965, when it made its first step to diversify outside of the textile industry. By that time it had built a sales volume up to about $150 million, net profit to over $3 million, and net worth to over $25 million without any dilution of common stockholders' equity, as all acquisitions had been made with cash, notes, and straight preferred stock.

I had persuaded Jim that diversification outside the textile industry would certainly benefit his stockholders as it had Textron's, although Indian Head just could not find the right deal to accomplish this goal. Finally, with my help, an opportunity to acquire Detroit Gasket and Manufacturing Company developed, and this automotive parts company was acquired in early 1965 for $20 million in cash.

Then, in rapid succession, several other companies were acquired by Indian Head to form a substantial automotive and metal parts group. In 1967 and 1968, five glass companies were acquired to form an outstanding glass container group. Indian Head common and convertible preferred stock, listed on the New York Stock Exchange, together with cash and notes, were used in this diversification program.

What finally happened to Indian Head? It was sold to a European company, with all stockholders getting a good price for their stock in cash.

In September 1973, Thyssen-Bornemisza NV, a privately owned European industrial holding company, made an offer to the nine thousand shareholders of Indian Head to purchase shares of Indian Head common stock at $27 net cash, about 50 percent over the market price. The high market price that year for Indian Head common, trading on the New York Stock Exchange was $27.50 in January; the low $15.25 in May. Thyssen-Bornemisza bought

1,213,619 shares from the public and an additional 750,000 shares from the corporation, also at $27, giving it 34 percent of the stock.

By the second quarter of the next year, despite increased sales and profits, the market price of the Indian Head common, still trading on the NYSE, had drifted back to as low as $17.25, or about five times earnings and about two-thirds of book value.

Later, in July 1974, Thyssen-Bornemisza made another tender offer for all remaining shares, also at $27, and ended up with 90 percent of the outstanding stock. This, of course, resulted in delisting from the NYSE. Finally, in November 1976, the balance of the stock was taken out at $32 per share, giving Thyssen-Bornemisza 100 percent ownership.

The buyer ultimately paid about $190 million for all the Indian Head securities purchased, or approximately eight times earnings and a substantial premium over book value. Nevertheless, this European company, like many others, made a very good purchase. Many astute European investors are buying up American companies at prices well above what American investors value the companies at as reflected in the market prices of their securities.

In 1974, Indian Head had sales of $615 million, net profit of $22 million, and net worth of $170 million. During the previous ten-year period, the company earned an average return on stockholders equity in excess of 14 percent. Earnings per share of $1.74 and book value of $12 per share in 1965 had approximately doubled. Yet the market price of the stock had gone nowhere. It was about $20 in 1965 and less than that in 1973 and 1974.

Jim Robison had always stated that the basic objective of the company was to increase the *intrinsic* value of the common stock. His theory was that the *market* value would ultimately reflect true intrinsic value. He was wrong. In the 1970s, market prices of most companies whose shares are publicly traded do not reflect true intrinsic values. The many tender offers for shares of public companies at prices well above their quoted market prices is clear proof that this is true.

In any event, when the Thyssen-Bornemisza offer came along Jim Robison was realistic enough to feel that the marketplace would not put an equivalent price on the shares in the foreseeable future. Being very conscious of his responsibility to all of the shareholders (including over two thousand employee shareholders) he thought it best that management cooperate with the buyer and let all shareholders decide whether or not to sell.

Here is a fine example of what happens in a case of a divestiture when key management is permitted to have a substantial piece of the action. Within a few months after the spin-off in 1953, the officers of Indian Head acquired over 30 percent of the total Indian Head shares then outstanding. With a subsequent offering to employees at $5 per share, stock options, and an employee stock purchase plan, management and employees all down the line ultimately had a very big stake in the company. They did very well for themselves and the other Indian Head stockholders. With stock splits and dividends, the tax basis of those original $1.00 shares was down to $.14.

How about Textron and its owners?

In the first place, Textron realized a profit on the sale of assets for which it had difficulty in finding a buyer.

At the time of the spin-off in 1953, Textron was selling at $11 per share. A Textron shareholder with 100 shares would have received 10 shares of Indian Head as a tax-free dividend. With subsequent stock splits and stock dividends, these original 10 shares would have become 69 shares. If held until the first or second tender offer, the stockholder received $186.30 for each original Indian Head share, and on the final take-out, $220 per share. Many of the original Indian Head stockholders did hold their stock until the end. (Incidentally, if a stockholder also held his Textron shares, the original 100 would have become 400 shares with a market value of about $11,000 in 1976.)

Another way of putting it is to compare total market values. At the time of the spin-off, Textron had 1,196,540 shares outstanding, which at $11 per share was a market value of only $13 million for the entire company. The 119,654 Indian Head shares that the Textron stockholders received finally were sold for over $22 million, or nearly double the market value of Textron at the time of the spin-off. There was no way that comparable results could have been achieved by keeping Indian Head as part of Textron.

*ADVICE: This is an excellent example of how a tax-free spin-off can create more value for the stockholders.*

# *Textron, 1954*

The merger of American Woolen Company and Robbins Mills, Inc. into Textron Inc., now Textron American, Inc., was negotiated in 1954.

For the year ending January 1, 1955, consolidated net earnings of Textron Inc. were $1,262,000 on sales of $99,717,000. During the last year, earnings from our non-textile operations amounted to $4,298,000. Losses incurred in subsequently discontinued textile units, however, amounted to about $2,000,000.

During the year ending January 2, 1955, American Woolen Company's sales were $28,191,000 and losses amounted to $18,-817,000. In 1954, fifteen plants were closed and only nine small units, seven woolen and two worsted, were in operation at the year-end.

Imagine taking on a headache of this sort just to get capital for the further acquisition of unrelated diversified companies! At the time this entire idea of merger was considered ridiculous by most investment banking firms who could not see the long-range potential advantage.

For the year ended November 28, 1954, Robbins Mills, Inc., showed a loss of $7,250,000 on sales of $49,364,000. Again the financial community could not understand what in the world Textron was up to in taking on companies that had experienced such fantastic losses.

An audit of the consolidated companies was made as of February 24, 1955, the date of the merger, and showed working capital of $48,068,000 and net worth of $79,706,000. This compared with Textron's working capital on December 31, 1953, of $10,344,000 and common stock equity of $25,119,000. It was primarily because of this enormous increase in capital and the combined loss carry-forward of close to $45,000,000 resulting from the merger that made it possible to proceed with plans to become a widely diversified corporation.

*"This is the part of capitalism I hate."*

We have one of the most effective pension plans in the country, for salaried employees of the former textile divisions of American Woolen, Robbins Mills, Textron, and Burkart, numbering in the aggregate over 1,450. This plan is sufficiently overfunded so as not to require any current company contributions even for future services of these employees. As a result of merging the pension funds of the three companies into the Sixty Trust, the combined net worth of the trust was in excess of $25 million.

Ten idle plants of the American Woolen Company were sold for $2.1 million for delivery on May 2, 1955. The carrying charges, not including depreciation for these properties, was at the rate of approximately $2 million per year. Although the price received was exceedingly low for the 6 million sq. ft. of floor space involved, losses on these plants ceased.

This indicates the problems that the New England textile industry faced in disposing of its huge plants during this period, when southern textile mills produced identical fabrics at far lower costs. The price of $2 million for these ten plants included large amounts of obsolete machinery as well as the floor space. It is no wonder that the American Woolen stockholders welcomed the merger with Textron.

Because our security holders (numbering with debenture holders, more than thirty thousand) were scattered throughout the country, we anticipated that only a handful of owners would attend in person the annual stockholders' meeting on May 18, which we were required by law to hold in Rhode Island. To keep everyone better posted about our affairs we held the following informal regional meetings that year, at which an interesting presentation was made: Boston, May 18; Philadelphia, May 19; New York City, May 24; Chicago, May 25; Los Angeles, May 26. The SEC would only permit these after the annual meeting.

Over two thousand security holders showed up at these meetings. This plan was one that I felt strongly about personally. In my opinion, it is important to hold stockholders' meetings in various parts of the country from time to time, and I have been pleased to see that many of our larger corporations are now changing the location of their annual meeting each year so as to get greater stockholder participation.

## DALMO VICTOR

In January 1954 we purchased the Dalmo Victor Company, whose principal owner, Tim Moseley, had done a wonderful job in building up a small company to become the largest supplier of airborne radar antennae to the government. The fixed part of the purchase price was $1,500,000 of which $300,000 was paid in cash and $1,-200,000 was paid by notes in equal monthly installments over the four years (1955, 1956, 1957, and 1958). An additional $1,500,000 was to be paid on or before December 31, 1963, out of one-half of the earnings of Dalmo Victor after Textron had received repayment of its $500,000 working capital loan and dividends totaling $1,500,000.

This was a complex agreement combining a fixed price installment sale plus a contingent payout. A combined transaction of this sort will no longer qualify for capital gains by the IRS.

In 1956, Dalmo Victor, in addition to maintaining its top position in the field of radar antennae for aircraft, substantially broadened its product base by entering two new fields, electro-hydraulic valves and in-flight refueling. In October 1956, Dalmo Victor completed its expansion program when it moved into its new, multimillion-dollar plant at Belmont, California, and brought together under one roof all operations, which were previously scattered through six different buildings in two cities.

Tim received his final payment long before the 1963 deadline and was for the first time in his life pretty well off. Thereafter, he devoted a lot of time to outside real estate investments and ulti-mately bought a fine sailing yacht, the *Orient*. After he had been paid off, he said to me, "Roy, don't ever buy another company on an incentive basis and put a top dollar limit on the price." I said, "Why not, Tim?" He said, "I never took any chances in building up a bigger business for you. I just played it safe, to be sure to get my three million dollars. As a result, that division is not nearly as big and as important as it could have been. I had no incentive to work hard after we had our three million dollars in the bag. If Textron's contingent payout had been open-ended for ten years, Dalmo Victor would have been a far more profitable division."

*ADVICE: When you make the owners of a small business you purchase wealthy, try to have some meaningful incentive so that they will continue to work hard for you in building up the business.*

Besides being a person of great charm, Tim was an extraordinar-ily capable engineer, an excellent manager, and a real entrepre-neur. As a result of my lack of foresight, Textron lost millions of dollars of potential earnings at Dalmo Victor by not adequately motivating Tim through an unlimited long-term contingent payout.

## MB MANUFACTURING COMPANY

The next business we bought in our diversification program was MB Manufacturing Company in New Haven, Connecticut. This company had recently earned $1 million pretax, and was for sale at $2 million. The company was the leading producer of vibration eliminators for piston engine aircraft and also was the leading pro-ducer of vibration shakers, a form of special equipment that was used to test all sorts of parts and materials to accelerate the time in which they could be destroyed or be useless. This operation, again, was a leading company in a small industry and therefore fitted our pattern. We soon came to terms with the owners and the purchase was made on March 25, 1954.

MB had an order backlog of about $6 million, which assured ca-pacity operations for the balance of the year with a satisfactory profit margin. It was operated as a subsidiary under the former owners' management with Rollin W. Mettler, president, and George H. Mettler, treasurer.

For the next year or so, sales and earnings held up, but when jet engines began to replace piston engines, the vibration elimination devices were no longer needed and the business gradually became unprofitable. The remaining business in vibration testing equipment did not have sufficient volume to carry the overhead.

*ADVICE: Here is a good example of how one can make a mistake by not having some outside firm like Arthur D. Little, Inc., check the industry's future. It was obvious that the owners were selling out because they knew that within a few years jet engines would replace piston engines and that their principal line of product would no longer be needed. If such a study had been made, we never would have bought MB Manufacturing.*

## AMERICAN WOOLEN COMPANY

Textron had made only two non-textile acquisitions in its unrelated diversification program by January 1, 1954. Both of them required cash since the price/earnings ratio on our common stock was so low that it was impossible to use it for acquisitions. At this time there was a lot of publicity in the New England papers about the problems American Woolen Company was having.

American Woolen was the world's largest woolen and worsted manufacturer with, at one time, seventy New England plants, many of them over one hundred years old, in small towns where there was water power available in the days before electric power could be purchased.

In addition to the very small mills, there were several huge plants in Lawrence, like the Wood mill with three million square feet in one building. The American Woolen Company had never built a new low-cost plant in the South the way their principal competitors, Deering Milliken and J. P. Stevens, had. They did have two small plants in the South, which were not well equipped, but they had missed the boat entirely on following the obvious southern trend of textile production.

The past record of American Woolen Company showed that the only time they really made big money was during wars. For instance, in the World War I period they had enormous earnings, and again during World War II. At the end of 1952, they had just finished another short but very profitable period during the Korean War, but by the end of 1953, they had suffered heavy losses again. The reason that their record was so spotty was that, basically, their plants were inefficient and they could not compete in normal times with the low-cost southern producers. However, when the government came into the market for hundreds of millions of yards of woolen and worsted fabrics for the services, this extra demand was so huge that it filled up all of the low-cost facilities and even the high-cost plants of American Woolen. In other words, American Woolen made money only in times of extreme shortage when their facilities, even though they were obsolete, were essential to supply the government's needs.

At the time we became interested in taking a good look at American Woolen, they were losing $1 million a month and the directors were split in opinion as to what should be done. There was one group that felt that the property should be liquidated while they were in a very strong financial position with over $20 million in cash and excess working capital. There were others, most of whom were presidents of companies doing business with American Woolen (like the Bangor and Aroostook Railroad; the New York, New Haven, and Hartford Railroad; and the Central Vermont Public Service Company), who wanted the company to continue operating. These directors were obviously interested in keeping the mills running in New England because they were providing services to the company.

There had been a stockholders meeting in 1953 that had been quite controversial, for which a man from Trenton had solicited proxies. Since Textron had really run out of money to make any further major acquisitions with cash, to carry out its long-range objective of buying companies completely unrelated to each other (primarily manufacturers that were leaders in relatively small businesses), we looked upon American Woolen as a possible source of capital for the further expansion of our program.

Even though we had indicated through the spin-off of the Indian Head operation that we were headed toward getting out of textiles entirely, we not only saw American Woolen as a source of capital, but we were also attracted by its huge tax loss carry-forward.

We approached the American Woolen board and tried to persuade them to work out a merger, but the majority (who had special interests to protect) knew that Textron would move the operations into modern new plants in the South, and they therefore opposed any association with Textron.

We were very fortunate, however, in having the company's secretary, whose law firm had formerly represented the company, give us a list of the shareholders so that we could approach them directly. I believe the reason he did this was that he was convinced that the present management of American Woolen would dissipate the assets and that the shareholders would lose everything. He had been one of the directors unsuccessfully recommending complete liquidation. I think another motivation was that his firm had lost the American Woolen account to Ely, Bartlett, Thompson and Brown, a firm headed by former Governor Joseph B. Ely.

At any rate, now having the list of shareholders, we prepared a registration statement and mailed a prospectus to all the American Woolen shareholders offering to exchange one-fifth share of 4 percent preferred, one-half share of common, and $5 cash for each share of American Woolen common.

While we were making the offer, the American Woolen board finally agreed that they should use their surplus $20 million cash to pay off the two preferred stock issues that American Woolen had outstanding, aggregating that amount. A stockholders meeting was called for January 23, 1954, with this as the principal purpose. Fortunately, in our prospectus we had stated that if the preferred stock were called and the surplus money used to retire the American Woolen preferred, our offer would be withdrawn. The special meeting was to be held at the Statler Hilton Hotel in Boston, and while the proxies were coming in for this meeting we were getting quite a few shares of American Woolen tendered under our offer. We, of course, realized that there would be very little objection to the directors' plan to call preferred shares unless we could find some American Woolen common shareholder who wished to exchange his common stock for our Textron package.

Using Claude Branch of Choate, Hall and Stewart, a law firm in Boston, to help us in this situation we finally were successful. Claude had found an American Woolen stockholder, Blin W. Page, up in the little town of Skowhegan, Maine, who was prepared to seek an injunction against the preferred stock plan in order to preserve his right to swap for our shares. We were quite sure that the court would at least give a temporary injunction if this request were made. However, the day turned out to be a bad one when Mr. Page was to drive to Boston and sign the legal documents in Claude's office. Heavy snows had fallen all day, and Mr. Page called Claude from Skowhegan and said that it would be impossible for him to drive down for the meeting so he therefore would have to give up the whole project. The meeting was called for ten o'clock the next morning, and when I dropped in to see Claude at six o'clock the night before, he said "Roy, we're licked. There has been a bad snowstorm up in Maine and Mr. Page just won't come down to sign the documents. I have been to the court and put them on notice that we plan to bring in a request for a temporary injunction before ten o'clock tomorrow morning, but I see no way that we can do that now."

I said, "Claude, I don't agree with you. If you will give me the documents you want signed in order to present them to the judge the first thing tomorrow morning, I will go over to the airport and see if we can find a pilot who will fly these papers up to Maine tonight and get them back in time to present them to the court first thing in the morning." Fortunately the heavy snowstorm was now over. It was a clear bright night so that there should be no problem in flying to Skowhegan, which had a small airstrip. It took me until ten o'clock that night to rout a pilot out of his home and get him over to the airport to start on his way to Maine with the papers to be signed and Mr. Page's name and address.

Next morning, I went to Claude's office but he had not heard from the pilot, so I decided to go over to the special meeting and find out what was going on. There must have been over a thousand stockholders at the meeting, which was called promptly at ten o'clock. There was a certain amount of routine procedure that had to be handled, like checking on a quorum. Then a motion to call the two preferred issues was put to the meeting. The chairman read the proposal that was to be voted on and said that before he took a vote, he would like to open the meeting to discussion. Well, it happened that Lewis Gilbert was attending that meeting in person, as well as several others who were opposed to the company's calling the preferred and, in effect, throwing in the sponge and going out of business. He and several others began asking questions and tied up the meeting for about half an hour. Meanwhile, our pilot had arrived back at the Boston airport. The airstrip in Skowhegan had not been plowed out so he had to land at another town fifty miles away. He took a taxi to our plaintiff's house, woke him up at four in the morning, got him to sign the papers, rode back to the airport in the taxi, and took off again for Boston. This was why he was delayed in getting back. When he called Claude, Claude told him to rush over to the courthouse immediately with the papers while he, Claude, went to see the judge to tell him that the documents would be there momentarily. You can imagine how I felt when the chairman was about to put the motion to a vote and the temporary injunction had not been delivered.

All of a sudden, during these hectic proceedings, with only seconds to spare, a messenger came in from the court with the injunction and handed it to the chairman. Then all hell broke loose. The chairman and all of the officers and directors who were on the stage got up and sneaked out the back door, leaving the meeting in an uproar. Lewis Gilbert went up to the lectern and for the next couple of hours, Lewis had a field day running the meeting and letting everybody have a chance to be heard. Incidentally, I have had years of experience with Lewis and had found him to be a very honorable and bright person. He has achieved many of his goals, things that most chief executives didn't approve of but which in the long run, Lewis persuaded them and the stockholders to go along with. As a result of his efforts, many large companies now hold their annual meetings in places where the greatest number can attend rather than in Flemington Junction, New Jersey, or Dover, Delaware. Also, I believe that he was responsible for changing the method of reporting of leading New York City banks, which used to have their annual meetings so close to the end of the year that the annual reports were not mailed out in advance but were presented at the meeting. As a result of Lewis's efforts, this practice was changed.

To continue our story—the calling of the preferred was now dead, so we went to work in earnest to get shares in. After some time, I realized that we were not going to get control of the company as a result of our exchange offer. I then went to Albert List, a wealthy textile operator whom I had known for many years, and persuaded him to lend Textron sufficient money to buy enough shares for cash so that with what we had received in our exchange offer we would have control of the company. Albert, of course, required that we use as collateral not only all of the shares we purchased but also those we had received in the exchange; so, in effect, he had a substantial margin on his loan. I always suspected that he hoped we might not be able to pay off his loan so that this would be a neat way for him to end up in control of American Woolen.

About this time, Joe Ely, who was the leading spirit in the battle against Textron, had called the annual meeting to elect directors. American Woolen had a staggered board in which only one-third of the board was elected each year. In addition, he had set the record date for voting at the annual meeting ahead of the date that we had acquired any shares so we couldn't vote our stock. It looked as though American Woolen directors would be reelected without our having anything to say about it. The only defense we had, therefore, was to refuse to attend the annual meeting and to hope that Ely could not get a quorum to reelect his board.

As a result of this tactic, American Woolen had to recess their meeting time after time after time—some thirteen times in all I believe—before they could get a quorum. Some of the shareholders who were in favor of our taking over the company organized a committee to call a special meeting of the shareholders to amend the staggered board provision and permit the election of the entire board at one time. This committee's special meeting happened to coincide with one of the recessed annual meetings. When we did not have a quorum for the special meeting, even with all our shares, I made a deal with Joe Ely to recess that meeting so that we would have a chance of getting a quorum. He agreed to do so, but then, when he announced to the group that it was going to be recessed, the shareholders present were so upset that the plan wasn't going to be voted on that Ely quickly changed procedures and asked for a motion to adjourn the meeting. He promptly got a second and announced the meeting adjourned. I rushed up in front of the meeting and said, "Joe, you can't adjourn this meeting. I'm voting Textron's proxies to recess it, not adjourn it." He said, "Roy, I'm the chairman of this meeting and I'm ruling that on the matter of adjournment, it can be done on a voice vote and I therefore will not count your proxies as voting on this matter." I said, "Joe, you know we made a deal before the meeting started and you agreed to recess." He said, "Roy, if you want to question my ruling as chairman you can always go to court." By that clever move, Joe Ely had killed the plan of many of the shareholders to eliminate the staggered board requirement at American Woolen Company.

As I have said before, recessed meeting after recessed meeting went on. Then in the spring of 1954, a man from Trenton, New Jersey, who was in the undertakers' supply business, came to see me. He said, "Mr. Little, in this little black bag I've got seventy-five thousand votes that can put you over the top. There are only a million American Woolen shares outstanding. You already have forty-seven percent, my seventy-five thousand votes will let you elect some representatives to the board of American Woolen." He offered to sell these proxies to Textron for $25,000, to which I said, "You know its illegal to sell proxies. Textron wouldn't think of

paying anybody for proxies." He said, "Well, if you don't buy them Joe Ely will," and with that he departed.

This episode made me wonder how in the world this man had gotten any proxies for the annual meeting. He had not directly solicited proxies, but I finally recalled that he had been prominent in soliciting proxies for a prior meeting in 1953, so I was suspicious that there was "something rotten in Denmark." We hired an investigator to go to Trenton and see what he could find out.

Believe it or not, in a garbage can, out on the sidewalk, they found dozens of American Woolen proxies that apparently the Trenton man had been signing names on and throwing away. When I saw these proxies, many of them signed with the same name, I realized what had happened—the Trenton man had gotten a batch of blank proxies from the company, and he was practicing forging signatures on the new proxies from the old ones of the 1953 meeting, which apparently the company had let him take home with him. With this information, we waited to see what would happen. Sure enough, on April 20, 1954, the recessed meeting was called to order. Governor Ely asked if there was a quorum. He was told there was, even though Textron's shares were not represented. His board was voted in.

In the meantime, we had put a handwriting expert into the National City Bank while they were counting proxies. The bank hesitantly permitted us to examine all the proxies. Our handwriting expert was able to prove that many of them were forgeries. Apparently, Joe Ely had bought the forged proxies.

With this information, we took American Woolen into federal court in Boston, and Judge Bailey, based on the testimony of our experts, threw out the results of the annual meeting. Finally the directors of American Woolen agreed to negotiate with us to merge. During the negotiation meetings with Governor Ely, I said, "Joe, how did you ever come to buy those proxies? You know that's

"*You have many more proxy fights left in you.*"

illegal." To which he replied, "Roy, I suspected there was something wrong, and I never did pay him."

In the final negotiation, American Woolen insisted that it be a three-party merger instead of two. They wanted to take in Robbins Mills, which Textron then controlled, since Robbins had some very efficient operations in the Carolinas, which really supplemented the production that we had in our low-cost southern plants. To show how fortunate American Woolen stockholders were, their stock was selling at $15 a share at the time. Textron was selling for $12 a share. The three underwriting firms representing the three parties at issue decided that a fair exchange for each American Woolen share would be two shares of Textron common stock. If we had not moved in to American Woolen, I am convinced that their shareholders would have lost everything.

What happened to them as a result of the merger? In 1968, when Textron sold for $57 per share after having been split four for one, the American Woolen shareholders, whose stock had been as low as $10 in 1953, had Textron shares at its highest price, worth $456.

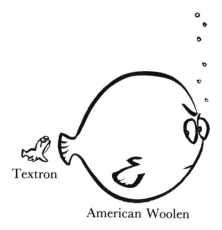

Textron

American Woolen

The information from the Textron 1953 annual report is interesting in retrospect:

On April 5, 1954, the Board of Directors authorized the acceptance of approximately 163,000 shares of common stock of American Woolen Company deposited or committed for deposit under our offer to exchange $5 in cash, one-fifth (1/5) of a share of 4% preferred stock Series B, and one-half (1/2) of a share of Common Stock for each share of American Woolen common. We have already purchased 50,200 shares for cash which brings total holdings to 213,200 shares in the aggregate, sufficient in our opinion to provide the base for ultimate control of American Woolen Company and for new management which will have a very large ownership interest.

The Directors at the same time extended the exchange offer until July 20th on condition that an additional 50,000 shares be deposited prior to 3 P.M. on April 19th and that hereafter, the cash part of the offer be reduced to $3.50 on April 20th to May 20th, $2 from May 21st to June 21, and no cash June 22 to July 20. The offer, however, may be withdrawn at any time upon 5 days' written notice to the depository bank.

If we obtain control of the board of directors of American Woolen Company, we are confident that the experience, the 'know-how' and the enthusiasm of our organization assures eventual rehabilitation and success for this fine old company. Our Industrial Building Department is particularly well-equipped to bring in fast-growing diversified industries to replace highly marginal textile mills. The record with respect to locating vital new industries in plants in Nashua and Suncook, New Hampshire, and in North Smithfield and East Greenwich, Rhode Island, formerly operated by us, demonstrates what can be done for the New England communities in which textile mills are forced to close.

You will notice that at no point have we stated the real purpose of our proposed merger of the American Woolen. Since we were

doing everything possible to get out of the textile business, it certainly looked a little ridiculous for us to be buying control of the largest woolen and worsted operation in the world. Our net worth was only $35 million, while American Woolen's net worth was over $77 million. They were loaded with cash and had a $30 million loss carry-forward so the obvious attraction to us, since we had made only three diversified acquisitions and had run out of money, was to merge with this source of capital and continue our acquisition program on a more aggressive scale through the use of their capital and tax-loss carry-forward.

The American Woolen merger enabled us to build the world's largest woolen mill in Barnwell, South Carolina, and consolidate all of their operations in that plant. We were then able to get rid of all their high-cost New England plants and stop their $1 million a month losses. As a result of this merger and the use of their surplus cash, loss carry-forward, and losses of millions of dollars on the sale of fixed assets that were later liquidated, Textron was able to continue its unrelated diversification program. Without the American Woolen merger, Textron would never have amounted to anything. It would have been a very small company with three or four diversified operations still primarily in textiles.

*Textron Balance Sheet, January 2, 1954*

| | |
|---|---|
| Cash | $ 4,708,000 |
| Accounts Receivable | 6,511,000 |
| Inventories & prepaid items | 11,879,000 |
| Total Current Assets | 23,098,000 |
| Fixed Assets (Net) | 28,272,000 |
| All Other Assets | 5,485,000 |
| Total Assets | $56,855,000 |

| | |
|---|---:|
| Current Liabilities | $12,754,000 |
| Long-term Debt | 8,664,000 |
| Total Liabilities | $21,418,000 |
| | |
| Total Capital Stock and Surplus | 35,437,000 |
| Total Liabilities and Capital | $56,855,000 |

*American Woolen Company Balance Sheet*
*December 31, 1953*

| | |
|---|---:|
| Cash | $11,782,066 |
| Receivables | 11,714,124 |
| Inventories | 22,043,395 |
| Other Current Assets | 148,192 |
| Total Current Assets | 45,687,777 |
| Fixed Assets (Net) | 25,662,914 |
| All Other Assets | 9,331,429 |
| Total Assets | $80,682,120 |
| | |
| Total Liabilities | 3,148,559 |
| Capital Stock and Surplus | 77,533,561 |
| Total Liabilities and Capital | $80,682,120 |

As you can see from the balance sheets of the two companies, the American Woolen directors could have used their surplus cash to gobble us up. Textron's entire common stock issue was selling for less than $15 million at the time.

*ADVICE: This is an interesting concept since our 470,000 shares of American Woolen would have been extinguished, 100 percent of Textron would have been owned by American Woolen, and there would thereafter have been only 530,000 American Woolen shares in public hands. If you are planning to make a tender offer for some company three times as big as you are, be sure to pick a company whose board of directors isn't smart enough to take advantage of a reverse acquisition of this sort.*

The three-way merger of American Woolen and Robbins Mills into Textron created great interest in the press. Even *Fortune* had an article, "Merger by Judo."

# *Textron, 1955*

On February 24, 1955, American Woolen Company and Robbins Mills, Inc., were merged into Textron Inc., which, as the surviving company, took the name Textron American, Inc.

Consolidated net earnings from January 2, 1955, through December 31, 1955, were $9,497,000 on sale of $189,214,000.

On July 9, 1955, all the outstanding shares of the Homelite Corporation of East Port Chester, Connecticut, were acquired on a part cash and part contingent installment purchase plan. Homelite was one of the country's leading producers of gasoline powered chain saws, generators, and pumps.

On September 30, 1955, we purchased for cash and a ten-year purchase money mortgage all of the assets, subject to liabilities, of Coquille Plywood Company, located in Coquille, Oregon. This company was a low-cost producer of quality Douglas fir plywood.

On September 30, 1955, we also purchased all the stock of Camcar Screw & Manufacturing Corporation of Rockford, Illinois, and certain affiliated companies on a part cash and part contingent installment purchase plan. The Camcar companies were efficient producers of small metal fasteners made primarily by the cold-flow process.

On October 13, 1955, we purchased 100 percent of the outstanding stock of Kordite Corporation of Macedon, New York, on a part fixed price and part contingent installment purchase plan. Kordite was a producer of plastic clothesline, polyethylene bags, freezer supplies, and plastic garment bags.

With the merger of American Woolen completed, Textron was affluent for the first time in its life; and all the surplus cash was burning a hole in my pocket. Between April 15 and October 17, we bought five different companies using $16,680,746, or 80 percent, of the money acquired in the merger in a little over six months. In our rush, I made two bad mistakes and Textron as usual ran out of money. We had to raise $20,000,000 of additional capital in

1956. Homelite and Camcar, however, proved to be among the best acquisitions Textron ever made. The current sales of these two divisions have increased tenfold.

Textron's long-range objective of 20 percent aftertax earnings on common equity had been set, but wasn't achieved until 1967— long after I had retired.

*ADVICE: If you're on an acquisition binge—slow down! Be more careful than I was in checking industry trends, the competition's profit margins, and particularly the management of the company to be acquired. If you're not 100 percent satisfied with the people involved—forget it. Management is the name of the game.*

## AN UNNAMED COMPANY

An unusual situation occurred when Textron bought all the stock of a company that was primarily involved in Air Force business.

The activities were confined to high-priority, classified defense work.

Textron paid $2 million down plus a contingent payout for this business, making approximately $1 million pretax, and again, the company was a leader in a very small industry. The company had a substantial backlog of orders, but immediately after we purchased it, we were alarmed to find that the Air Force would not give us any new business. We approached the buyers at the Air Force but got no satisfaction whatsoever as to why no new business was being awarded.

After a year, all the orders ran out and heavy losses were suffered. Being a highly specialized business with no place to go, we had to liquidate the operation. It was nearly two years later, when one of the partners of the engineering firm Rath and Strong, with whom I discussed the situation, found out from a close friend of his who was a general in the Air Force why the company had been taken off their approved list of vendors. It seems a couple of months prior to our acquisition, someone from the company had given a big dinner for a lot of civilian employees and officers at Wright Field. After dessert he had gone around the table trying to hand out large amounts of cash in plain white envelopes to those who attended the party. Apparently everyone present refused to accept these cash payments but it is now easy to understand why the company was put on the black list.

*ADVICE: When buying a company that is doing business exclusively with any of the services or government agencies, it is imperative that you check in advance as to whether there may be a problem with that company as a future source. It is my opinion that if we had gone directly to the Air Force before making the purchase we would have been advised to stay away from the situation, even though they might not have disclosed all of the details that caused the company to be eliminated.*

*ADDITIONAL ADVICE: When you have a contingent payout such as we had at this company, be sure you have a walkaway provision in the contract if the division loses money in any year. Otherwise you can have a real hassle if things go sour and the former owners insist that you keep the operation going for the full term of the contract.*

## HOMELITE

In 1954, I heard that a company called Homelite, which had originally been in the power-driven generator business to supply light and power to farms and homes in remote areas where utility power was not available, was for sale. This company had been built up from a tiny concern into a big operation during the war because the government needed thousands of two-cycle engine-powered generators. During this period, a very able MIT graduate, Allan Abbott, managed the company for the family that owned it.

When the war was over, he realized that they had a serious problem because of the cancellation of government orders and the consequent lack of business for their tremendously enlarged facilities at East Port Chester, Connecticut. Allan saw an opportunity to develop a power saw, using Homelite's lightweight two-cycle engine to drive the chain. He realized that the days of the big two-man handsaws were over for cutting timber. He was determined to design the finest chain saw in the market. Being a skilled engineer, he developed products that he personally used to cut down dozens of trees before releasing them for the market. His program was a lifesaver for the owners of Homelite, and by 1954 the business was successful.

We heard from G. H. Walker and Company in 1954 that the County Trust Company of White Plains, New York, were acting as agents to sell the business for the owners, who had retired from active management by that time. Allan, who owned no stock himself, did not want to go public with the company. He did not want to

have all the problems of dealing with several thousand public owners. Also, Allan felt that he should be permitted to buy the business from the family, in view of the wonderful job that he had done for them, and County Trust agreed. We were unable to persuade him that the business should be sold to Textron. So, rather than lose this opportunity, we came up with a plan whereby Textron's pension trust, the Sixty Trust, financed the purchase of the business by setting up a new highly leveraged corporation that bought the assets of the old company and permitted Allan Abbott, other key management people, and a few of Allan's friends to acquire a substantial equity position for a nominal investment in relation to the real value of the business.

The company did very well for the next year, and then we proposed to Allan that he sell the business to Textron for a cash down payment plus contingent payout based on future earnings. This idea appealed to him and his key management group. So, as a result of the Sixty Trust intermediary financing, Textron was able to acquire Homelite. It would have been completely impossible for them to have done so originally. The plan was to pay all cash to nonmanagement stockholders. Allan and his employee shareholders were offered half as much cash per share, but to provide an unusual incentive, an additional 25 percent of the pretax earnings over the next ten years—all as capital gain to them. The result was that the Sixty Trust and a few of Allan's friends who had participated in the equity ownership of the company made a substantial cash profit. All the management group took the low cash fixed price with the contingent payout.

After Textron took over, Allan and his management team then had access to almost unlimited capital to expand the business. As a result of Allan's superior engineering know-how and the organization that he built up, the sales soon far exceeded the capacity of the East Port Chester plant, and we built a beautiful new single-story, windowless factory for them in Gastonia, North Carolina, with a saving in labor cost alone of over $900,000 annually. Sales continued to expand, and the new low-cost plant with its highly productive labor enabled Homelite to increase its market share at the expense of industry leader McCullough, whose plant was located at the Los Angeles Airport—an unusually high-cost area in which to operate any business.

The Gastonia plant was soon operating very efficiently with about five hundred workers, averaging twenty-five years of age, and no union. We decided that it would be advisable to build another plant, but in a new location. The second unit was erected at Greer, South Carolina, the same size as Gastonia and far larger than was immediately needed. By that time, we were convinced that we had a real winner in Allan Abbott and Homelite.

The management group were not only motivated by the contingent arrangement, which enabled them to receive substantial payments each year as capital gain, but they were determined to replace McCullough as the industry leader. Although Textron had only $4 million invested in the division when they first took it over, Allan Abbott had done such a fantastic job in expanding the business that after four or five years we had $16 million tied up in divisional net worth. I had made a very serious mistake in not having provided in the contingent payout a more substantial charge for the extra capital than just 6 percent interest. The management group had done such an outstanding job that they were now receiving large contingent payments. They were getting too big a share of the earnings made with our additional capital.

I went to Allan and explained our problem. If we continued the contingent payout on the basis of the contract, it would be very unprofitable for Textron to put up more millions for further expansion of their division and have them receive half the aftertax earnings as contingent payout. To show what an understanding and loyal person Allan Abbott was, he agreed to renegotiate the contract so that the future payments would be limited to a fixed amount to be paid each year for the balance of the contract. If we had not been dealing with a man of his character, this could have been an impossible situation to resolve. As a result of his willingness to cooperate and his continuing drive to build Homelite in spite of the elimination of the contingent plan, Textron put more and more capital into his division, with the result that Allan Abbott, during his active life with Textron, built tiny little Homelite into the world's largest and most profitable producer of power-driven chain saws.

Of all the division presidents who worked for Textron, Allan Abbott was my favorite—a man of intense energy. When I visited plants with him, he always went up two steps at a time and practically ran from department to department. He had the complete loyalty of everyone who worked for him, and there is no question but that Allan Abbott did one of the most outstanding jobs of any division president. One of the many things that impressed me most about him was that after he was well-to-do, he never let up for one minute on the quality of his work or in his determination to make Homelite the best and biggest in the industry. If we had been fortunate enough to have bought ten other companies with management like Allan Abbott, Textron today would be doing $5 billion in sales.

*ADVICE: The mistake that I made of not charging adequately for the additional capital poured into the Homelite Division could have been a disaster for Textron. Textron would have paid the management shareholders many millions of dollars more than they did if Allan Abbott had not been fair-minded and allowed the contract to be rewritten. It is important, therefore, if anybody plans a contingent payout in connection with an acquisition, to provide that the sellers be charged interest at 20 percent per annum for any additional capital the buyer puts into the division before computing contingent payout.*

## CAMCAR

In retrospect, based on our experience in a few cases to be mentioned, it shows how difficult it is to have only lawyers prepare a contract that will not end up with serious differences of interpretation when a joint audit is to be made by the auditors for both parties to determine the price for the buyers and sellers.

As an example, Camcar Screw and Manufacturing Corporation was privately owned by Bob Campbell, Ray Carlson, and Bob's brother who was head of sales. Their principal operations were in Rockford, Illinois, and the company had been very successful in supplying small metal fasteners of various types to the automobile and aircraft industries and to other users of such parts. They showed me their balance sheet with a complete disclosure of net worth as they had computed it in the past, and, of course, we had their sales and earnings for many years to determine the steadiness of their past earnings record. We bought Camcar on October 1, 1955.

The contract was drawn by the lawyers, without our auditors being present, on the basis of determining the net worth under sound accounting principles, but when the joint audit was made at closing both their auditors and ours added $1 million to the net worth figures that had been shown to me. They claimed that the company had been incorrect in the past in writing off over $1 million worth of dies and tools, which both auditors claimed should have been capitalized. While we had assumed the net worth would be as shown to us during negotiations, Textron had to put up $1 million more than we had anticipated.

In spite of this mistake on my part, Camcar has been an excellent acquisition for Textron.

*ADVICE: Never let your lawyers prepare a purchase and sales agreement for an acquisition without having auditors representing both sides present to prevent a misunderstanding of this sort.*

## COQUILLE PLYWOOD COMPANY

The next acquisition that Textron made was Coquille Plywood Company of Coquille, Oregon, on October 3, 1955. The principal stockholder and manager, George Ulett, told me during negotiations why he was willing to sell the company, which was earning $2 million a year before taxes, for $4 million. "Roy," he said, "I've had a rule all my life that any time I can double my money in any deal I'll sell. Our group only put two million dollars into Coquille a few years ago. If Textron buys it for four million dollars, we'll make a hundred percent profit."

This looked to us like a terrific bargain, paying only four times aftertax earnings for a leading producer of plywood, operating in the heart of the Douglas fir country where plenty of raw material was available. At $4 million, this was a steal. How could we go wrong? Well, we managed to find a way.

The Coquille Plywood mill at Coquille, built in 1952, was one of the most modern plywood operations in Oregon. After its purchase in September 1955, Textron acquired two additional plywood plants to round out and diversify the Coquille operations; one in Norway, Oregon, formerly owned by Myrtle Point Veneer Company, located about five miles from Coquille; and the other in Bandon, Oregon, formerly owned by the Bandon Veneer and Plywood Association, located about eighteen miles from Coquille.

With its modern plants and acquisitions, Coquille became the fifth largest producer in the country of Douglas fir plywood, with an annual capacity of over a quarter of a billion square feet. In terms of quality, Coquille was always rated among the industry's top ten.

Before agreeing to the purchase, we asked Arthur D. Little, Inc., to make a survey of the industry to see whether they saw any problems. They noted that the business was highly cyclical since it tied in with the home building industry, which varied materially in the number of housing starts from year to year. They stressed that the greatest danger in the acquisition was Coquille's lack of large reserves of timber to back up their productive capacity with low-cost material. Coquille was dependent on purchases made at the government auctions of Douglas fir from our national forests. In spite of that warning, we went ahead with the acquisition.

The plywood industry suffered a sharp reversal in the middle of 1956, nine months after we bought Coquille. Prices dropped from $88 to $68 per thousand, plants were shut down completely in the months of November and December 1956, and we lost over $1 million that year.

There were two things that we discovered later. There were many small private plants in the northwest that were run as cooperatives. In effect, the workers owned the plants. When business was good and they were making big profits, they would pay themselves tremendous wages. When things got tough, the workers, as the owners, would take far lower wages than our union workers demanded in order to keep the plants running. This was a type of competition we had never experienced in any other industry.

What really convinced us that we were in the wrong business was that shortly after we bought Coquille, Georgia Pacific and U.S. Plywood began acquiring huge tracts of Douglas fir by purchasing the stock of timber companies. As a result, they could put logs into their plywood plants at one-half what it cost us to buy at the government auctions. Both these companies bought enough timber during this period to be protected on all their converting operations on a perpetual yield basis. Another thing we discovered in analyzing their annual reports was that they were paying an average tax rate of only 27 percent against our 50 percent. Companies in the timber business for many years got a special tax break. In processing logs for any purpose, the difference between their cost of timber and the market price, namely the government's auction price, was treated for income tax purposes as capital gain at the then low 25 percent tax rate. Therefore, they were able to operate their plywood and other conversion facilities at cost and still make money. Their 27 percent average tax rate proved there was no way Coquille could show a profit in bad times without owning huge tracts of fir.

Since we had a $6 million investment at Coquille, we had a survey made to determine how much we would have to spend to buy timber holdings sufficient to put our operations on a perpetual yield basis. Based on prices of timber tracts that were available for sale we were amazed to find that it would cost us $64 million to protect our initial investment. At that point we were willing to admit our mistake and sell out.

*ADVICE: When an outside consulting firm warns you about a problem that may develop in an acquisition, you'd better listen! In addition, the plywood business is even more cyclical than textiles, and Coquille certainly wasn't a leader in a small industry.*

## KORDITE

Kordite Corporation was a manufacturer of plastic clotheslines, polyethelene film, and many other products such as bags, shower curtains, and so forth made from film. We purchased the business from the Samuels brothers on October 17, 1955, and everything went fine for a couple of years. Then our principal competitors were gobbled up by Union Carbide and Dow Chemical, both suppliers of polyethelene raw material. With these two giants now completely integrated, I panicked and sold Kordite to our supplier, National Distillers. Howie Samuels left and went into politics—he ran unsuccessfully for governor of New York. The Justice Department soon forced Union Carbide, Dow, and National to divest, so my haste in disposing of Kordite cost Textron shareholders millions of dollars. Kordite today is probably producing $200 million in sales.

*ADVICE: Since the Justice Department will not permit industry mergers with customers, suppliers, or competitors, don't panic the way I did in a simi-*

*lar situation. Wait a while to see what the government does. It may be safe to ride it out.*

# *Textron, 1956*

For the year ending December 29, 1956, consolidated sales and net earnings were $245,794,000 and $6,503,000 respectively. Based upon an average book value of $15.92 per share, we only showed a return of 10.8 percent on the common stock equity.

On February 1, 1956, Textron sold, through a large group of underwriters headed by Blair and Company and Scherck, Richter and Company, $20 million worth of 5 percent convertible subordinated debentures due January 1, 1971. This was an unusually successful offering, which was immediately oversubscribed.

On April 2, we acquired all the stock of General Cement Manufacturing Company of Rockford, Illinois, on a part fixed price and part contingent installment purchase plan. They distributed radio, television, and other electronic parts, tools, liquid cement, and certain chemicals.

On April 2, we also purchased on a part fixed price and part contingent installment purchase plan all the stock of a leading producer of extruded aluminum products, consisting primarily of storm windows, doors, awnings, and siding.

On April 11, we purchased for cash and short term notes all the assets, subject to certain liabilities, of Myrtle Point Veneer Company of Norway, Oregon, and on June 20, for preferred stock, the assets, subject to certain liabilities, of Bandon Veneer and Plywood Association of Bandon, Oregon. Both of these plants were integrated with Coquille Plywood.

On April 20, we acquired for cash, substantially all the assets, subject to certain liabilities, of Campbell, Wyant and Cannon Foundry Company of Muskegon, Michigan. Campbell, Wyant and Cannon was a leading producer of alloy iron and steel castings for the automotive, railroad, agricultural implement, refrigeration, marine, and other industries.

On May 1, we acquired for cash all the stock of Carolina Bagging Company of Henderson, North Carolina, as an addition to the F. Burkart Manufacturing Company Division to supplement its six other plants with an operation in the rapidly growing southeast.

On June 29, we purchased for cash all the assets, subject to liabilities, of Hall-Mack Company of Los Angeles, California, and at the same time we acquired the business of its affiliate, Peat Manufacturing Corporation of Norwalk, California. Hall-Mack manufactures and distributes a distinctive line of bathroom accessories and fixtures.

On July 10, Textron purchased the *S.S. LaGuardia,* which has since been rechristened the *S.S. Leilani.* This is an 18,500 ton, single class, tourist passenger liner with accommodations for about 650 persons. She has been bare boat chartered to Hawaiian Steamship Company, Ltd. on a long term net lease under which all costs and responsibilities of operation are borne by Hawaiian Steamship. Regular sailings between the West Coast and Honolulu started February 5 the following year. Three-quarters of the purchase price and reconstruction costs have been paid for through nonrecourse mortgage notes held or insured by the government.

On August 31, we acquired, on a common stock for assets basis, the business of the Federal Leather Company (now Federal Industries) of Belleville, New Jersey. Federal Industries manufactures vinyl resin-coated fabrics for automotive interiors, as well as for use in railroad cars, planes, and ships, and for luggage, handbags, shoes, furniture upholstery, and wall coverings.

We missed our earnings projection by 40 percent, barged ahead with too many acquisitions, ran short of working capital, and had to cut our dividend—a very erratic performance. I also made several more mistakes.

In 1956 Rupert C. Thompson and G. William Miller joined Textron as officers and added greatly to the strength of management of the company. Each one later became chief executive officer.

## GENERAL CEMENT MANUFACTURING COMPANY

When we purchased General Cement Manufacturing Company of Rockford, Illinois, we got a surprise. We had been shown a balance sheet and sales and profit figures for the previous five years. Again, this was a situation in which the lawyers drew the contract on the basis of paying net worth as the cash down payment, plus a contingent based on future earnings.

The owner had done an excellent job in building this operation from practically nothing. He, his family, and a few friends owned all the shares. It was therefore possible for us to purchase 100 percent of the stock, which would not have been possible had it been publicly owned. The close relationship also made it possible to have a contingent payout since the management owned most of the shares and, therefore, would be motivated to do a good job in the future. Both the $1,943,000 cash down payment and the future contingent payments would be treated as capital gains to the sellers at the 25 percent capital gains tax rate in effect at that time. Capital gains treatment was far more attractive than some plan to pay management bonuses based on future results.

General Cement was a true pioneer in its field. It started in 1929 as a resource for chemical and cements for the infant electronics industry. It manufactured and sold repair parts and accessories for use in radio, television, and industrial electronic repair work. Its products included liquid cement, paints, electronic chemicals, resistors, and antennae, as well as fittings and a comprehensive line of repair tools and kits for television service and installation. Outstanding products were hi-fi speaker kits for rear seats in automobiles and station wagons, as well as servicing tools for color television—an industry first. This highly comprehensive line (which runs into thousands of items) was sold through forty major manufacturers' representatives, who in turn distributed through about two thousand radio, television, hardware, and electronic parts dealers.

A forceful program of merchandising and vigorous trade advertising and selling displays enabled General Cement to keep up with this changing field. Great emphasis was placed on "selling aids" of all types and description to help the distributor. Even in a lagging economy, General Cement could achieve greater sales on service items, primarily because the consumer would be using his television, radio, and other appliances longer and, therefore, would require more service.

After the contracts had been signed, the president said to me, "Roy, you're going to get an unexpected pleasant surprise when your auditors do the joint audit to take over our business and determine the initial down payment."

I said, "How in the world can that be?"

He said, "The way the contract is drawn we must have the auditors determine our net worth based upon the accounting procedures that we had used in the past, which means that instead of valuing our inventories at the lower of cost or market, our inventories will be priced the way I have priced them in the past."

"What possible difference could that make?" I said.

He replied, "Well, Roy, being a small company, we set up substantial inventory reserves—probably five hundred thousand dollars."

"That is just great," I said. "Don't you realize that since we are buying your shares, and our auditors will be taking inventory with your auditors, our auditors will make us at closing write up the inventory to cost or market, and will require us to pay a quarter million dollars in taxes, because of the way you priced your inventories in the past. What you thought was going to be a pleasant surprise for us means that we are going to be stuck with extra taxes."

*ADVICE: Here is another case where if both auditors and both lawyers had been in on the negotiations in drafting the contract, we would have undoubtedly required the seller to accrue the taxes he should have paid, and reduced the purchase price by a quarter of a million dollars. So far as Internal Revenue Service was concerned, they came out better than they would have had General Cement valued inventories at cost or market. The corporate tax rate had gone up in the interim, so that no one but Textron got stuck on that transaction.*

## AN ALUMINUM PRODUCTS COMPANY

The next company we acquired was one which made extrusions from the ingots bought from the basic aluminum suppliers like Alcoa and Reynolds, and also made doors and windows. It had shown a very good earning trend for the last couple of years. The acquisition closing was April 2, 1956.

It was one of the nation's leading producers of aluminum storm doors, prime windows, metal awnings, metal siding, and a variety of accessories of vinyl plastic. The future of aluminum was most promising, and the company was an important supplier for the home building trade. Among the variety of featured products were shower doors, tub enclosures, awnings for residences and for industrial uses, aluminum siding for the construction industry, and frames for windows, doors, and casements. Its activities were fully integrated from extruding aluminum pig to the sale of fabricated aluminum products.

Having been badly burned on the Camcar acquisition where we stated that the net worth should be determined by sound accounting principles by the auditors, we decided this time to solve that problem by having the net worth determined exactly the way the company had determined it in the past.

Again this acquisition involved a $3 million down payment equal to the estimated net worth plus a percentage of future earnings in the next ten years to provide the incentive that had been lacking in the Dalmo Victor acquisition for the management to stay on and work hard. The incentive would be capital gain to owners, since it was a way of determining the purchase price of their shares.

When the audit was finally made, our auditors discovered a half million dollars of accounts payable in the president's right-hand top drawer, which had not been included in the past in determining his net worth. I said, "How in the world can we determine the purchase price without having your payables included to reduce the net worth?"

He said, "Well, Roy, remember the way you drew the contract? You specified the net worth would be determined exactly the way we had done it in the past. I never put our payables on the balance sheet until I paid them, so you are out another half million dollars." And sure enough, he was right. I didn't have a leg to stand on.

Although the company had an excellent past earnings record, after a year or so the profits turned to losses, and we ultimately sold the business back to the former owners. The only reason that they had made large profits previously was because they had an assured supply in a time of shortage. As soon as the aluminum industry built new capacity and overproduced, they could no longer make money since they were in competition with the basic producers, who were selling extrusions to the door and window manufacturers at low prices and giving long terms. The producers were interested primarily in making a profit on their basic aluminum ingot production and were supplying extrusions with no additional profit mark-up on those operations. In addition, since doors and windows could be made by hundreds of small shops requiring very little capital, that end of the business became unprofitable.

*ADVICE: Beware of buying businesses where the basic producer of the raw material is in direct competition with you on your converting operations. When*

*business is bad they will invariably provide that additional processing opera-*
*tion to their customers at cost in order to sell their basic product at a profit.*
    *I also advise you to take a look in the seller's right-hand top drawer before*
*you sign the contract of sale.*


## S.S. LEILANI

In 1956, Textron was approached by a group that had raised $1 million of working capital to take over the operation of the converted troop ship *S.S. LaGuardia* to compete with the Matson Line in the California-Hawaii passenger service. The Maritime Commission would finance most of the reconversion cost and then sell the ship. The new operating company wanted Textron to buy the ship and charter it back to them.

This whole idea had been originated by Tom Cuffe, who was president of the Pacific Far East Steamship Company. He had started with only a quarter of a million dollars capital in 1946 and had done an outstanding management job by building up his net worth to $13 million by the time we were approached to make our investment.

Tom Cuffe's company operated freighters on a government-subsidized basis. The Pacific Far East Steamship Company was therefore not permitted, as a subsidized line, to operate steamships between U.S. ports; that is, they could not carry passengers or freight between the West Coast and Hawaii.

On the other hand, they had the management know-how to be the managers of a privately financed company to operate such a vessel. Money for the proposed Hawaiian Steamship Company was raised by some individuals plus a lot of the suppliers to Pacific Far East Steamship Company. The *LaGuardia* was being rebuilt by the Todd Shipyard Company in New Jersey, and the ship was to be purchased after completion of the conversion by Textron for a $1,-837,000 down payment plus two nonliability mortgages totaling $5,513,000 to the Maritime Commission. Here was a situation where the new operating company needed $1,000,000 for working capital, but could not raise sufficient funds to buy the ship. An outside investor was required to complete the transaction.

The mortgages on the vessel provided that subject to the fulfillment of certain statutory requirements, the sole recourse against Textron was limited to repossession of the vessel. The vessel was

bare boat chartered to Hawaiian Steamship Company, Ltd., for a fifteen-year term at a net rental of $1,320,000 a year.

The net lease that Textron made would have returned over 35 percent after taxes on the original investment, and although this was a departure from our plans to stick to manufacturing operations, it really looked like an opportunity to achieve a better return than our long-range objective of making 20 percent after taxes on our capital, as opposed to the 5 percent that we had been making in the textile business. So we signed up.

The ship had to be taken from New York through the Panama Canal around to San Francisco. The operators decided that instead of running bare boat they would put on a full list of passengers with a lot of publicity, and invite all of the country's newspapers to send their travel editors for a free ride.

The initial trip was a complete disaster. The Todd Shipyard had workmen on the voyage trying to make last-minute adjustments to toilets and other necessary equipment. The refrigeration system for food storage was out of commission. Many passengers and crew were taken off with ptomaine poisoning and put in hospitals in Panama. The editors, who got a free ride, wrote the story exactly like it was! That poor ship, which was about to go into competition with the prestigious Matson Line, never had a chance.

The publicity made it extremely difficult for the company to sell tickets for their future runs between California and Hawaii. Within a year the million dollars of working capital was completely dissipated and Hawaiian Steamship Company was hopelessly in debt.

Pacific Far East Steamship Company, as managers, had no financial responsibility, but they were certain that if Textron were willing to put up some more money the ship could be sold as a going operation and we would get our initial investment back. The alternative was to let the Maritime Commission foreclose and lose $2 million. As usual, I made the wrong decision.

We did attempt to keep the *Leilani* going in Hawaiian Textron, Inc. (a new wholly-owned subsidiary), despite continuing losses, hoping that some other steamship company would bail us out— but that never happened. In December 1957, Hawaiian Textron took over the operation of the *Leilani* from Hawaiian Steamship Company, Ltd., to whom this 650-passenger vessel had previously been chartered. The *Leilani*, one of the largest ships in the Pacific run, was completely upgraded. Its Hawaiianization program included extensive redecorating and betterment of its public rooms and general facilities.

It ran alternately between Hawaii, San Francisco, and Los Angeles, and there was a temporary increase in its popularity with the traveling public and shippers. The *Leilani* was promoted throughout the travel agents fraternity as a "fun ship" with a full and exciting program of activities for adults and children. For those who were budget minded in their travel plans, the *Leilani* offered excellent values in gracious accommodations, cuisine, and comfort. In our desperation to drum up business we even suggested a holiday trip to the Hawaiian Islands on the *Leilani* to our stockholders. Finally, after losing another $6 million on the operation, the ship was turned over to the Maritime Commission and Textron took its loss.

*ADVICE: Here is an excellent case to prove that if an investment goes sour, the first loss is the best loss. If Textron had thrown in the sponge at the time the operating companies could no longer pay the rent, the loss would have been limited to the initial cost of $1,837,617. Because of my persistence in trying to keep the ship afloat, hoping to resell it while it was in operation, we finally lost $8 million. As a result of this disaster, we had a huge picture of the Leilani hung in our main office in Providence. Whenever I was considering a new acquisition, Rupe Thompson and Bill Miller would escort me to the picture and say, "Roy, do you still want to go ahead with this new deal?"*

# Textron, 1957

For the year ending December 28, 1957, consolidated sales amounted to $254,575,000 and net earnings were $8,696,000.

On September 10, the business of California Technical Industries (CTI) of Belmont, California, was acquired by the issuance of 7,410 shares of Textron common, 67 percent of CTI having already been owned by us.

On October 25, 1957, 100 percent of the stock of Accessory Products Corporation, of Whittier, California, was acquired on a contingent installment basis.

On January 24, 1958, but as of December 31, 1957, we acquired on a common stock for assets basis the businesses of the Fanner Manufacturing Company of Cleveland, Ohio.

To divert the stockholders' attention from some of my diastrous acquisitions, I put some pretty charts in that year's report. Actually six divisions lost over $6.7 million. While we had used up $12 million of our loss carry-over, twenty million dollars would expire in 1958, $3.1 million in 1959, and $8.5 million thereafter.

## FANNER MANUFACTURING COMPANY

The Fanner Manufacturing Company of Cleveland, Ohio, was the country's principal producer of chills and chaplets essential to every grey iron foundry's operations. As the leader in a small industry, Fanner certainly qualified as an acquisition for Textron.

The company had been started by the Raible family, who had completely controlled it until the second generation took over. As usually happens in such family-owned concerns when most of the stockholders no longer work for the corporation but are dependent upon it for dividends, dissension ultimately occurs. Those family members who are drawing large salaries don't need additional income in the form of dividends, so the management tends to be parsimonious and retain most of the earnings in the business for future expansion. Resentment develops and ultimately the company goes public so that the nonmanagement shareholders can bail out.

That is exactly what happened at Fanner. All the Raibles except Grief, who was president, sold out through a public offering, with the First Cleveland Corporation heading the underwriting syndicate. Soon afterwards the new board of directors became disenchanted with Grief and fired him even though he still owned 37½ percent of the stock.

Grief Raible was replaced by a professional manager, Tom Butz, who had been with the company for some years. With limited marketability for his shares in this relatively small over-the-counter stock, Grief was looking for a sucker to unload on. Unfortunately, that's where I came in.

Textron exchanged 130,396 shares of its stock for his 325,990 Fanner shares or four-tenths for one. We assumed that we could persuade the several thousand public shareholders to accept the same exchange. No way! Emile Legros, head of the First Cleveland Corporation, was now chairman of Fanner and had complete control of the board. As a relatively small underwriter, he relished the prestige of the chairmanship and its perquisites and he wasn't about to give them up. We were allowed two directors on the board and were assured that we would be very pleased with our fine investment.

Since Textron was an operating company—not a closed-end investment trust—we wanted to acquire 100 percent of Fanner so that it could become a division of Textron. From September 1956 through January 1957, we bought 84,200 shares of Fanner in the over-the-counter market for $972,120 which was an average of $11.55 per share and succeeded in pushing the price way up without gaining control.

After a long period of dickering with Legros, we finally reached an agreement on January 24, 1958, to take over all the assets and liabilities in a tax-free deal for 395,145 of our common shares with a total market value of over $4 million at the time. Legros really made us pay through the nose. His shareholders received much more than Grief did.

If all the Fanner shareholders (including Grief) had held their Textron stock until 1977, it would have been a bonanza for them, as by then it was worth over ten times its value at the time of merger, or $58,000,000 with an annual dividend of $5.60 on each original Textron share received.

*ADVICE: Don't buy a minority position in a company you wish to acquire unless you are prepared for a knockdown, drag out fight and an expensive, unfriendly tender offer.*

*FURTHER ADVICE: If there is any likelihood that an acquisition you want to make may go sour, insist on using cash, not stock, if at all possible. Out of the many different operations that Fanner ultimately had, not a single one has made the grade in Textron. Every one has been sold. However, the 526,541 shares used in the Fanner merger are all still outstanding with no earning power from the acquisition behind them. A company can survive some pretty bad cash mistakes but when stock is used to buy a failure permanent dilution cannot be avoided.*

## AMERICAN SCREW COMPANY

One of the oldest and most respected companies in Rhode Island was the American Screw Company, which was founded over a hundred years ago, and operated in the center of Providence. For many years this company was one of the principal suppliers of screws and other small metal fasteners. They were leaders in this industry, having built up a fine reputation for quality and service. However, the old buildings that they occupied were multistoried with narrow post spacing on all floors, and not really suitable for modern manufacturing procedures. As a result of this inadequate floor space, the company was wise enough to purchase from United Aircraft a plant built by them during the Second World War, to take advantage of the government program known as Certificate of Necessity. Any company that was a large supplier to the government could build modern factory space and charge off the entire cost through depreciation over a five-year period, at a time when excess profit taxes were as high as 95 percent. More and more of American Screw's manufacturing operations were transferred to Willimantic from the older buildings in Providence. Like many of the old, established businesses in Rhode Island with unlisted securities and several thousand shareholders, its stock sold at a very substantial discount from net worth.

In 1960, conservative Rhode Island was shocked to have a New York company, Nomalite, make an unfriendly tender offer for a local company's shares. This was the first time anything of the sort had occurred to a Rhode Island concern. The management was most unhappy and approached Textron to see if we would enter a bid for their shares so that the company could still be controlled in Rhode Island. After long negotiations, we finally made an offer of $50 per share, provided we got 51 percent of the stock.

In the meantime, Nomalite and its president, Sadaca, had already obtained 20 percent of the shares, so it was becoming difficult for us to make much headway. We were unwilling to buy shares in American Screw unless we obtained 51 percent. After realizing we had very little chance to get control, we discovered that Sadaca's shares, listed on the American Stock Exchange, were selling at a very low price. We were amazed to discover that the total market price of his entire capitalization was less than the aggregate price we were offering for American Screw Company.

So I wrote a letter to Sadaca saying that we noticed that if we made an offer to buy all his stock that we could get control of both his company and the American Screw Company at a real bargain price. When Sadaca received that letter, he panicked. He made an arrangement with a group of Canadian banks to lend his company millions of dollars, which he used to buy his own shares, thereby pushing the price up from four dollars to ten dollars. As a result of getting so heavily in debt, Nomalite ended up in serious financial difficulties and ultimately had to dispose of American Screw Company. Many years later, Textron purchased a plant in Virginia formerly operated by American Screw. It is currently a successful part of the Camcar Division.

One of the hilarious things that happened as a result of Textron's participation in this venture was that they ended up achieving the headline of the year in the *Bawl Street Journal* which reprinted the *Willimantic Chronicle*'s famous

"TEXTRON, INC. MAKES OFFER
TO SCREW COMPANY SHAREHOLDERS."

*ADVICE: If you try to purchase a business in a small community, be sure the local newspaper editor has a sense of humor.*

# *Textron, 1958*

When the stockholders, in 1952, authorized a change in business purposes to permit wide diversification into unrelated, non-textile operations, there was general skepticism regarding the ultimate success of the project. Since then a total of twenty-four non-textile companies had been purchased and six had been disposed of. We had seventeen major divisions. Although we had made several errors in our acquisitions, we now had a fine group of wholly-owned companies, all of which contributed to future earnings. It was not until 1958, however, that our basic concept of unrelated diversification had its first real test. The recession year of 1958 confirmed the validity of our theory. Although sales dropped 4 percent to $244,277,000 from 1957's all-time high of $254,575,000, earnings increased 24 percent to $10,756,000 from $8,696,000 in the previous year.

We were far from satisfied with the 15.3 percent pretax return on average common stock book value, but progress was being made toward our long-range objective of 20 percent earnings after taxes on equity. The following charts indicate graphically the results achieved through non-textile diversification:

**PER CENT OF NON-TEXTILE SALES TO TOTAL SALES 1952-1958**

**NET EARNINGS, 1952-1958**

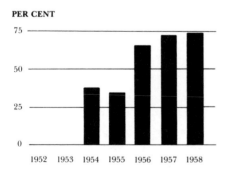

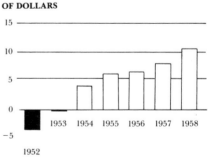

On June 28, 1958, we acquired for $7,135,000 cash all the assets, liabilities, and business of the Waterbury Farrel Foundry and Machine Company. Waterbury's average pretax earnings for the past ten years had been $1,400,000. This business was a valuable addition to our operations.

On August 1, 1958, we sold the assets and business of Kordite, our polyethylene converting company. With the industry trend toward complete integration, we were faced with the alternatives of a substantial investment for production of required raw materials or a profit squeeze from existing integrated competition. We chose instead to sell Kordite to our principal raw material supplier, National Distillers and Chemical Corporation.

On September 26, 1958, we purchased Shuron Optical Company for $5,511,000 cash.

On October 31, 1958, we took over the business of Precision Methods and Machines, Inc., for 65,027 shares of our common stock. This company had been a consistent earner and closely supplemented the operations of our Waterbury Farrel Foundry and Machine Company.

By 1958, I admitted my bad batting average: six mistakes out of twenty-four acquisitions. But I was still boasting about the basic concept of unrelated diversification and put in a neat seven-year chart to prove it.

# Textron, 1959

In each of the last seven years both total earnings and earnings per share of common stock increased over the previous year. In 1959, sales were $308 million (excluding Textron Electronics) compared with $244 million in 1958. Earnings of $16,643,000 showed an increase of 55 percent over the $10,756,000 earnings of the previous year.

Joe Collinson (currently the chief executive officer of Textron), formerly a partner of Arthur Young and Company (certified public accountants), was elected vice president and treasurer, and Bill Miller was elected vice president and assistant to the president,

Rupe Thompson. There were only seventy persons employed in the company's corporate office with overhead cost representing less than ½ percent of sales. The rest of the twenty-one thousand employees were employed at the divisions.

I was still gung-ho for acquisitions. On March 16, we acquired 88 percent of the stock of Nuclear Metals, Inc. This company operated metallurgic research and prototype manufacturing operations in Concord, Massachusetts, for the Atomic Energy Commission and industrial companies that were primarily in the field of atomic energy fuel elements and special metals and materials.

On March 23, 226,000 shares of the Townsend Company were acquired and subsequently an additional 36,000 shares were purchased, bringing Textron's holdings to 99 percent of the outstanding stock. Townsend Company operated seven plants in various parts of the country and one in Canada. It produced metal fasteners, rivets, ball studs, and stampings.

All the assets, subject to liabilities, of the Pittsburgh Steel Foundry Corporation were purchased on May 29. This company produced steel castings for valve manufacturers, railroads, and heavy equipment producers. In addition, it designed and built special heavy machinery and equipment for basic metal industries.

On June 18, the net assets and business of the Randall Company were purchased. Randall supplied the automotive industry with special parts and interior metal trim. Its Wagner Manufacturing Division produced and distributed cast iron and aluminum cooking utensils under the Wagner and Magnalite trade names.

The business of Amsler Morton was purchased on November 11. It designed and installed furnaces, soaking pits, and related equipment for the basic steel industry. This company complemented our Pittsburgh Steel Foundry operation.

On January 29, 1960, we purchased all the outstanding shares of Terry Industries Limited of Canada. Terry manufactured and distributed products of our Homelite Division in Canada.

All of these companies cost Textron $21,679,000—quite a spending spree for one year!

By the fall of 1959, I realized some of our loss carry-forward was going down the drain. I decided to sell three profitable divisions to a newly created subsidiary at a substantial profit thereby using up the expiring loss carry-forward and increasing the depreciable base for future tax savings.

Everyone except Bill deWind of Paul, Weiss in New York City

said it couldn't be done. The tax law said, "No loss could be taken selling to a sub"—nothing about making a profit, so it stood up. That minor loophole was closed in the 1976 tax law.

## AN ALMOST ACQUISITION

When my children were young we had a place on Rose Island in the Bahamas. It was very isolated, about ten miles from Nassau by boat. All our food, mail, and other supplies had to come to our place on the beach in our small boat called the *White Gull*.

The swimming was fantastic—beautiful beaches and clear water without any heavy surf. In front of our house were many coral reefs with fish of amazing color—possibly as many as one hundred different species of small fish with varying hues.

My son Arthur, who was then eight, and I began to do some snorkeling, and he was fascinated by this new sport. Then we met Stan Waterman, whose boat *Zingaro* was equipped with aqualungs, masks, swim fins, spears, and so forth. We used to take lunches everyday and Stan would take us abroad and go out to see coral gardens that nobody had ever visited before. The amazing thing was that in these areas where the fish had never been speared, they showed no fear whatsoever of us as we swam around amongst them. Many times the fish would swim by within inches of our masks. We actually found that after they got used to us they would swim up and take food right out of our fingers. As a result, my son and I both became so fascinated with this new experience that Arthur was provided with a small aqualung and soon became expert, even at age eight, in diving with us. We later began to take underwater movies, since Stan had a globelike watertight device into which the fifty-foot magazine movie camera could be placed and protected from moisture while it took pictures. With this case, it was possible to start and stop the camera and change the exposure and distance setting on the lenses. Stan was one of the most graceful underwater swimmers that I have ever seen, and I took a lot of footage of him spearing groupers, lobsters, and other edible seafood. I once got a picture of him pulling a ten-foot shark by the tail out of a coral cave in which it was hidden. To my amazement, Stan didn't get bitten. Another time, a huge manta ray swam by with Stan and me in close pursuit, but it was so large that although Stan hit it twice with powerful spears the ray just swam away without being stopped. Stan later gave up his regular business and, like John Jay who for years made and showed marvelous ski movies, Stan did the same with underwater pictures and was in great demand at clubs throughout the country. He and his family spent one whole year in Tahiti and came back with fabulous underwater movies. He later did much more professional work and was one of the producers of the movie *Blue Water, White Death.* Stan's influence on my son and me was very great; Arthur, now an expert diver, often goes down to depths of 150 feet or more in the Bahamas.

I became convinced that snorkeling and aqualunging would become great sports in the States, and that Textron should try to buy the leading company that produced the equipment and become an important factor in this leisure sport activity.

The leading company in this field manufactured diaphragms, tanks, fins, masks and all equipment required for aqualunging. This company was controlled by a Frenchman, who was in a position to market all of these products throughout the United States.

When I visited the owner, he allowed as how he might be willing to be taken over by Textron. When I asked him for a balance sheet and earnings statement, he showed me pretax earnings for the prior year of only $250,000, which was quite a low percentage of profit on sales. I explained to him that since we were buying for cash we could not afford to pay over $1 million for his company, which would be eight times aftertax earnings. That was the basis on which we were acquiring many other businesses.

He said, "Mr. Little, that price is ridiculous. When you own this business you will have far greater earnings than I am showing." I said, "How so?" He said, "For example, my sister lives in Paris and she is technically our European sales agent. I pay her $50,000, which she turns over to my Paris bank account, so that raises the earnings which you would get to $300,000." I said, "Will we have to continue that arrangement if we buy the business?" He replied,

"Of course not, she doesn't do any work. That is just the way that I divert profits over to my French account." At that point, I said, "And what else?" "Well, Mr. Little, I have a Swiss bank account and that bank holds some patents that I own, and the American company pays to my Swiss account $50,000 a year in royalties for the use of those patents." I said, "Well, I suppose we will have to continue to pay royalties on those patents." "Oh, no. Those patents are really worthless. This is just another way that I transfer funds from the United States to my credit in Europe." I said, "Then you claim that your pretax earnings will be $350,000 if we take the company over, so we should pay you $1.4 million instead of $1 million for your business." "Oh, no, Mr. Little. This is just the beginning. We operate only five days a week. Every Saturday morning I pull up in a small truck at the plant when nobody is around, and I take out $5,000 worth of our finished products and sell them for cash, keeping the money myself. That means that there is another $250,000, or a total of $600,000 pretax, $300,000 after taxes; eight times that is $2,400,000." I was amazed by this disclosure, and said, "Don't you realize that in this country there are informers who turn people like you in to Internal Revenue and collect a fee for so doing? You are in great jeopardy of not only ending up owing more taxes but also a good chance of going to jail," to which he replied, "Mr. Little, that is outrageous. In France, everyone does things like this."

*ADVICE: When someone admits tax frauds of this sort, the only way to handle the situation is to require both the individual and the corporation to file amended tax returns for all the years involved, and pay all back taxes due over a ten-year period. Needless to say, Textron didn't buy this one.*

# Textron, 1960

Based on its annual rate of sales for 1960, Textron ranked among *Fortune*'s one hundred largest U.S. industrial corporations. By 1977, a company with only $450 million in sales would have ranked only 427th. Textron employees numbered twenty-nine thousand; Textron plants, ninety, in twenty-one states and Canada; and Textron securityholders, fifty thousand. Quite a change from the three employees, one plant, and three stockholders at Special Yarns in 1923!

Rupe Thompson was now chairman and chief executive officer, and Bill Miller was president. Two years before I retired, I had turned over the chief executive position to Rupe Thompson and had become chairman of the executive committee—a plan I recommend for all companies.

On May 13, Textron purchased the Weinbrenner Shoes Company of Milwaukee, Wisconsin, which manufactured work shoes and other special footwear, including official Boy Scout shoes.

On June 10, Dorsett Marine was acquired, and on September 16, E-Z-Go Car was acquired. Dorsett was a leading designer and manufacturer of fiberglass pleasure boats, and E-Z-Go produced electric golf carts.

On July 1, Textron made its most important acquisition of all times. It bought all of the defense operations of Bell Aircraft Corporation, which had total sales of $100 million, and got in the helicopter business. *Forbes Magazine* (May 1, 1960) reported this acquisition:

Chairman Royal Little of Textron Inc. has long practiced the corporate art of diversification as another man might play poker—picking up and discarding cards, thriving in an atmosphere of risk. Since 1952 Little has bought 26 companies, sold all or substantial parts of 5 major operations plus a flock of little plants. All in all, he has been on balance a winner. From an unprofitable textile operation, he has parlayed the pot he controls in Textron into a profitable and widely diversified industrial enterprise.

HORNSWOGGLED? Last month, Little once more sat down to play his favorite game—this time with a man famed as a shrewd poker player in his own right: President David M. Milton of Equity Corp. When he emerged, it was with a deal that left Wall Street visibly wondering whether Little had finally lost his old sure touch. The deal: an agreement to buy from Equity Corp.-controlled Bell Aircraft the biggest part of its business, a group of companies doing defense work. The price: full book value, or around $32 million. The $32-million question with which Wall Street was instantly abuzz: whether for once veteran trader Royal Little had not been slickly hornswoggled.

In September 1960, Textron financed Photek, Inc., to enter the office copying and equipment field, utilizing secret chemical processes for photocopy and thermocopy papers, permitting its president to acquire a 20 percent stake. A similar arrangement was made with management to enter the pharmaceutical business.

Textron Pharmaceutical, Inc., was organized late in 1960 as a means of entering the ethical and proprietary drug fields, initially through acquisition of existing companies. Again, the president bought 20 percent.

In 1960, shareholders approved an employees stock savings plan under which shares of Textron common stock were purchased in the open market. Eligible employees could contribute up to 10 percent of base salary. The company contributed an amount equal to one-half of participants' payments. The purpose of the plan was to assist employees in obtaining a proprietary interest in Textron, thereby gaining an added incentive for profitable operations. This plan became so popular that nearly 20 percent of the company's common shares are currently owned by it.

Although I was no longer chief executive officer, I continued to work on acquisitions. I had four disasters that year: Weinbrenner Shoes, Dorsett Marine, Photek, Inc., and Textron Pharmaceutical, Inc. Little E-Z-Go Car's sales, however, are currently forty times original volume. Our all-time best acquisition, Bell Aircraft, was made that year and has frequently earned more after taxes in a year than its entire cost. Even a blind pig occasionally picks up an acorn!

## DORSETT MARINE

After World War II the use of fiberglass material became most effective for construction of small sail and power boats. Since we in Textron were interested in acquiring one of the leading companies in this relatively small industry so as to participate in the leisure market, we found a company in California called Dorsett Marine. It had an excellent record, so we seriously considered buying it. Before doing so, however, we checked other leading companies in the industry and found Glasspar Company had an excellent record, with constantly increasing sales and earnings. Sales jumped from $6.5 million in 1958 to $11.8 million in 1959. The stock was a spectacular winner, going from $.50 when offered in 1954 to a high of $9.50 in 1958, and to $25.00 in 1959—all adjusted for a two-for-one split in the latter year. Glasspar had too high a multiple to be readily available for acquisition.

Dorsett, however, was owned by a couple of young men who had

started the company and had built it up to its present size. They were young enough so that we felt they would wish to continue to work hard even after selling out to Textron. We finally made one of the few early acquisitions in which Textron used common stock. I can recall that one of our directors was somewhat worried about the industry, saying that it had been overexpanded and that there were too many small builders in it. He thought that we should wait another six months before committing ourselves. As usual, however, I insisted on going ahead right away. Our timing could not have been worse. The acquisition was made June 10, 1960, and by that summer there was such an overproduction of boats that Dorsett never made substantial profits again.

In desperation, to create a new product we built boats without outboard motors into which they put high pressure pumps that forced out strong jets of water behind the boat just above the waterline. The force of this water jet moved the boat forward rapidly. This type of propulsion had many advantages: it was relatively quiet, and it could navigate in very shallow water as there was no propeller down behind the boat. For a while, it appeared as though this new device was going to save our investment in Dorsett. Unfortunately, the whole idea of the water-jet boat was never widely accepted by the boating public, even though it had the advantage of eliminating the exhaust odor involved in high-speed two-cycle marine engines. We finally threw in the sponge after losing a couple of million dollars. As I recall, we sold the business back to the former owners.

ADVICE: Don't be in a rush to close an acquisition in a rapidly expanding field—perhaps too many people are getting into the business, with resulting overproduction. Also beware when hundreds of small shops enter a new field, *as they did with fiberglass boats. If I had listened to our cautious director, we would have proceeded more slowly, discovered the overproduction and market collapse, avoided this bad mistake, and saved $2 million.*

## PHOTEK

Having missed the purchase of Apeco (a copy-paper business we almost bought) feeling that the price was too high, we decided to start a company in the wet process copy-paper field in competition with Apeco and 3-M (bear in mind that this was prior to Xerox and their superior dry process system). Also remember that prior to the development of paper copying systems, the old method of making copies required multiple carbon paper inserts between sheets of paper. This was very cumbersome and soon became obsolete when the original wet copy paper systems were evolved.

We found an inventor who had developed a process that appeared to produce a product superior to that of either Apeco or 3-M. We set up a subsidiary named Photek, Inc., in which Textron owned 80 percent of the common stock, and the manager was permitted to buy 20 percent for $50,000. We also agreed to lend the company at least $1,000,000 in subordinated loans so as not to reduce management's equity position when additional capital was required.

After many tests and sample runs we were convinced that we had a winner, so we built a plant especially for this process near the Kingston, Rhode Island, railroad station and also near the University of Rhode Island where it would be possible to get scientific assistance. The finished product from the plant proved to be very acceptable. The problem, however, was that the inventor was not satisfied with the product he was making, although it was completely salable. He was always experimenting with improvements rather than turning out substantial tonnage of satisfactory material to the trade. Before we finally threw in the sponge on this one, Textron lost a couple of million dollars.

Rupe and Bill were smart enough to get rid of my $2 million Photek mistake before it became a disaster.

*ADVICE: Don't ever make an inventor president of the company you are financing unless his name is Land. Very rarely will it be successful. The inventor will constantly be experimenting with possible improvements of the product*

*rather than settling upon a formula and producing big tonnage for an estab-
lished market.*

## TEXTRON PHARMACEUTICAL

At Textron, we felt that it would be advisable to get into the pharmaceutical business since a study of the industry indicated that the
return on sales and return on capital in the well-managed companies far exceeded that of most other manufacturing businesses.
With the low multiple on Textron stock, however, there was no opportunity for us to acquire an important company in that field.

We therefore decided to start small and try to build up a pharmaceutical company of our own. To accomplish this, we hired an
able young man, Bob Grant, from Plough and, again, set him up
with a 20 percent equity interest costing him $50,000 in a subsidi-
ary that Textron would finance with subordinated loans while retaining 80 percent of the equity itself. In this way, Bob was
protected against dilution of his equity position. Our plan was to
pick up several small pharmaceutical companies for cash, most of
them privately owned, and then, with Textron's financial strength,
to build up a really big pharmaceutical operation in our subsidiary
called Textron Pharmaceutical, Inc.

Again, this plan of establishing Textron in a high multiple business, hoping that if we were unusually successful the market place
would give Textron itself a higher multiple because of the pharmaceutical activities, failed. This attempt to enter a new market
was unsuccessful, and before we stopped this program it had cost
Textron well over $2 million, with practically no recovery on its
investment. Incidentally, Bob Grant is now head of American Bak-
eries and is doing an excellent job.

*ADVICE: If your company's shares are selling at a low multiple, there is no
way you can become an important factor in a high multiple business because
you cannot use shares for an acquisition. At the present time, many of the top
drug companies are selling with multiples of 13 to 18. Also, if one attempted
to purchase a big drug company for cash, the price would have to be substantially over current multiples—possibly as high as 20 times earnings. Even if
one could borrow long-term money at 10 percent for such an acquisition, the
earnings of the acquired company would not even cover the total interest cost.*

# *Textron, 1961*

Nineteen sixty-one's annual report was signed by George William Miller, president, and Rupert C. Thompson, Jr., chairman of the board.

During 1961, Textron continued its expansion, notwithstanding the retarding effects of the recession during the first half of the year. Sales for the year rose to $473 million, an increase of 23 percent from the previous year's volume of $383 million. Net earnings for the year were $10.5 million, compared with $14.1 million in 1960. Earnings per share of outstanding stock in 1961 were $2.06, compared with $2.93 the previous year. This was our first drop in earnings since starting diversification and came as quite a shock.

In each of the previous two years, Textron had the benefit of certain credits that reduced the amount of federal income taxes. Some credit would remain available to subsidiary companies in 1962. Textron's effective consolidated federal tax rate, which was approximately 27 percent in 1961, was expected to be about 40 percent in 1962. We anticipated that the full corporate rate would be applicable to 1963 earnings. The tax benefits from the American Woolen merger were vanishing fast. We would soon be like everyone else—paying full taxes.

In January 1961, Textron purchased Modern Optics of Houston, Texas, a producer of multifocal lenses. Modern's production was moved into the new Shuron plant in South Carolina.

Textron became a supplier to the gas utility industry with the acquisition in April of Sprague Meter Company of Bridgeport, Connecticut, for cash. Sprague was a leading manufacturer of gas meters and regulators, and also produced a line of marine fittings.

To broaden further its earnings base and to enter the promising agrochemical field, Textron, in July, made one of its principal acquisitions: Spencer Kellogg and Sons, Inc., an old and established Buffalo company, was acquired in exchange for 1,038,718 shares of Textron common stock, of which 771,885 shares were purchased at

SCHOCHET

$28 a share from its shareholders through an invitation for tenders, and the balance of 266,833 shares from treasury stock previously purchased at lower prices. This plan was a neat way for Textron to avoid dilution while giving selling shareholders a tax-free deal.

At the end of September, a second supplier to the public utility field, M. B. Skinner Company of South Bend, Indiana, a producer of clamps and service fittings for gas and water utilities, was acquired for cash.

In December, Tubular Rivet and Stud Company of Wollaston, Massachusetts, which manufactured tubular rivets and rivet-setting machines, was purchased in a cash transaction to round out the product line of our Townsend Company.

With sales running at an annual rate in excess of $550 million, Textron had attained a base sufficient to produce a creditable return on its shareholders' equity. Energies, therefore, were being directed toward the further refinement of existing operations, with emphasis on improvement of profit margins.

The book value of the net assets of Spencer Kellogg and Sons, Inc., at date of acquisition exceeded the market value of the Tex-

Hoo-BOY!

I RETIRED AND NOBODY KNOWS THE DIFFERENCE—

9-24

BRICKMAN

Washington Star Syndicate, Inc.

tron common stock issued therefor. The balance of $6,858,960 was being taken into income ratably over a period of ten years from date of acquisition—the opposite of goodwill write-off.

This handling of excess value over cost (so-called negative goodwill) that was possible in 1961 can no longer be done. The effect of this practice was that it was a method of offsetting goodwill resulting from excess cost of assets acquired.

On December 30, 1961, subsidiaries of Textron, Inc., had unused federal income tax loss carryovers of approximately $6 million that were available to offset taxable income in future years.

By this time, the tax losses acquired from the American Woolen-Robbins merger had been largely used up and the company now would begin to pay a higher tax rate on its earnings in future years. Since the merger, the use of these tax savings had added $43 million to Textron's cash flow—not bad for an amateur tax expert.

Nineteen sixty-one's annual report stated: "Effective January 1, 1962, Textron's founder, Royal Little, who became 65 on March 1, 1961, retired as a Director and Chairman of the Executive Committee. This action was at his own wish as expressed when he resigned as Chairman of the Board and Chief Executive Officer in July 1960. At that time he announced he would leave the board at the end of 1961."

Retiring from Textron's board was one of the smartest things I ever did. I had complete confidence in both Rupe Thompson and Bill Miller, whom I had picked to succeed me. They did a fabulous job in building the company to a $3 billion operation after I left, without any interference from me.

## BROWN AND BIGELOW

One of the companies that Textron hoped to buy was Brown and Bigelow, of St. Paul, Minnesota. As was basic to our long-range concept of buying leading companies in relatively small industries, Brown and Bigelow was a perfect fit. They were the country's leading producer of business calendars and gifts for business purposes. The company had been established many years before by the Brown and Bigelow families and had been built up to a very substantial, profitable operation. The president of the company, Charlie Ward, had been in some kind of trouble many years before and ended up in Leavenworth. When he was in prison he came to know one of the original family members from the company. When Charlie was released he was offered a job at Brown and Bigelow. He moved ahead very rapidly in the organization, building the business up from $1 million a year in sales when he first joined it, to over $50 million in sales with excellent profits at the time we were negotiating the merger.

I came to admire Charlie very much because, in addition to running the company successfully, he had spent a great deal of time over the prior years in helping rehabilitate people who had been in jail and finding important new jobs for them in business. He worked with groups all over the country and spent time talking to businessmen about helping with his project. He had contacts with the wardens in all of the principal prisons and got recommendations from them as to which people, when they were released, would be most likely to adapt and become successful citizens again.

The approach to acquire Brown and Bigelow was made some years after the Tobey hearings, when Textron and I had received quite a lot of adverse publicity. Charlie knew about this situation and, when I explained what had happened, was still willing to proceed with the proposed merger. After some weeks of negotiations with the auditors and lawyers, we prepared a final merger plan that was to be presented to our respective boards for approval.

Just before our meeting, Charlie said, "Roy, I think it is only fair for me to tell you that as a result of what I have done all over the country in rehabilitating people who have been in prison, there are several others besides myself in Brown and Bigelow who have had this unfortunate experience. I can assure you that they are all first-class and doing a terrific job. You've got nothing to worry about."

I said, "Charlie, I certainly appreciate your being frank about this situation, and with your permission I will explain this to our board and ask them for approval of our plan."

He said, "Roy, I think you must explain this because I wouldn't want them to hear about it indirectly. I want it to come straight from me."

When I took the merger proposal to the board, I got an enthusiastic response, and even when I explained to them what Charlie had told me, they still backed me up and voted to go ahead. However, when Charlie took the proposal to his board, he was turned down. They didn't want to be associated with me.

*ADVICE: If you are ever the subject of a Senate investigation and have received a lot of unfavorable publicity nationwide, don't expect everybody to want to merge their company with yours.*

# *Other Mistakes*

## *HOMELITE FOUR-CYCLE ENGINE*

In those days the only other well-known outboard motor company was Champion. Allan Abbott spent some time with them and tested some of their motors but decided against buying the company which, incidentally, had a negative net worth at the time.

A lightweight four-cycle engine was originally developed for the small Crossley car, which was to have been made right after World War II. Somehow or other the engine got to Twin Coach where its development was carried on further by Lou Fageol. Finally Twin Coach decided they couldn't handle it, so Lou Fageol and a partner, Crofton, took it over and carried on the development.

Lon Casler somehow heard of Lou Fageol and got enthused about their engine. In addition to the four-cycle outboard, Lou apparently had a design for an inboard-outboard motor and may have had a patent; and, of course, Homelite made a deal that involved a purchase and some royalties. This was done at my insistence with Allan Abbott objecting and predicting failure—but I was determined to get into outboards. Later there was some litigation between Lou Fageol and Twin Coach. Twin Coach contended that Fageol and Crofton had made an inside deal and the result of the litigation was that the royalties we paid went in part to Fageol and Crofton and in part to Twin Coach. Incidentally, Lon Casler was Textron's acquistion vice-president and a tower of strength to me.

The lightweight four-cycle outboard engine had many advantages: it was much quieter than two-cycle engines, it eliminated the regular outboard's exhaust problem (it wasn't "a stink pot"), and the engine could be run efficiently at any speed. The owners loved them but it cost so much more than the two-cycle engine that its market was very limited.

This deal was made in 1957, but after about three years, Homelite concluded the project should be killed. But I decided that Homelite should continue—at least for another year—which again was against their better judgment. Among our reasons for asking Homelite to continue was the fact that the engine had been featured on the cover of Textron's annual report. How's that for an excuse to continue a loser?

When we all agreed to let Homelite abandon the outboard business, Dick Fisher, who was the founder and principal owner of the Boston Whaler Company, was reluctant to see the engine go out of production, so he formed a new company, which bought it for some cash and some notes.

So the Homelite four-cycle engine was a hell of a development, which lost a lot of money for a lot of people. Allan Abbott tells me it cost Textron at least $5 million.

*ADVICE: Don't force a division president to take on a product that he's not sold on. He will undoubtedly know more of its potential than you ever will.*

## RAEFORD MILL

Another example of the sort of problem that develops in the purchase and sale of a business occurred when Burlington Mills wished to buy our Raeford Mill in North Carolina. The Raeford Mill, which was one of the units in the Robbins group, was a very modern plant making synthetic blended and worsted fabrics, which were sold to garment manufacturers. It became part of Textron when we merged with American Woolen and Robbins Mills.

The transaction was worked out between Spencer Love of Burlington Mills and myself, with lawyers representing both companies present. The deal was a fixed price for the fixed assets, with inventories to be priced under standard accounting principles by a joint audit at closing. When the closing took place, the auditors came up $1 million apart on the valuation of the inventory.

Spencer phoned me and said, "Roy, we're not going to pay your price for the inventories."

I said, "Why not? Those inventories are valued at the lower cost or market and we insist on being paid that price."

Spencer then said, "Roy, we have always carried our inventories at raw material and labor cost only, with no factory burden. In Textron you price at raw material, labor, and factory burden. At Raeford you have a million dollars of factory burden involved in your inventory cost. If we should buy the inventory on the basis of your cost, we would immediately have to write off a million-dollar loss the day after we purchase it so as to standardize our inventory valuation procedures. We just can't afford to do that." As a result we had to compromise the situation and lose $500,000, which we had not anticipated, on the sale.

*ADVICE: If Spencer and I had required both auditors to be present with the lawyers when we negotiated this deal we would have avoided this unpleasant situation. When you are working on an acquisition be sure to have both the auditors and lawyers attend the meetings.*

## TEXTRON VS. BURLINGTON

Spencer Love and I were good friends and often discussed our future hopes and goals. He had started a small rayon weaving plant in Burlington, North Carolina, on a shoestring in 1923, the same year that Special Yarns began operations. In 1953, when I told Spencer about plans for unrelated diversification, he, like most everyone else at that time, thought I was crazy.

He told me that his goal at Burlington Mills was to diversify completely within the textile industry and to build the world's largest and most profitable company in that field. One day he said to me: "Roy, let's get together every year when our figures are available and compare notes." "Spencer," I said, "that's a great idea. Perhaps I can someday convince you that the textile business can't make a fair return on its equity." Spencer said, "Roy, Burlington will beat Textron. I still think your idea is crazy. Nobody has ever done it. You can't possibly manage thirty different kinds of businesses that you've had no experience in." To which I replied, "We'll see, Spencer."

We did compare results for years, but unfortunately, Spencer dropped dead playing tennis some years ago. Here are the results of our comparisons through 1977:

*% Return on Net Worth*
Based on income before preferred dividends

| Year | Textron | Burlington Mills |
|------|---------|------------------|
| 1954 | 1.8% | 5.6% |
| 1955 | 6.9 | 9.2 |
| 1956 | 8.9 | 10.3 |
| 1957 | 11.0 | 7.4 |
| 1958 | 12.3 | 4.6 |
| 1959 | 15.7 | 10.0 |
| 1960 | 12.0 | 10.8 |
| 1961 | 8.6 | 6.4 |
| 1962 | 11.3 | 10.0 |
| 1963 | 12.6 | 10.5 |
| 1964 | 13.9 | 12.5 |
| 1965 | 16.7 | 13.6 |
| 1966 | 21.0 | 15.1 |
| 1967 | 20.4 | 10.4 |
| 1968 | 16.7 | 13.1 |
| 1969 | 16.0 | 11.8 |
| 1970 | 13.5 | 9.9 |
| 1971 | 12.5 | 5.4 |
| 1972 | 14.8 | 6.5 |
| 1973 | 15.6 | 10.3 |
| 1974 | 15.3 | 11.6 |
| 1975 | 13.2 | 4.5 |
| 1976 | 18.2 | 11.2 |
| 1977 | 16.4 | 9.0 |
| 1978 | 18.1 | 6.9 |

I'm sorry that Spencer couldn't have lived to see that our system of diversification was far better than his. After 1956, he never came close.

## DEERING MILLIKEN COMPANY

The next transaction involving a problem of this type occurred in 1963 when Textron sold all of its remaining textile operations to Roger Milliken of Deering Milliken Company. He agreed to pay the full book value of fixed assets and inventories at closing, which amounted to approximately $45 million.

Because of the experience we had with Spencer Love, we checked in advance and found that there was no difference in the accounting procedures so far as inventory valuation was concerned. However, neither of us thought of the fact that South Carolina operated on the merit system in their unemployment compensation program. Textron, because of the steadiness of all its operations, had built up hundreds of thousands of dollars of credit in the state unemployment compensation fund, and since Textron had a new Shuron Optical plant in Barnwell, South Carolina, and another new plant for its Homelite division at Greer, South Carolina, we felt those credits should remain with Textron to benefit the employees of the two remaining operations. However, when it came time to close, even though this matter had not been discussed and had not been thought of by Deering Milliken, Roger Milliken refused to make final payment on the transaction until this matter was compromised. It was finally settled at a cost of several hundred thousand dollars to Textron.

*ADVICE: Here was a case where even the auditors and lawyers didn't think of the problem in advance. Well, you can't win 'em all!*

# Lost Opportunities

In addition to losing money for Textron through mistakes, I lost millions for the shareholders by not paying the asking price on several most attractive acquisitions. There must have been at least a dozen cases where the seller and I were a few hundred thousand dollars apart, where I would not budge and refused to meet the seller's price.

## TOM HUSTON

One of those I recall was the Tom Huston Company of Columbus, Georgia, a peanut butter manufacturer with an excellent distributing organization, who felt that they needed to be taken over by a company that was strong financially in order to be able to expand their production and market more rapidly than they could on their own. I can remember meeting with the owners in Columbus. We apparently could not get together on price so this company, which could have been built into one of the leading consumer product divisions of Textron, was lost forever. It was later purchased by General Mills.

## TUPPERWARE

One of the most interesting opportunities I had was that of purchasing the Tupperware Company from Earl Tupper, its founder. His original plant was in Milford, Massachusetts, but as his success through the introduction of the "Tupper Party" method of sales built up his volume, he needed large additional manufacturing facilities. He took over our old Blackstone Mill, which had formerly been part of Lonsdale, and put in injection molding equipment to make the products that his sales organization was distributing so successfully all over the country. He indicated an interest in becoming a part of Textron, so I offered him $10 million for the entire business. Again, we were far too conservative. Dart Industries made him a better offer. Again here was an opportunity that Textron lost by being too chintzy on price. If Tupperware had been purchased by Textron at that time, it certainly would be one of their most important consumer product divisions now. Tupperware sales last year were reputed to be $500 million with pretax earnings of over $100 million.

## JOSTEN

The outstanding case of where I got stubborn and would not meet the offering price concerned Josten. Josten was a competitor of Balfour in making rings for students in schools and colleges. Balfour originally was the leader in this industry, but Josten now far exceeds them in volume and profits. The offering price was $13,-000,000, and I finally came up to $12,500,000 but wouldn't go the last half million dollars. As a result of this lost opportunity, this mistake on my part undoubtedly cost the Textron stockholders over $30,000,000 in lost values. Dan Gainey, who controlled the company and was at the time treasurer of the Republican Party, then made a public offering. In 1976, sales were $163,700,000, net profit after taxes $9,525,600, net worth was $43,000,000, and their 5,040,000 common shares at $25 had an aggregate market value of $126,000,000.

Josten would have been an ideal acquisition for Textron since it fitted our basic concept of being a leader in a relatively small industry. Today Josten is the undisputed leader in the school ring business, and their performance is so superb that their shares are selling at a price/earnings multiple of 12, whereas Textron stock has recently been selling at only 6 times. In retrospect, of the many situations that Textron missed by being too conservative in the price we were willing to pay, the outstanding examples have got to be Tupperware and Josten.

*ADVICE: If you have an opportunity to purchase a company as outstanding as Josten, don't let a mere $500,000 stand in the way. If a business such as Josten's with its tremendous future potential is worth $12,500,000 it certainly is worth $13,000,000. Refusing to meet the firm offering price in this case was one of the worst mistakes I ever made at Textron.*

## SCOTT-ATWATER OUTBOARD MOTORS

Observing the success of Outboard Marine, and being determined to increase our participation in leisure activity industries, I decided that Textron must get into outboard motors. Mercury and Scott-Atwater were number three and number four in the industry after Outboard's Johnson and Evinrude. At that time E. C. Kiekhaefer of Mercury was unwilling to consider a merger with Textron but the controlling shareholders at Scott-Atwater were intrigued with the idea. We worked out a plan, which appeared to meet their requirements, and invited them to join our directors, officers, and division presidents at a get-together we were having in South Carolina. We wanted their management to be exposed to our division presidents so they could learn of the high degree of autonomy that we gave our managers. Everyone was enthusiastic about the plan. Textron directors approved the acquisition. The sellers seemed to be happy. Then we played golf and socialized. The party broke up Friday afternoon. The following Monday Scott-Atwater announced that McCullough—our principal chain saw competitor—had bought them.

*ADVICE: Don't count your chickens before they're hatched!*

# Product Liability

## ELECTRIC BLANKET

The product liability problem that companies now have reminds me of a couple of cases that happened years ago at Textron.

One day, the president of a prominent bank in New Jersey called me, and since we were in the process of lining up credits with some new banks, I said after he introduced himself: "Mr. Smith, are you calling to offer to take a position in our line of credit?" To which he replied, "Hell, no, I've got a serious complaint." I said, "Are you making a complaint as a stockholder, Mr. Smith?" And he said, "No. I have a serious complaint about one of your products." "What is that, Mr. Smith?" He said, "We've always used your electric blankets with great satisfaction over the years, but last night one of your blankets burned up my mother-in-law." "That's terrible, Mr. Smith. How is your mother-in-law this morning?" "She's dead," he said. "I'm so sorry, Mr. Smith, to hear this bad news. I certainly offer my humble apologies," and so forth. "Mr. Little, one of your blankets burned up my mother-in-law and I want to know what you are going to do about it." This remark was followed by a long period of silence. Normally, matters of this sort are handled by Textron's Legal Department; so for once in my life, I was struck dumb.

## POSIES

Another interesting case was one involving a most attractive new product for which we had gotten exclusive North American rights. This was a replacement for bras. The patent covered a new adhesive material that could be used on the inner ring of a bralike cup that fitted over each breast and stayed snugly in place without any straps or other fasteners. These cups could be used repeatedly

without causing irritation even to the most sensitive skin. Since we were at that time producing women's blouses, lingerie, and housecoats we saw this as an opportunity to replace bras entirely and become a dominant factor in this new field. We decided to call the product "Posies." The material on the outside of the "Posie" was a beautiful flower sewn on the basic fabric, which was held in place by the inner adhesive ring. We made these in five sizes: small, medium, large, droopers, and superdroopers. Although a small size could hold only one flower, such as a rose, hibiscus, or a carnation, we were able to get an entire flower garden on the superdroopers. We designed these five sizes in a multitude of floral patterns and built up an extensive inventory so that when we did our massive promotion we would be able to make prompt delivery to the leading department stores all over the country.

The idea was so new and the design so alluring that we got off to a terrific start and received tremendous publicity for this product. Everything was going beautifully until one day a lawyer came to the office and brought a suit against us for a large sum of money as the representative of a famous nightclub performer who had used our "Posies." It seems that in the midst of her act one of her Posies fell off, and she was arrested for indecent exposure. That was the end of our attempt to put the bra manufacturers of the country out of business.

*ADVICE: Don't always count on a little glue to hold things in place.*

## OTHER PRODUCTS

Golf cart manufacturers have been sued by golfers who are careless and drive the cart with one foot over the side. This is the surest way to break a leg. In spite of the fact that each cart has a sign requesting that feet be kept inside the cart, builders get sued for this carelessness on the part of the driver.

I understand that golf ball manufacturers are sued by careless golfers who hit a stone wall with the ball, which bounces back and puts out an eye. In neither of these cases is the manufacturer at fault. Unfortunately, juries now make large awards even in product liability cases of this sort.

*ADVICE: Check your product liability policies to be certain your coverage is adequate to meet the awards currently being made in your industry.*

# Epilogue

I have always felt that too much credit has been given to me for what has happened at Textron. In 1952, when our original concept was to build a company with completely unrelated divisions, no banker, no insurance company, no broker, indeed, no one in the entire financial community thought that the basic plan was feasible. Time after time, financial people would say to me, "Roy, this idea cannot possibly work. How can any one person run twenty or thirty different businesses?"

The financial community was so skeptical about the whole idea that I decided that for the company to get any acceptance it would be necessary for me to bring in as my successor someone who could gain their confidence and convince them that the Textron program was sound. That's why we were so fortunate in having the opportunity to persuade Rupe Thompson and Bill Miller to join Textron in 1956 after we had completed the American Woolen acquisition, and finally had the capital to expand our ideas beyond the three initial acquisitions. Rupe, as a conservative New England banker, was able to do something that I never could have possibly done. He convinced the investment community that Textron's basic concept was sound, and as a result, he was able to get the backing of leading banks (particularly their trust departments) to invest in Textron. Rupe felt strongly that we should not encourage mutual funds to buy our stock. They are not stable investors, they tend to get in and out fast, and are not as long-range in their planning and thinking as the trust departments of big banks. Without Rupe, Textron would never have become the important diversified company that it is today. He brought some top companies into the fold: Gorham, Bostitch, Speidel—none of which could I have acquired for Textron.

When Rupe turned over control to Bill Miller, Bill in turn made tremendous contributions. It was Bill who worked closely with me for a year during the American Woolen acquisition, and without his constant help, I doubt whether that merger would have been accomplished. In addition, without Bill taking over the Bell Aircraft negotiations, that company might never have been acquired. Since Rupe's death, Bill has refined the operations and has brought the company to its present position of achievement and reputation.

I would like to stress the fact that where I made many very bad mistakes in acquisitions in the early days, Bill and Rupe never made a single one in which the company has ever lost money—an unusual performance for any management. To show what a fantastic job Rupe Thompson and Bill Miller have done for Textron, the following information from the 1961 annual report compared to 1978's report will give a better idea of the relative contributions that the three of us made to the company. For the year 1961, sales were only $473,120,000 and net income was only $10,545,000. Textile sales that year were close to $70,000,000, so that by the time I retired we had been able to develop only about $400,000,000 of unrelated diversification volume in the company.

In 1978, sales were $3,230,640,000 with a net income of $168,-075,000. That year the net return on average common equity was 18.6 percent compared with only a return of a little over 8 percent in 1961. From these figures, you can see what a wonderful job the management who succeeded me at Textron has done for the shareholders. The basic concept of unrelated diversification has been soundly proven. There is no way, in my opinion, that Textron with its wide diversification could ever lose money overall in any one year.

Textron has an advantage over most other diversified companies in having more top companies in small industries within its fold. For example: Bell helicopter, Gorham silver, Homelite chain saws,

Polaris snowmobiles, Sheaffer pens, Shuron eyeglasses, Speidel watchbands, Talon zippers, Fafnir bearings, Bostitch staplers, E-Z-Go golf carts—just to mention those that are well known.

Although Textron's sales of non-textile products have increased 6½ times since my retirement, I have been amazed to learn that the divisions acquired prior to January 1, 1962, contributed 61.1 percent of the company's total divisional pretax profits in 1977. The sales of four of these operations: Bell, Homelite, Camcar, and Townsend are now each ten times their volume prior to acquisition. E-Z-Go has increased forty times.

So my crazy idea in 1952 of unrelated diversification was perfected by Rupe and Bill. Lucky me! And now Bill Miller has become chairman of the Federal Reserve Board. Lucky United States! Bill as usual is doing a super job for all of us at a tremendous financial sacrifice personally.

At the present time Textron is in the capable hands of Joe Collinson as chairman and chief executive officer and Bob Straetz as president and chief operating officer.

TEXTRON 1976 Annual Report

*Since Bill Miller was a graduate of the Coast Guard Academy, and he was the one who really closed the Bell deal with Helicopter becoming Textron's most important division, it was particularly appropriate for the company to use this cover on its Bicentennial year report.*

# Some of My Other Mistakes

# Narragansett Capital

$T$o prove that I practiced what I preached, turning over control to successors prior to final retirement, the Textron directors permitted me to start a small business investment company in 1959 so that I would have an established business in operation when that time came.

In 1958, Congress passed the Small Business Investment Act, "An act to make equity capital and long-term credit more readily available for small-business concerns, and for other purposes." The statement of policy is as follows:

It is declared to be the policy of the Congress and the purpose of this Act to improve and stimulate the national economy in general and the small-business segment thereof in particular by establishing a program to stimulate and supplement the flow of private equity capital and long-term loan funds which small-business concerns need for the sound financing of their business operations and for their growth, expansion, and modernization, and which are not available in adequate supply: *Provided, however,* That this policy shall be carried out in such manner as to insure the maximum participation of private financing sources.

To attract more equity capital in small business investment companies (SBICs), investors' losses on such stock were granted unlimited deduction for tax purposes against ordinary income. In addition, dividends received by SBICs were exempt from any federal corporate tax. The biggest advantage was that the Small Business Administration (SBA) would sell to institutional investors completely subordinated long-term debentures of SBICs with full government guarantee in a maximum amount up to four times the issuer's equity capital. Some leverage!

For years I had difficulty raising capital for Special Yarns Corporation. I was particularly interested in helping other entrepreneurs in financing their businesses. As a result, Narragansett Capital was organized in Rhode Island in 1959 and on September 7, 1960, G. H. Walker and Company and Blair and Company underwrote a 500,000 share public offering of Narragansett Capital, Inc. at $11 per share with proceeds to the company of $5 million.

In organizing Narragansett Capital, I felt certain that my experience at Textron, where I had made so many mistakes, would enable us to invest Narragansett's funds safely. The record indicates that I was unduly optimistic. I just found a lot of new ways to make mistakes.

Our first mistake was in the prospectus, where under the heading "Investment Policy" a sentence said: "Narragansett will not invest more than 20% of its combined capital and surplus in the obligations or securities of any single concern." If we had been foresighted, we would have added the following: "unless approved by the SBA" and would have avoided a most embarrassing minority stockholder's suit.

In 1966 Sydney Garwin, representing Jeffrey M. Green, the owner of one hundred shares of Narragansett, sued the directors and officers for having invested more than $2 million in Bevis Shell Home Company, even though we had obtained specific approval to do so from the SBA. This suit dragged on for a couple of years, taking a lot of executive time in depositions and winding up with a court-approved settlement.

*ADVICE: If you've raised capital with a public offering, be certain that you review frequently your statement of business purposes to avoid the careless mistake we made in the Bevis case. After the derivative action was brought, we even went to the expense of calling a special meeting of the Narragansett stockholders to give us retroactive approval of the transaction.*

*Even though we got overwhelming approval, the court refused to dismiss the case. If we had not obtained the assistance of Abe Pomerantz in dealing with Mr. Garwin, this action could have been far more expensive. If we had not settled the case, the directors and officers could have been found guilty of having violated one of the "Stated Business Purposes" in the original registration statement, and would have been required to pay the company $2 million. The Bevis investment was a dilly!*

*In derivative suits it is usually advisable to make a reasonable court-approved settlement that permits the corporate defendants to have the company reimburse them for all legal expenses. Otherwise you run the risk of having to pay not only the judgment but also all your legal expenses out of your own pocket.*

Narragansett's files indicate that we have made investments in 110 companies since 1960. In spite of nearly sixty years of business experience, I have managed to make some appalling mistakes. Some of the real beauties are included in the following section.

## BEVIS

Bevis Shell Home Company was organized by a group in Tampa, Florida. They built and sold so-called shell homes, which were basically the framework of a house to be completed by the owner. Since the buyer put in his own time to complete the house, the ultimate cost was much lower than having to buy a finished home from a builder.

When Narragansett Capital became involved in this situation, Bevis sold these small units for around ten or eleven thousand dollars with a 15 percent front-end load and seven-year paper with 6 percent interest for the balance of the payment. The salesmen, who were on commission, received practically all of the front-end payment so that the cash flow to the Bevis Shell Home Company came only after subsequent payments were received.

It was customary in this industry for the company to borrow very heavily against its future paper—possibly up to 75 percent—so the whole situation was highly leveraged, and Bevis needed to raise additional capital to supply the funds required to expand, build homes, and carry the installment paper.

As a result of a public offering made by G. H. Walker and Company in May 1961, this was one of the very first investments that Narragansett Capital made after its own public offering.

Narragansett bought $1.1 million of long-term subordinated debentures with some warrants to purchase Bevis's common stock. We had representation on the board and within a year and a half, Bevis was in trouble. Its principal competitor, Jim Walter, had been very successful in this field and had been very careful in checking the ability of people to whom they sold houses to pay their future obligations. This credit activity was centralized in Jim Walter's home office. On the other hand Bevis made the mistake of letting the salesmen, who were getting an immediate commission when making a sale, check the credit.

When the banks and insurance companies who financed Bevis realized there was a serious problem under the terms of their agreement, they gave the necessary two-weeks notice to take a specific lien on all the receivables. Since the receivables represented the principal assets of the company and since we at Narragansett were subordinated to the senior creditors, we knew that our $1.1 million would be wiped out if we permitted the senior creditors to take over all of this collateral.

We therefore petitioned the company into receivership under chapter 10 of the federal bankruptcy laws. In receivership there was a trustee appointed by the court to operate the company, and it was his responsibility to come up with a reorganization plan that was satisfactory to the equity owners and to each separate class of creditor.

However, since Narragansett was the sole owner of the subordinated debenture issue, no plan could be approved by the court without our acquiescence. The trustee tried to get us to approve the plans that he concocted, but right from the start we offered our own plan, which involved receiving 80 percent of the common stock in exchange for our canceling our $1.1 million investment. We also wanted to be sure that the senior creditors would give the company at least five years to work out their problems instead of having immediate liquidation of all the receivables and other assets.

I was fortunate in getting the services of my former classmate at Harvard, Lloyd Garrison, who is an expert in reorganization matters from the firm of Paul, Weiss, Rifkind, Wharton and Garrison, to assist us in carrying out our plan. It actually took two years before the other creditors, the trustee, the court, and the SEC, which also got involved, accepted our program.

In return for going ahead with our plan, Narragansett agreed to use its best efforts to find profitable businesses to put into Bevis to use up some of the tax loss carry-forward that the company had developed prior to reorganization. As a result of the adoption of the plan and our 80 percent equity ownership, we were immediately looking for possible acquisitions. We bought Newman-Crosby Steel Company of Pawtucket, Rhode Island, as an unrelated line, and later Marshall and Williams Company, manufacturers of textile finishing machinery and plastic stretching equipment.

A couple of years later we were having too much trouble in collecting our shell home receivables, which had been taken back from many house buyers, some of whom had put houses on land they did not even own, so that we felt it was advisable to liquidate that part of the business and concentrate on our recent acquisitions. James Talcott, Inc., one of our largest creditors, agreed to buy all the receivables and thereby clean up all the outside indebtedness. The substantial loss carry-forward of some $7 or $8 million created by the sale of this paper would be used up by the earnings of the businesses that we had put into Bevis.

Things went along fairly well for a while, but then in February 1969 we had an opportunity to merge Casper Corporation, a substantial house-to-house greeting card manufacturing and selling organization, into Bevis, issuing the owners of that company 1,034,-955 shares of Bevis stock.

The management of Casper Corporation was very ambitious. They had ideas that they could, through their extensive house-to-house sales organization, build up a huge volume of sales of additional products not made and sold by the original company. To raise more capital for the house-to-house sales and catalogue business, which appeared to us to have unlimited expansion potential, we sold off both Newman-Crosby and Marshall and Williams. To raise additional capital we made a rights offering to Narragansett shareholders to purchase Bevis stock at $10 per share. The public market had risen from practically nothing at the time of the receivership to over $10. The company by then had used up its loss carry-forward and was entirely out of the shell home business.

Then the management of Casper expanded to the point where it appeared that they were over their heads, and it was necessary for us to make a management change. At this point, after an extensive search, we took on and made president a man who had been the chief executive officer of an important division of a diversified company. This man put up a substantial amount of his own money to buy shares and then built up a large organization to try to reach our long-range goal of building up something like Avon with many, many products to be sold through house-to-house canvassing, plus catalogue sales and direct mail advertising sales.

This was a major expansion requiring tremendous amounts of seasonal financing because many of the products that were being sold were made in the Orient at very low cost. Since this was a cash business where hundreds of checks were coming in with firm orders for merchandise daily, we found as the company expanded it was becoming an extremely difficult one to manage properly, because when the buyers made commitments for merchandise from the Orient it often took six months to get delivery. When we struck upon a really successful item we would be very quickly sold out, and it would be impossible to replace inventory fast enough to hold the customers' money. The state law in New York required that any checks received must be returned within thirty days unless specified merchandise could be supplied since no substitutions were permitted.

The problem soon became very serious. When we made a mistake on purchases, obsolete inventories built up with no chance of being sold at a profit. With the hot items we never could replace merchandise promptly enough to avoid having to return to customers hundreds of thousands of dollars of cash.

Every year we built up huge inventories, borrowed very heavily from the banks to finance the foreign purchases, then at the end of the year cleaned out as much of the merchandise as possible and paid off the banks so that we could then get credit to go ahead and order again for the next year's requirements.

Unfortunately, with the large plants we acquired in Baltic, Connecticut, and Webster, Massachusetts, and the big overhead at the White Plains, New York, home office, the company just never made an adequate profit and in later years showed enormous losses. The ultimate result was that we finally had to shrink the business down to just some retail stores that were selling under the Dione Lucas name specialized equipment for home kitchens and household use. As of the end of 1976, the loss carry-forward amounted to $11 million. In 1977, we transferred the profitable Greenville Tube operations into Bevis and this year MD Pneumatics is being sold to Bevis so we are finally making some progress in using up the loss carry-forward. At least I'm persistent.

*ADVICE: When you invest in a situation that really gets into difficulty, it is far better to take the first loss instead of struggling as we have in Bevis for fifteen years to try to recoup our original investment. As a result of our attempt to make a success out of this one bad investment, Narragansett invested an additional $3,340,000 and Narragansett stockholders, through subscribing for rights at $10 per share, put up another $1,000,000 of equity capital. The stockholders, creditors, and Narragansett lost close to $10,000,000 in Bevis. We should have written off that $1,100,000 loan when the company went into receivership. The grief we are going through is unbelievable!*

## MASSLITE

In 1961, George Macomber and two other individuals named Anthony Larusso and Herman Protze, the former the owner of a large shale deposit in Plainfield, Massachusetts, the latter a professor at MIT, approached us with a brand-new idea that seemed incredibly secure and certain to make a fantastic return on an investment. This group told us that all of the lightweight aggregate being used by the building trade in New England came from plants in Pennsylvania and New York State, particularly in the Hudson River Valley where several of them were located. It is used in place of gravel to mix with cement to reduce the weight of the combined material for foundations, blocks, and other structural uses.

The lightweight aggregate was made in the Hudson Valley plants by taking shale and heat treating it in a rotary kiln that changed the structure of the solid shale by burning out the inflammable material in it so that it became much lighter in weight and extremely porous in structure. This porosity was another big advantage when mixed with cement since it gave a better bond than did solid gravel.

At the time that Macomber and his group came to us he explained that they needed about $1 million to build a plant at the quarries in Plainfield where the shale would be obtained as a raw material. The process they were going to be using was different from the normal kiln method and was one that was used successfully only in the Midwest for making lightweight aggregate. This new process was called sintering. It consisted of treating the shale after crushing on a continuous conveyor, which passed through a heat chamber that burned off the volatiles and made the resulting product both porous and lightweight. The key to success of this whole operation was the freight differential. There was a market of perhaps a million tons a year of lightweight aggregate in all of New England, with much of it within reach of this new plant, theoretically on a highly profitable basis, since the freight rate was $4 a ton from the Hudson Valley into Boston.

The group was convinced that the process itself was certainly as efficient, if not more so, than the kiln method. With an unlimited supply of shale available to the plant for the cost of quarrying, namely about fifty cents a ton, the new Masslite plant would be able to sell its product at the market price of ten dollars per ton and make a profit at least equal to the freight differential. One other feature that made this proposal attractive was that there apparently was no other quality shale deposit anywhere else in New England except in northern Vermont. Therefore, once this operation was started and they had obtained control of the entire eastern New England market, there would be no local competition to interfere with the profitability of the operation.

The plant was built and put into operation, but the sintering process proved to be somewhat unreliable and there was a high percentage of downtime on the equipment because of constant repairs and adjustments to the sintering machine. This problem slowed down the startup of the operations. We had figured that we would have pretax earnings of four dollars per ton, protected taxwise by high depreciation on the plant and depletion allowance on the quarried shale. These figures indicated that we certainly had a sure thing, with the possibility of paying off the entire cost within two years.

George Macomber was in the construction business and gave the new plant some contracts at the ten-dollar price, meeting the competition of the outside New England producers. The limit of our freight advantage extended about one hundred miles from the plant in a westerly direction and therefore gave us the opportunity of taking all lightweight aggregate business as far west as Hartford and Springfield. We had a substantial advantage in Maine, New Hampshire, and Rhode Island. However, the total volume of construction in these three states at that time was far below that of other parts of New England.

As we increased our production and became more aggressive in taking over business from competitors, to our surprise, they began to cut prices to meet our competition. Within six months the price per ton was nine dollars. Within a year it was down to eight dollars. The competitors were unwilling to sit back and let us pour tons of lightweight aggregate into the market at ten dollars per ton as we had anticipated. Some of our competition in the Hudson Valley were plants owned by large corporations who had the muscle to run, if necessary, at a loss in order to maintain their market share.

For example, one of the largest facilities was a division of U.S. Steel and we found that they were not prepared to throw in the sponge and let our little company put them out of business. When we finally got up to full production, and had taken away all the business in eastern New England from the established competition, the price had been reduced to six dollars per ton and from then on the company never made money because the four dollars a ton profit that we had counted on because of the rail freight differential was gone forever.

*ADVICE: When new production is brought into any market, it is bound to cause severe price competition. No competitor is going to stand idly by and let his share of market evaporate. All our forecasts of sales, profits, and prices had been made on the assumption that the $10 market price would continue even after our large production became available. Any businessman who overlooks the effect of competitors' price reductions when enormous new capacity is added to the market, will have a rude awakening. It is impossible to start a new operation like Masslite and throw many tons of capacity on the market without creating an uncontrollable price situation. The Masslite investment was a disaster.*

The whole Masslite operation was ultimately sold back to the former owner of the shale deposit for practically nothing. Since he therefore wiped out the entire original cost of the plant he has been able to prosper. The market has finally risen to $13.25 per ton, which enables him to make a tidy profit on his limited operation.

## CABLE TELEVISION

Back in the early days of Narragansett Capital, about 1962, Bill Daniels from Denver, Colorado, came to see me in Providence and said, "Mr. Little, you ought to invest some of your money in cable television operations." I said, "Bill, what's cable television?" He said, "This is a brand-new industry that has fantastic potential that all started back in 1946 in a small town in one of the deep valleys of the Pennsylvania coal mining regions. A distributor of radios and television sets found that while the radios he sold worked beautifully down between the hills, his television customers got no reception at all. He couldn't sell any television sets. Before giving up, however, he went to the top of a nearby mountain with one of his better sets and just pulled out the built-in antenna.

"To his amazement, he got perfect reception. He then had the bright idea that is now revolutionizing the industry. He went back to town, got a contractor to build an antenna up on the mountain, and ran a cable from the top of the mountain down into town. He leased pole rights from the telephone company to give him access to all of the houses along the main streets. He then took television sets from door to door, hooked in the drop wire from the cable and showed the homeowner a new miracle—television with beautiful reception. As a result of that bright idea he had soon sold hundreds of sets. He was now not only making money selling television sets, but since he was charging each subscriber on the cable five dollars per month the cash really started rolling in. There was very little operating expense involved running this first television cable installation. As a result of that experience others all over the country began to do the same thing in towns hidden behind mountains and in out of the way places." Bill continued, "So, Mr. Little [he soon was calling me Roy], you and Narragansett should finance some of these projects. A lot of them have been started and have run out of money. They need someone like you with venture capital to buy them and complete the installation."

"Bill," I said, "how do you make your money?"

"I am a broker," he replied. "I get a commission on all of these sales."

By that time I was really fascinated and said: "I'll tell you what I am willing to consider, Bill. To be sure that you bring us only the good ones, I'll make this kind of deal. For every location where you can bring us a cable television station costing a million dollars or less, we will put up $80,000 for 80 percent of the equity, you put up $20,000 for 20 percent of the equity, and we'll lend the operation the balance on a subordinated long-term loan." This plan appealed to him. He said, "Roy, you're on. Let's go." As a result of that unusual visit, Narragansett Capital, with Bill's help, financed many cable television installations in small communities where the reception was impossible without it.

Then some years later, after we had acquired a large enough group to consider going public, we discovered that suddenly the investing public had heard about this marvelous new opportunity. Hundreds of thousands of investors in the country wanted to invest in cable television. There were only three or four companies that were exclusively involved in cable. Many of the others were part of huge corporations where an investment in their stock would not really represent much of a stake in cable. The result was that with a limited number of pure cable companies demand was greater than supply. Cable television stocks in the sixties began to sell at a hundred times earnings—in our case at a hundred times losses.

We picked this time to put all our stations together into American Television and Communications and go public. The offering was very successful. The only problem was that the underwriters wanted to sell far more shares than the company wished to offer, so Narragansett had to sell a couple of hundred thousand shares of its own stock to make the underwriters happy. As a result of this transaction, Bill Daniels overnight became a very wealthy man and he permitted us to take Monty Rifkin, his able manager, to be the president and chief executive officer of our new company.

Prior to the public offering, we worked out a plan for Monty to pick up a substantial number of shares so that he too would have a piece of the action. This small venture has become very exciting. Monty Rifkin has done the best job of anyone in the industry and has bought out many other operations, including some of Time's investments and those of other large companies that lacked the management skills he had. Today, American Television and Communications Corporation has over 750,000 subscribers in ninety-seven systems in thirty-one states and is currently building big systems in large cities like Orlando, Florida; Jackson, Mississippi; Albany, New York; Portland, Maine; Fresno and San Diego, California; Shreveport, Louisiana; Birmingham, Alabama; and Charlotte, North Carolina.

But during the years when American Television and Communications Corporation (ATC) was being expanded through acquisitions, we had an unusual situation arise involving their best efforts to file a registration statement for the sale of common stock.

On February 22, 1972, ATC signed a contract to purchase Jefferson Carolina Corporation, which controlled a large number of cable television operations in the South. Half the stock was owned by the Jefferson Standard Insurance Company and half by United Telecommunications, a public utility in Kansas.

In addition to a cash payment, each of the partners was to receive 175,000 shares of ATC common stock and wished to sell their shares. The contract carried a provision requiring the company to "use its best efforts to cause such registration statement to become and remain effective." The closing was on August 16, 1977, and on that same day United demanded the registration statement be filed. On September 28, ATC filed a registration statement for a total of 500,000 shares including the 350,000 which Jefferson and United wished to dispose of.

Shortly after this filing, ATC had an opportunity to merge with Cox Cable Communications, a subsidiary of Cox Broadcasting of Atlanta, Georgia. Since this merger would have caused ATC to become the second largest cable operator in the country everyone, including Jefferson and United, was enthusiastic about the idea since it was felt that this merger would improve the marketability and price of ATC. As a result, on November 8 the registration was held up so that the Cox financials could be included. There were some technical problems, which further delayed the filing of the amended material, but the coup de grace came when the Justice Department stepped in and brought an action to prevent the merger. Everyone was amazed at the Justice Department since the company, after merger, would have had a combined net worth of only $40 million and would have had less than half the subscribers of Teleprompter, the industry's leading cable operator.

As a result of the Justice Department's action, the Cox merger was called off. The price of ATC had dropped from $45.25 on November 8, and the underwriters were no longer willing to sell the shares in the falling market. By December 5, 1973, the price of ATC had dropped to $7.75 per share, and United filed a claim against ATC for a total of $8,718,750 covering the difference in price of the shares plus some interest costs. On March 17, 1975, the claim was reduced to $7,483,219. The basis of the suit was that ATC had not used its best efforts to cause the registration statement to become effective and that United and Jefferson thereby were severely damaged.

Among the witnesses that we produced was Frank Wheat, the former chairman of the SEC, who explained to the court that in the financial community a best efforts agreement had no financial responsibility whatever. The court decided otherwise, and awarded $2,012,000 to the plaintiffs. ATC appealed the case and lost again, finally settling in 1976. In addition, ATC had very heavy legal costs.

An interesting sidelight on this case is that the court did not require the plaintiffs to sell their shares when the settlement was made, with the result that if they had continued to hold the shares until today, when ATC is currently selling for more than the $45.25 price of November 8, 1972, they would now be in a position to have their cake and eat it too, because of the $2,012,000 settlement.

*ADVICE: If you are an investment banker, have no fear of the financial responsibility for signing a contract involving your best efforts to file a registration statement to sell securities. If market conditions become adverse, you are off the hook. However, all other businesses should be extremely wary of becoming involved in a "best efforts" commitment for the sale of securities as a result of our sad experience.*

ATC has been taken over by Time as a result of their recent tender offer of $50 per share or 1.55 shares of Time convertible preferred.

## SAM SNEAD ALL-AMERICAN GOLF

When I came to live with my uncle and aunt in Brookline in 1911, I spent the summers with them at various resorts like Mount Kineo House at Moosehead, the Mansion House at Poland Spring, the Rockend at North-East Harbour on Mt. Desert Island, and, in the summer of 1911, at the Equinox House in Manchester, Vermont.

One of the finest golf courses in the country was the Ekwanok Country Club at Manchester. In those days the hotel had the privilege of letting their guests play that course. As a result I took my first golf lessons and played Ekwanok during the summer of 1911. I'm sure that it must have taken me 150 strokes to get around the course at age fifteen. It is interesting that the course today is very similar to the original layout, and I've played it many times since 1911.

When I went to work at the Lustron Company and later at the Special Yarns Corporation in South Boston during the 1920s I played at the Chestnut Hill Golf Club, a nine-hole course, par 36, but only 2,640 yards long. I used to go out and play practically every evening in the summer, and I remember that when it began to get dark we would often put a white handkerchief in the hole in order to putt out.

On the weekends, I often played fifty-four or sixty-three holes, and since I was never proficient at tennis, I spent most of my spare time on the golf course.

When my son Arthur was thirteen years old, he started taking golf lessons from George Kinsman, the pro at the Point Judith Country Club in Narragansett, Rhode Island. George had done an excellent job with youngsters at our club and really enjoyed teaching them more than he did the adults. My son rapidly became enthusiastic about the game. I started to play with him whenever we could arrange it. He gradually improved his game so much that every time he had a vacation coming up he'd say, "Dad, let's go off on a golfing trip for the next couple of weeks."

We would go to Pittsburgh for a week and play Oakmont, Chapel Hill, and other fine courses. Then the next time, we'd go west and play Olympic, San Francisco Country Club, and then to Pebble Beach, Monterey Peninsula, Del Monte Country Club and, of course, Cypress Point. Arthur got to be a very capable golfer, shooting anywhere from 75 to 80 on practically any course. He used to say when he was younger and not quite so good, "Dad, you

## ST. ANDREWS LINKS
## HANDICAP TABLE for OLD, NEW, EDEN and JUBILEE COURSES

| | |
|---|---|
| 1 | 8 |
| 2 | 5 11 |
| 3 | 2 8 14 |
| 4 | 3 7 11 15 |
| 5 | 2 5 8 12 16 |
| 6 | 2 5 8 11 14 17 |
| 7 | 2 5 8 11 13 16 18 |
| 8 | 2 4 6 8 11 13 15 17 |
| 9 | 2 4 6 8 10 12 14 16 18 |
| 10 | 1 3 5 7 9 10 11 13 15 17 |
| 11 | 1 3 4 6 7 9 10 12 14 15 17 |
| 12 | 1 3 4 6 7 9 10 12 13 15 16 18 |
| 13 | 1 2 4 6 8 9 11 12 14 15 16 17 18 |
| 14 | 1 2 3 5 6 8 9 10 11 13 14 16 17 18 |
| 15 | 1 2 3 5 6 7 8 9 10 11 13 14 16 17 18 |
| 16 | 1 2 3 5 6 7 8 9 10 11 12 13 14 16 17 18 |
| 17 | 1 2 3 4 5 6 7 8 9 10 11 13 14 15 16 17 18 |

know what I like best? Beating you at golf." This relationship with my son was great and it lasted until he discovered girls.

For many years one of our most famous golf courses had this sign at the first tee:

### NOTICE
ATTENTION IS CALLED TO THE FOLLOWING
EXCERPT FROM THE RULES
LADIES ARE PERMITTED TO PLAY ON THE
COURSE BY COURTESY—SUCH MATCHES
MUST ALWAYS STEP ASIDE AND ALLOW
A PROPERLY CONSTITUTED MATCH TO
PASS REGARDLESS OF POSITION ON
THE COURSE—UNLESS STRICTLY
OBSERVED MORE RESTRICTIVE RULES
WILL BE ADOPTED
EXECUTIVE COMMITTEE

The women's liberation movement finally prevailed, and the sign was removed last year.

American golfers will be intrigued with the unique handicap system used at St. Andrews in Scotland. In the United States, it is customary for strokes to be assigned to specific holes, usually odd strokes on front nine, even on back nine, with the result that in a

| HOLE | NAME | MEDAL LENGTH IN YARDS | PAR | HANDICAP | CHAMPIONSHIP LENGTH IN YARDS | PAR | | | | LADIES' LENGTH IN YARDS | PAR | HANDICAP | SCORE |
|---|---|---|---|---|---|---|---|---|---|---|---|---|---|
| 1 | Ailsa Craig | 354 | 4 | 9 | 361 | 4 | | | | 331 | 4 | 9 | |
| 2 | Mak Siccar | 377 | 4 | 13 | 426 | 4 | | | | 354 | 4 | 13 | |
| 3 | Blaw Wearie | 392 | 4 | 5 | 467 | 4 | | | | 391 | 5 | 5 | |
| 4 | Woe-be-Tide | 158 | 3 | 17 | 168 | 3 | | | | 146 | 3 | 17 | |
| 5 | Fin'me oot | 406 | 4 | 3 | 482 | 5 | | | | 383 | 5 | 3 | |
| 6 | Tappie Toorie | 236 | 3 | 15 | 242 | 3 | | | | 213 | 4 | 15 | |
| 7 | Roon the Ben | 465 | 4 | 1 | 520 | 5 | | | | 413 | 5 | 1 | |
| 8 | Goat Fell | 391 | 4 | 11 | 427 | 4 | | | | 361 | 4 | 11 | |
| 9 | Bruce's Castle | 405 | 4 | 7 | 449 | 4 | | | | 361 | 4 | 7 | |
| OUT | | 3184 | 34 | | 3542 | 36 | | | | 2953 | 38 | | |
| 10 | Dinna Fouter | 409 | 4 | 6 | 453 | 4 | | | | 337 | 4 | 6 | |
| 11 | Maidens | 135 | 3 | 18 | 178 | 3 | | | | 118 | 3 | 18 | |
| 12 | Monument | 386 | 4 | 8 | 390 | 4 | | | | 352 | 4 | 8 | |
| 13 | Tickly Tap | 375 | 4 | 14 | 381 | 4 | | | | 326 | 4 | 14 | |
| 14 | Risk-an-Hope | 395 | 4 | 2 | 441 | 4 | | | | 384 | 5 | 2 | |
| 15 | Ca Canny | 162 | 3 | 16 | 210 | 3 | | | | 149 | 3 | 16 | |
| 16 | Wee Burn | 366 | 4 | 10 | 412 | 4 | | | | 336 | 4 | 10 | |
| 17 | Lang Whang | 481 | 5 | 4 | 498 | 5 | | | | 387 | 5 | 4 | |
| 18 | Ailsa Hame | 373 | 4 | 12 | 431 | 4 | | | | 363 | 4 | 12 | |
| IN | | 3082 | 35 | | 3394 | 35 | | | | 2752 | 36 | | |
| TOTAL | | 6266 | 69 | | 6936 | 71 | | | | 5705 | 74 | | |

Marker's signature ......................................

Player's signature ......................................

| GROSS | HANDICAP | NETT |
|---|---|---|
| | | |

four-ball match, the two partners always duplicate strokes up to the lower handicap player's allotment. At St. Andrews, the team gets a break. For example, if one partner gets three strokes, and the other player twelve, there is no duplication. Three strokes come on the second, eighth, and fourteenth holes, and as you can see, the partner with twelve has the advantage of getting his strokes on different holes. This is a great advantage in four-ball competition. Perhaps the USGA should consider adopting the St. Andrews plan. If they did, all the country clubs in America would have one hell of a problem making up new handicap systems. In addition to St. Andrews, I have played many courses in Scotland including Rosemont, Carnoustie, Muirfield, and Gleneagles and then Troon, Preswick, and Turnberry on the west coast.

American golfers will be intrigued by the way the Scots name the holes at Turnberry's Ailsa course (see above).

As a result of having visited clubs in various parts of the country, I have played with quite a few professionals. For example, on April 4, 1960, Jim Robison and I played a round with Chi Chi Rodriguez who was then assistant pro at Dorado Beach and later became famous on the golf tour. At the time he weighed about 115 pounds and could hit the ball off the tee 300 yards. That particular day he accomplished something that I had never seen before. On the back nine, which is 3,500 yards in length, par 36, he started out birdie 3, birdie 3, par 5, birdie 2, birdie 3, birdie 4, par 4, birdie 2, and then hooked his drive deep into the palm trees to the left of the last fairway. I went into this dense growth with him and said, "Chi Chi, why don't you chip out onto the fairway and hopefully get your four for thirty." He said, "No, Mr. Litter [he couldn't pronounce Little], I've had a thirty, I want to get a twenty-nine." The hole was 455 yards and he had an opening of less than two feet between two trees in order to land on the green. He took out a three iron and, believe it or not, hit the ball onto the green fifteen feet from the pin, and sank his putt for twenty-nine. This was the first time I had ever seen anybody in the world get a twenty-nine in nine holes—seven birdies and two pars.

I had gotten to know Sam Snead well through George Denton, who was the financial adviser handling his common stock investments. I used to go down to Greenbrier and play with Sam. On June 29, 1960, playing in a best ball match with my son Arthur and me, Sam had a 32 and 31 for a 63—the lowest score I had ever seen.

In the first week of June 1961 the International Golf Championship, at that time called Canada Cup Matches, was being held at Dorado Beach. There were thirty-three teams from thirty-three different countries, and the United States was represented by Sam Snead and Jimmy Demaret. I followed Sam around most of the time during these matches, and was amazed at the consistency of his golf. Every round was under 70. He won the low individual score for the four rounds and the United States won the team championship.

In October 1970, Sam Snead asked me to be a member of his pro-am team with himself and two other amateurs. The tournament was played on the famous Cascades course at Hot Springs, Virginia. Sam's foursome was the last to finish and there must have been one hundred spectators at the clubhouse around the last hole watching Sam come in. The tee is elevated with a pond about 125 yards in front of the tee, and the green at least 50 feet above the level of the pond. Sam hit a beautiful drive right on line about 20 feet short of the pin, but I skied my drive and just barely got over the pond in the hollow below the green. Taking out a wedge, I played a shot that looked pretty good and suddenly heard all the spectators cheer. I decided I must have had a pretty good shot.

When I walked up the hill I noticed that my ball was leaning against the pin, and when I took the pin out of the hole the ball fell in for birdie 2. The interesting part of this story is that Sam missed his 2 and when we turned in our scores we found that our team for the entire tournament had the lowest score by one stroke; so that, in effect, I had won the tournament for Sam, for which he received first prize of $1,250.

In 1974, the Lyford Cay Club had a member-guest four-ball event. Each member was permitted to bring three partners who were dues-paying members of any legitimate golf club. Since I knew that Sam was a dues-paying member at Pine Tree, of Daytona Beach, Florida, and played regularly in their club championship, I invited him to join Chuck Mauro (a former Rhode Island State Amateur Champion) and Ronnie Quinn (a Rhode Island State and New England Amateur Champion) on my team. The only prize that the winners were going to get was a nicely engraved pewter plate with the Lyford Cay insignia on it. Since this was strictly an amateur event, no expenses could be paid or cash prizes awarded. Sam flew back especially from Brazil, where he'd played an exhibition match, and arrived dead tired just before the tournament started.

I was amazed at his performance, where there was no money involved and where he played as carefully and as hard as if he had been after a $50,000 first prize. He shot successive rounds of 64, 68, 66, and 65, and had only one five in 72 holes in four days of golf on this tough 72 par course. The result was that Sam on his own ball was 25 under par, the lowest 72 hole score that anyone had ever recorded on that course. Our team won the low gross for the tournament by 22 strokes. I did not help a single stroke.

I have gone into great detail about golf and Sam Snead to lay the background for my venture in building golf courses and how I lost over $2 million doing it.

As a result of my great interest in golf, I discovered a new trend that was taking place in various parts of the country. Par 3 golf courses were being built that gave one an opportunity to use every club in the bag, with holes from 100 yards all the way up to two or three par 4 holes over 300 yards. These courses could be played in one and one-half hours. They were built with automatic watering systems and lighted for night play. They were very often on leased land near large population centers.

I visited several of these courses and suddenly got a terrific idea.

Why not put up a chain of par 3's all over the country so that golf could be played day and night all year around? I would get the best architect in the country and best known pro involved with us in this enterprise.

Having known Sam Snead well for many years, he would be the ideal partner for this wonderful new project. I visited him at White Sulphur Springs and suggested that we form a new company to be financed primarily by Narragansett Capital, in which he would have a stock ownership. When he accepted we decided on our name "Sam Snead All-American Golf." Robert Trent Jones, the leading golf architect, was particularly excited about the idea and also wanted a "piece of the action." Narragansett Capital would have half the equity and would lend over $1 million initially to the company to finance the first few golf courses. Sam Snead actually put up $60,000 and Robert Trent Jones $30,000.

We had an architect design a standard clubhouse, with colored roof and painted much like Howard Johnson's basic idea. As a highway advertising sign we had a large pole with a huge golf ball and Sam Snead's straw hat sitting on top of it to identify our location. We then got a real estate broker, who also invested in the project, to select our sites. We had a wonderful location in San Diego, right in the heart of the city. In Florida we had a site on Route 1 opposite Cape Canaveral. We bought land right next to the airport at Colton, California, halfway between Los Angeles and San Bernardino. We had another site just south of San Francisco Bay in the San Jose area. More land was purchased in Orlando, Florida; Dallas, Texas; and Fresno, California.

Trent Jones then got busy and we went over the land in each area together, laid out the eighteen holes, and actually built courses at San Diego and Colton in California, and at Sharpes in Florida.

We started another course which was approximately half completed in the San Jose area when to our dismay a northerly storm struck San Francisco Bay and our whole new golf course was inundated with salt water. We then discovered that we had bought that land without checking to see whether it had ever been flooded before.

Just before we started construction at our Dallas site, which was located on a small river, there was a cloudburst. The entire acreage was covered with some twelve feet of flash flood water. Again we had not carefully checked the area for flooding.

These two experiences slowed us down a bit and we tried to operate just the three courses that had been completed to see, before going any further, whether they would be profitable.

It took about $800,000 to build a course. The land cost about $250,000 for the fifty-five or sixty acres required, the lighting system over $100,000, the automatic watering system another $100,-000, and the construction of the course the balance. After we put over $2,000,000 into this venture, we finally realized that none of the courses were really making money. Unfortunately, I had let my enthusiasm for golf affect my judgment as an investor.

After we made these investments, I finally went to work with a pencil and put down the total cost of the project and the annual operating expenses, and discovered why we weren't making money. To make a 10 percent return after taxes on each golf course, I found that it would be necessary to have a thousand players per week with a $3.00 greens fee over each course every week in the year regardless of weather. We discovered from experience that it was completely impractical and impossible to get that much traffic over any of our courses. So our investment of over $2,000,000 was lost.

*ADVICE: Don't invest in a project in which you are personally influenced by association without sitting down and figuring out how much you are going to have to gross to make a fair return on your money.*

*ADDITIONAL ADVICE: If you pull a blooper like this, try to make some recovery by using the loss carry-forward. In addition to Narragansett stockholders, I felt a real obligation to Sam and Trent. After I persuaded Sam to put up $60,000 for stock in our "Sam Snead All-American Golf" and the*

*venture went broke and lost a couple of million dollars, Sam never once men-*
*tioned to me the loss on his investment. Trent also was very understanding.*
*I'm delighted to report, however, that after we cleaned out the golf courses we*
*used the corporation with its big loss carry-forward with Narragansett to pro-*
*vide new capital to purchase three successful Pepsi-Cola franchises in Spring-*
*field, Ohio; Sacramento, California; and Winston-Salem, North Carolina.*
*Later we went public in order to have a market for our shares. Finally, we*
*merged that company into General Cinema, receiving their shares in a tax-free*
*exchange. Although I understand that Sam has sold his stock, I have never*
*discussed the matter with him but hope that he and Trent got out whole,*
*which they certainly would have if they had retained the General Cinema*
*shares.*

Several times when I went down to play golf with Sam at White Sulphur Springs, I was amazed to find that when I went to the cashier to pay my hotel bill I was told, "Mr. Little, Mr. Snead has taken care of your account." I have found Sam to be an excellent companion and a lot of fun; and, as a matter of fact, a very generous man in spite of his reputation for being a tightwad. I am a great admirer of Sam's, and we remain the best of friends.

## HYDROSYSTEMS

In early 1965, Republic Aviation Corporation was being liquidated. Their main plant was in Farmingdale, Long Island. Among the various activities that Republic had been involved in, besides building airplanes, was a very small operation in which they had financed a group of engineers to develop special equipment for the Navy to train submarine officers in handling the complex requirements of the submarine operation in specially constructed test facilities called "Submarine Simulators." This equipment was most complex but it did permit the simulation of all of the actions that a submarine could take underwater. The equipment was on land, and the Navy wished to have one unit in each naval base in the country. This system was so much safer for training the officers rather than actually aboard ship, where a mistake could be disastrous.

Republic had reached the point where it was about to receive a contract, but since the company was in liquidation, the Navy insisted that a new company be set up with the key management group outside the Republic corporate structure before they could qualify for a contract.

Narragansett Capital did incorporate a new company, with unusually high leverage, so as to give the key engineering group who were leaving Republic to join the new company, a chance to buy a substantial equity position. None of these young engineers had been able to accumulate any capital, with the result that they were able to put up a total of only $25,000 for half the stock of the company, which was to be called Hydrosystems, Inc. Narragansett purchased the other half of the shares and the balance of the capitalization was a Narragansett Capital subordinated loan— $450,000.

It was necessary for the group to move out of Republic's buildings, so they leased a small, single-story plant nearby and started up operations. They succeeded in getting contracts and actually made some money. Their sales and earnings since incorporation are as follows:

| Year ended | Net Sales | Earnings | |
| | | Pretax | Net |
| --- | --- | --- | --- |
| 2/28/66 | $1,430,703 | $ 118,149 | $ 67,149 |
| 2/28/67 | 2,034,437 | 225,165 | 117,165 |
| 2/29/68 | 2,917,800 | 252,809 | 131,809 |
| 2/28/69 | 2,680,097 | (228,549) | (174,850) |
| 2/28/70 | 1,719,890 | ( 39,969) | ( 42,526) |
| 2/28/71 | 2,172,882 | 81,441 | 48,841 |
| 2/29/72 | 2,233,168 | 224,614 | 110,614 |
| 2/28/73 | 2,578,601 | 274,649 | 140,649 |
| 2/28/74 | 3,756,806 | 289,001 | 148,001 |
| 2/28/75 | 6,235,515 | 656,934 | 316,934 |
| 2/28/76 | 9,619,746 | 1,090,044 | 520,044 |

On November 18, 1974, after receiving a proposal from the management to buy us out, and since we felt that they had built all of the submarine simulators that were needed, we made what we considered an unusually attractive deal with them in view of a couple of loss years. We were paid $400,000 for our stock ($100,000 in cash, $300,000 in notes) and consulting and noncompete payments of $35,000 a year for ten years, for a total payment of about $750,000.

*ADVICE: In a case like this, be careful not to sell out too fast without a thorough investigation. After buying us out, this group sold their company for $7 million of Gould, Inc., shares.*

## *TEXAS PEPSI*

The president of Pepsi-Cola Company, a subsidiary of Pepsico, was a good friend of ours. He brought to Narragansett's attention the possibility of investing in Pepsi-Cola franchises from time to time in various parts of the country. The situations that were brought to our attention were those where the owner had died or had not done the best job in building up the per capita consumption in the area. Pepsico wanted to get new owners involved with more competent management to improve those situations.

The first opportunity that came to us in this manner was located in Springfield, Ohio. The owner had died and the widow was attempting to operate the business and was losing market share in relation to Coca-Cola. Not only did Pepsico bring us this opportunity, but they also suggested that we take over Bob Haley, the manager of their Chicago office, who was an experienced soft drink man. His responsibility had been to supervise all of the franchise operators in the Midwest.

We worked out a plan whereby we used an existing corporation to purchase this franchise for $1,000,000, and let Haley purchase 50 percent of the equity for $50,000. Narragansett owned the other half of the equity and lent money to the company on a subordinated debenture to complete the purchase price.

Our partner in this venture did a fantastic job, and at the end of a couple of years, he had doubled the per capita consumption in Springfield and actually far surpassed the per capita consumption of Coke in that area. He had turned around a lackluster, low profit situation into a highly profitable one, and we were all extremely pleased with our experience in the Pepsi-Cola franchise business.

We next had the opportunity to purchase from former owners the Sacramento, California, franchise. Although that operation was also put under Bob Haley's supervision, the local management remained on the job. Again, the results were most successful and we built a very fine new bottling plant during our ownership.

Within a year or so thereafter, we had an opportunity to purchase the Winston-Salem Pepsi-Cola franchise—again to be supervised by Bob Haley. This franchise was operating far below the normal per capita in North Carolina, but within a couple of years was most successful.

At this stage, we all felt that it would be advisable to put the three operations together in one company and to go public both to get marketable securities for Narragansett and to get the manage-

ment involved in each place. The public offering was made in February 1970. The company raised $1.2 million and paid off most of its indebtedness, and everyone was happy.

We continued to keep in touch with Pepsico for more opportunities to expand our bottling operations. In 1972, an opportunity was presented to us by Pepsico to take over four bottling plants in the Southwest: Corpus Christi, Waco, and Beaumont, Texas; and Fort Smith, Arkansas.

These operations had been really run down and required tremendous investment for new trucks and vending machines. The amount of money we paid the former owners was minimal, since their debt was high. We had to put up more money to provide working capital to build up the operation. The big attraction in these franchises was the potential growth. Coke was then outselling Pepsi 9-to-1 in Texas and it looked as though there was an opportunity to increase greatly the Pepsi-Cola market share in those four locations. This was the big appeal.

On the other hand, because of the immediate success we had in Springfield, Sacramento, and Winston-Salem we did not carefully check the problems that would be involved in the Texas area. We just assumed that with our record there would be no problem in duplicating or even bettering those results. However, Bob Haley was to have no responsibility for Texas.

Again, Pepsico offered us one of their able young men to go in as president of the company, since at this time it was not advantageous for us to try to put this operation into our publicly owned Pepsi-Cola Bottling Company. Pepsico, through its leasing company, put up nearly $3 million to finance trucks and vendors so that the entire operation was modernized and really ready to go places.

Narragansett was called on time after time to put up more capital and ultimately got involved to the extent of $3.2 million before we finally realized the situation would require far more capital than we could afford to risk. After having made some progress in increasing the market share in the area, we discovered that the whole price structure was far lower on soft drinks in Texas than any other place in the country, primarily because the Coke bottlers were all very well-to-do, had low-cost plants, and really had control of the market. They were not about to let the price structure go up so as to make it easy for Pepsi or anyone else to increase their market share.

Another bad mistake we made was not realizing that when you are outsold 9-to-1 by a principal competitor, your drivers, who had to deliver the merchandise from the bottling plant to customers, were probably putting in five times as many miles to sell a truckload as the Coke drivers were.

Well, the final result was that after some five years of struggling with this operation, it was beginning to make a little money, but it got beyond the means of Narragansett to carry through and make a success of the operation. Finally, in 1976, Pepsico took over the liquidation of the operation, and Narragansett's entire $3.2 million investment was wiped out.

*ADVICE: Just because you have been extremely successful in an industry in one part of the country, don't assume it will be equally easy to succeed in some other area. Check very carefully the price structure and all other elements of the business before you commit an investment in another area in a business in which you have been successful elsewhere.*

## CORNER HOUSE

In the summer of 1969, an investment opportunity was brought to us at Narragansett Capital, which I should have turned down as soon as I heard about it.

The business consisted of sewing plants and a knitting plant to make garments for sale in some twenty retail stores scattered through New Jersey, Pennsylvania, Maryland, and Virginia. For the previous couple of years, before our acquisition, the business had been very profitable since there had been some staple styles of women's sportswear, which made it possible for the company to rely exclusively upon its own garment manufacturing plants for the products sold in the retail stores.

As soon as I saw the figures on this company and analyzed its operations, I had recollections of the disastrous integrated brand-name program at Textron. I should have remembered from that experience that it would be equally impracticable for a chain of retail stores to rely exclusively on their own manufacturing operations as their sole source of supply.

However, because of Corner House's excellent earnings record, we made a thorough investigation of their operations and found that they had purchased locations in residential areas so as to be near their potential customers. Many of these were on street corners, hence the Corner House name. Because they were completely integrated from purchased yarn through knitting, sewing, and retailing, they were not only able to undersell their leading competitors, but they also made it convenient for their customers by locating these converted stores in heavily populated areas.

We made the mistake of paying the owner $2,000,000 for his company, and then let him purchase for $100,000 a 50 percent interest in the new Corner House Corporation, which we financed, to buy the assets. We hoped that his investment would be sufficient incentive for him to duplicate in the future the fine earnings that he had shown in the past.

The new company was highly leveraged, with only $200,000 equity, or 10 percent of the total purchase price. Shortly after this acquisition, the staple sportswear, which had made it possible for him to operate efficiently, went out of style and it was then necessary for his sewing plants to make such a wide variety of high-styled goods that it was no longer profitable for him to produce the enormous variety of products required at the retail level. Meanwhile, he had not built up alternate sources of supply from other garment manufacturers, who were unwilling to sell their products, in effect, to a competitor who had his own sales outlet and therefore was in a position to undersell the affiliated retail outlets.

It wasn't long before we had a loss situation on our hands, but in this case, we were smart enough not to throw good money after bad. Finally, in January 1972, we found someone to bail us out. We received $500,000 of preferred stock of Apparel Affiliates, Inc., who owned and operated a large number of ladies' ready-to-wear clothing stores and therefore could take over the Corner House stores and liquidate the factories.

The final result of this fiasco, which I never should have gotten involved in after my Textron experience, was to lose over $1.7 million of Narragansett Capital's money.

*ADVICE: Almost anyone can afford to make a single mistake, but when you make the same identical mistake twice, it is time to visit the headshrinker!*

## AQUARIUS CORPORATION

Aquarius was a company that a group of investors financed in Albuquerque, New Mexico. They came to us at Narragansett Capital and had a wonderful sounding plan to convert the job shop printing plant that they had taken over into a highly sophisticated operation that would do quality color work for large industrial users throughout the Southwest.

In addition, the states of New Mexico and Arizona, which had to go as far as San Francisco or Chicago to get good color reproduction work for all their tourist folders and other promotional material, were excellent prospects. This type of business ran into very substantial volume and we were told that once the plant was equipped with new machinery bought with our money, there would be no question about their getting continuing orders from the contacts they had made in the area.

The principal investor, who was president of the company, was really a spellbinder in his presentation. I personally went out to New Mexico to see the plant, which had excellent floor space and was well located, and met the group of key personnel that had been assembled, some of whom had experience in this type of operation in other parts of the country. I remember saying to the promoter, "How in the world do you get a group of people who have had wide experience to work for you for lower salaries than they were getting in Chicago or New York?" He said, "Roy, this is a wonderful part of the world to live in. These people will work out here for two-thirds of the pay they were getting in other parts of the country. We have a great opportunity to build a most important printing business here and all of this group have put up some money to show their confidence in the venture. I can assure you, Roy, that this could be one of the finest investments that Narragansett ever made."

When this investment was brought to the board for consideration, my son, who had met the principal and thought he was too much of a promoter, tried to persuade me to take it easy and not rush the board into approving this transaction. In my usual manner (once I was sold on something, I insisted on getting the board to act on it that day), without having any consultant like Arthur D. Little, Inc., investigate the situation and check with the states of Arizona and New Mexico to see if, in fact, they were prepared to give millions of dollars of printing business to this new company), I rushed ahead. Believe it or not, without further investigation we made a total investment of $830,000 put up as follows:

| Date | Amount |
|---|---|
| 10/16/69–12/5/60 Original investment | $680,000 |
| 2/16/70 | 25,000 |
| 2/24/70 | 50,000 |
| 4/3/70 | 12,500 |
| 4/23/70 | 12,500 |
| 5/22/70 | 50,000 |

Within one year, the venture went broke and Narragansett took a complete loss.

*ADVICE: Don't let a super salesman con you into making an investment. This company was formed and named at the height of popularity of the musical* Hair. *Just the fact that someone would name his company after the principal musical hit of that show should have been warning enough.*

## ETEC

In May 1970, we heard that two brilliant Chinese engineers were trying to raise money to manufacture very complex optical equipment called SEMs (scanning electron microscopes) in California. An SEM "sees" with a very fine beam of high voltage electrons, which sweeps over the specimen in a scanning sequence similar to that used in television. It bridges the gap between the capabilities of standard optical microscopes and conventional transmission electron microscopes. The latter can give higher magnification than SEM but requires very expensive ultra-thin slices of specimen. An SEM, on the other hand, can give a three-dimensional picture of irregularly shaped specimens and thus eliminate the need for costly slicing or other preparation requirements for surface examinations.

We were particularly impressed with these engineers' program and began to finance their early engineering work and construction of this unusually complicated equipment. Starting in a small rented plant in Hayward, California, they soon were swamped with orders for this equipment, which in the past had been built by the Cambridge Company in England and by a scientific instrument company in Japan. Within a couple of years, our group dominated the market and we were called upon time after time to put up additional capital to finance their expanding business.

We had Arthur D. Little, Inc., make a study of their operations and were delighted to learn that half the equipment used in the country was actually built by Etec. All this had been accomplished in a relatively short time. The only problem was that the equipment was used primarily in laboratories for testing purposes and once all of the potential customers were equipped there would be very little replacement market. The SEMs sold in price ranges from $50,000 to $150,000, depending upon the exact specifications that the customer required. Although Etec was extremely successful in obtaining market share, we were disturbed by the fact that their earnings on the sales of these complicated precision instruments were not at least 20 percent before taxes.

One evening, when I attended a dinner party for Etec's principal customers, I found that the customers were completely satisfied with the quality of the workmanship and especially delighted with the service they received in the maintenance of the equipment after it was installed. But I was also told that Etec's prices were lower than their competition in spite of their being the principal domestic supplier and providing excellent service. With this tip-off, we realized that the president of Etec was so sales-minded that he was not pricing his product in a way that assured the company of a substantial profit. Unfortunately, about a couple of years ago, Etec had pretty well saturated the market for the high-priced SEMs and they were looking for new fields to conquer.

American Telephone and Telegraph's Bell Labs in New Jersey had recently taken out patents on a far more complicated piece of equipment called MEBES (manufacturing electron beam exposure system). This highly sophisticated machine using electron beam lithography is employed to increase the density of circuitry packed onto the surface of semiconductor chips. Such results have generally been achieved by using optical photography for generating a photoetched master mask. Such masks are then used to control the diffusion and etching processes required to produce integrated circuits. The use of the electron beam exposure system, however, allows masks of greater resolution and higher quality to be produced, thus making possible chips with substantially greater circuit density at greater production efficiency.

Bell Labs decided that Etec was the most advanced technical and scientific group capable of making this new very expensive equipment under license from them. The result was that Etec worked out a license arrangement under which they paid Bell Labs $500,000 and were assisted by Bell in starting to manufacture this new complicated equipment, including complete sets of drawings and personal help from their scientists.

Etec then got busy to sell these highly specialized units for a minimum of $1,250,000 initially and $1,750,000 currently to many of the leading scientific companies in the United States and abroad such as Fairchild, RCA, ITT, Siemens in Germany, OKI in Japan, and so forth. These contracts all called for progress payments but permitted the purchaser to withhold 20 percent of the total price after delivery until complete acceptance of the equipment.

For a small company like Etec to suddenly find themselves with $20 million worth of orders on the books and very limited working capital created a serious problem. Narragansett had made equity investments twice and had made a total of fourteen different injections of additional financing through the subordinated debt route. Our legal limit under the SBA for loans was approximately $2 million, so we were unable to provide further financing. Etec is, therefore, a prime example of what happens to companies that have enormous long-range potential when Narragansett Capital reaches its maximum investment limit. In this particular case, it appears that we have no alternative except to find some large corporation with sufficient muscle to carry this unusual scientific development through to its successful conclusion.

*ADVICE: Be careful about taking on the development of highly scientific ventures if you do not have the financial staying power to carry them through to their full potential.*

Etec shareholders last year granted an option to Perkins-Elmer to purchase the company for $20 per share in return for Etec's receiving a substantial working capital loan subordinated to the bank. Perkins-Elmer took up the option on May 1, 1979—an ideal solution for all concerned.

## ACRODYNE INDUSTRIES, INC.

We were approached by a promoter who had what looked like a viable idea to build equipment that could be used in the remoter school systems of the country to assist the teachers in bringing to their classes material that the teachers themselves might be incapable of handling.

This young man started manufacturing equipment in the Philadelphia area. He kept running out of money so that after our original investment of $225,000 he kept coming back for more and more until we finally got up to $1.8 million, and the company still wasn't making a profit. The following schedule shows how many times we dug up money:

| | | | |
|---|---|---|---|
| 7/16/71 | $ 50,000 | 10/4/73 | $ 25,000 |
| 9/13/71 | 50,000 | 10/12/73 | 75,000 |
| 11/23/71 | 30,000 | 10/31/73 | 63,171 |
| 12/2/71 | 230,000 | 11/1/73 | 50,000 |
| 1/6/72 | 50,000 | 12/7/73 | 50,000 |
| 1/18/72 | 25,000 | 1/15/74 | 50,000 |
| 1/28/72 | 25,000 | 1/31/74 | 60,000 |
| 2/10/72 | 60,000 | 2/27/74 | 50,000 |
| 9/11/72 | 35,000 | 3/6/74 | 20,000 |
| 10/20/72 | 45,000 | 3/12/74 | 50,000 |
| 11/9/72 | 45,000 | 3/26/74 | 30,000 |
| 2/28/73 | 58,770 | 4/16/74 | 50,000 |
| 6/14/73 | 10,000 | 4/25/74 | 50,000 |
| 6/18/73 | 25,000 | 5/6/74 | 50,000 |
| 6/22/73 | 150,000 | 6/7/74 | 180,000 |
| 9/21/73 | 50,000 | | |

At this point, we had a real problem. We had lost confidence in the original promoter. We were now in a position, with our loans overdue and interest unpaid, to act and bring in competent management to salvage the business.

We made contact with a successful businessman in Philadelphia who impressed us very much with his ability and record. We asked him to make us a proposal to take over the management and help us to bail out our $1.8 million investment. He made it very clear that if he were going to put up equity money behind us there was no way he would be personally liable for our debt. After many meetings, we finally compromised by agreeing to accept a long-term $1.8 million obligation with no fixed interest payments. He insisted, however, that he must have options to buy us out at a substantial discount. The first year he would be permitted to buy the $1.8 million note for $500,000. Under the option the price would go up $100,000 a year until thirteen years later he would have to pay the full amount.

New people were put in the operation, and within a year they had turned it around and were sending us reports showing substantial profits. To our surprise our loan was paid off in the second year at the $600,000 option figure, resulting in our taking a loss of $1.2 million on this situation, which we originally thought had great promise.

*ADVICE: No business, however promising, is worth backing unless the management is capable. This situation illustrates dramatically how one man can be a failure in a new business and another man can turn it around and be successful in two years. If you are smart enough—or lucky enough—always to back competent people, you will never lose money.*

## *VAREC*

In 1971, Rudy Eberstadt, president of Microdot, a large diversified company, called me one day and said, "Roy, I plan to cut back my Microdot operations to three major lines with the result that I wish to dispose of three divisions which are profitable, but which do not fit into our long-range plans."

I said, "Rudy, give me some idea of what these operations are because it may be possible for us to have Narragansett Capital finance the purchase of one or two of them, and at the same time give your divisional management an opportunity to have a piece of the action."

Eberstadt said, "One of the best is Varec on the west coast, a company that makes measuring devices for use in gas and oil and petroleum product measurement. In other words, if any storage area puts in our equipment, which measures the amount of product constantly in the tanks and reports it at a central control center, people no longer have to go around and measure how full each tank is. Varec earns about $700,000 pretax and we would like to get $3,200,000 for it."

"Rudy," I said, "this sounds to me like just the size of company that would qualify as a small business under the SBA's restrictions and we would like very much to send somebody out to meet the management to see whether we feel they are competent to run the operation; and, even more important, whether they are willing to put up a substantial amount of money to buy an equity interest in the highly leveraged new company that we will set up to take over your assets and liabilities."

Narragansett did a thorough investigation of the situation; had their auditors, Arthur Young and Company, check the financial aspects, and also had an analysis made of the markets served by Varec and their competition. Everything checked out, and Narragansett set up the following financial plan: an Industrial National Bank five-year term loan with a 50 percent balloon, $2,000,000; and a Narragansett Capital ten-year subordinated loan with no payment until the sixth year, $1,000,000. The equity was divided—$350,000 from Narragansett for 70 percent of the common stock (50 percent of the voting stock), and $150,000 from ten individuals in the management for 30 percent of the equity (50 percent of the voting stock). The acquisition was made May 14, 1971, and ran very successfully until early 1975, when we negotiated the sale of the company to Emerson Electric Company.

Emerson was extremely thorough in its investigation, and since Varec had a partnership operation in England and another one in Belgium in which the English partner participated, Emerson said that they would not go ahead with the acquisition unless we could get rid of the investment in England because of its socialistic trend and the severe severance pay problems. If an English company had to be liquidated in that country, Emerson wanted no part of it. As a result, before we could put the sale through, we had to go to England and Belgium and work out a swap with the English partners whereby they sold us their entire interest in the Belgian plant in return for our selling them our entire interest in the English operation.

Once this transaction was completed, Emerson negotiated with us to take over the Varec Company. Since Emerson's stock was selling at about a 30 multiple, they wished to use their shares for the acquisition, whereas we were more interested in cash since Narragansett needed a realized profit instead of an unrealized profit on this transaction to offset losses we had taken in other ventures. In addition, *Fortune* had published in February 1975 an article that I had written in October 1974 predicting the worst recession we had had in the country since 1932, so I was very skeptical about taking Emerson Electric's common stock. Their high multiple was due to the fact that they had a fantastic earnings record for the previous eighteen years. Every quarter, their earnings per share had exceeded that of the previous quarter. No other large company in the country could equal this record except for Beatrice Foods. With a price/earnings ratio of 30, and my conviction that 1975 was going to be a terrible year, I was sure that Emerson could not possibly maintain their record of increasing earnings every quarter during 1975 the way they had in the past. I was also certain that if their earnings per share in future quarters dropped, their multiple might easily drop to 10 times earnings, and we would be locked into a situation in which we would make no profit at all on the sale.

Emerson started off by offering us 170,000 shares and finally raised the ante to 200,000 shares, which at the time of our negotiations in 1974, would have amounted to $8 million. However, in a sale of this sort, it is possible to do a public offering only on half the shares received in order for the transaction to be tax-exempt. It would have been necessary for us to have waited until their 1975 first quarter figures were published before we could have sold half our position through a shelf registration. As a result, I was unwilling to run this risk, and we finally worked out an installment sale at $4,700,000 with 6 percent interest payable over a four year period. Since Emerson stock is presently selling for $35 per share, 200,000 shares would have been worth $7,000,000 even today. This was at least a $2,300,000 mistake on my part.

*ADVICE: When you are dealing with a company like Emerson, with a fantastic track record and, which is, in my opinion, the most efficient, highly di-*

*versified company in the United States, don't be worried about taking their shares on an acquisition even though the multiple is high. Where there might have been a serious drop in the value of their shares in 1975, even if they had failed to increase their earnings every quarter as they did, the management of that company is so superior that in the long run, taking their shares would have been far preferable to selling out at a low price the way we did. At the present time, Emerson has now completed twenty-one years with a perfect record of having increased their earnings per share every quarter over the prior quarter during that entire period.*

## CODATA

In April 1972, we heard about a group of engineers who were working on a system that would meet the requirements of the New York City Fire Department's ordinances to install in every office building over ten stories a complete fire control system. This group of bright engineers had found a way to use the existing wiring systems in buildings rather than having to install very expensive new wiring systems throughout the buildings to control the elevators, air conditioning systems, and stairwells.

We were very much impressed by this group headed by Bert Dorfman, and we advanced money many different times to keep their project going. Finally, after about $2 million had been spent for research and development work, Codata began to get some orders. Since they had no working capital left to finance the new business and we had loaned our legal limit of slightly over $2 million it was necessary to make arrangements with Wertheim and Company to raise additional capital.

Codata now had ample working capital to handle the business that was coming their way from most of the building owners in New York City. After having developed a backlog of over $12 million in orders and after having installed several successful systems, the entire business was brought to a grinding halt when one of the landlords sued the City of New York on the basis of the fire department's requirements being a confiscation of capital since the landlords by the terms of their leases were unable to pass the cost on to their tenants.

The result of the lawsuit has been a complete tragedy for Codata. Their customers not only stopped all work in progress but, in many cases, refused to pay for the partially completed jobs as required with their orders. It was customary for Codata to receive 10 percent of the value of the order at the time blue prints and specifications were submitted. Thereafter, progress payments were to be made so that at no time would Codata have to use their own capital to finance these installations. The lawsuit was brought in 1976, and after a year of litigation, the landlord's case was upheld in the lower courts and the City of New York has so far failed to appeal or to make a compromise to settle the matter.

In an attempt to find a solution, we suggested to our attorneys that the City of New York could get this case settled promptly by agreeing to reduce each landlord's future taxes for a ten-year period in order to reimburse them for the cost of this highly sophisticated equipment. Unfortunately, New York's financial affairs are in such dreadful shape that this settlement of the case, although realistic, was impossible to accomplish.

The result of this entire situation is that Codata, which at one time appeared to be the brightest star in our portfolio, has become an extremely difficult problem. There is no question that it is desirable for all tall buildings to have adequate fire control systems to protect the lives of those who work in the buildings, but it appears that it will be some years before this lawsuit will be settled. It is also obvious that Codata had a less expensive system, which did the job, than Honeywell, Johnson Controls, or other large manufacturers. To indicate the magnitude of the problem it is estimated that it will take at least $400 million in installation costs in New York office buildings over ten stories to meet the requirements of the fire department and the city. In retrospect, it is obvious that the building landlords were not going to take any such financial loss lying down.

*ADVICE: Where we made our original mistake in financing this small company whose product was excellent was in not anticipating trouble and potential lawsuits from the landlords. It was obvious that the high cost of installing fire control systems could not be passed on to the tenants under their long-term leases and that the $400 million cost therefore had to come out of the landlords' pockets.*

*It is vital, therefore, not to get into a similar situation involving regulations requiring building owners to absorb huge capital expenditures. Landlords are heavy contributors to the politicians in all cities, and they have too much political clout to accept any such huge cost as the fire department's regulations imposed upon them in New York City.*

*Our total investment in Codata was lost because I was not realistic in evaluating the potential danger of landlords' suits.*

## CUMBERLAND FURNITURE

In June 1972, a bright young man came to us with the idea of manufacturing unusually high quality office furniture on a special order basis. The sketches of his proposed work and some of the samples we saw impressed us with the design and quality features he planned to emphasize, so we launched him in business. After several injections of capital, we finally got involved to the extent of $527,500, and for five years this young man struggled valiantly to keep his head above water.

In spite of all our efforts to rescue him, this one appears to be a lost cause. We recently offered to sell out our position and take our loss providing he could raise some capital elsewhere. His efforts to do so have been in vain, so another small business has gone belly up!

*ADVICE: Don't count on a young entrepreneur being successful in a business like high-grade office furniture in competition with such giants as GF Equipment and Steelcase. It can't be done, and we have lost our entire $527,500 in the Cumberland Furniture venture.*

## MASONRY SYSTEMS

The next blooper was Masonry Systems. The man who had been one of the principal suppliers of bricks to the building trade in New York became alarmed over the drop in the use of bricks being used for construction in his area for the last few years. He felt that this was due primarily to the high union wages that the bricklayers charged for on-site work.

Glass, steel, tip-up concrete, and aluminum were being used to replace brick for the outside of buildings, largely because of the cost factor. This gentleman heard about a process that was being used successfully in Denver and Chicago. Large brick sections were being erected indoors and carried to the site on trucks. They were then hoisted into place on-site. In New York, bricklayers were willing to work at $2 per hour lower wages because of the year-round possibility of building these sections indoors. The union made this concession because they were convinced that tall brick buildings, as previously constructed, were a thing of the past. The company that controlled the patents was willing to give an exclusive license to Masonry Systems for all of New York State and New Jersey.

The key to the success of this operation was due primarily to a chemical adhesive that Dow Chemical made. When mixed with mortar, it was practically impossible to separate the bricks once they had been assembled. This adhesive was so strong that it was possible to pick up a large section of brick wall that had been assembled indoors, place it on a truck, and then lift it into position at the building with a crane. One other great advantage was that because of the strength of the sections built this way, a brick building could be constructed with a much thinner wall than normal. Therefore, the whole steel structure of the building could be lighter, with a substantial savings in cost.

Since engineers and architects who were designing modern buildings had discontinued specifying brick construction, Masonry Systems might now reverse that trend.

With the capital that Narragansett put into this venture, a plant was built on Staten Island a few years ago, which could conveniently service New York City and New Jersey, and the venture got under way after the exclusive license had been obtained from the parent company.

One of the problems that became apparent immediately was that buildings have to be planned far ahead. With a new type of material, it was necessary for both the architects and engineers to specify that product and recommend it to the building owner. This requirement caused at least a one-year lead time, and consequently the new company obtained very few orders except for limited quantities of their product.

The coup de grace, however, was the fact that we had an exclusive license in an area where in the last few years there had been practically no new building construction. We were faced with a dilemma. Should we put up more money hoping that building in New York would pick up, or should we admit that we had made a mistake and limit our loss to our initial investment of $875,000? This time we decided that our first loss was the best loss. Not one cent of our investment was ever recovered.

*ADVICE: Just because a new venture in the building trade is successful in some parts of the country like Denver where building expansion has been ex-*

*tremely rapid, don't make the mistake of financing that type of operation in a place like New York City where new building is practically nonexistent.*

## SOUTHWEST TUBE

In 1973, we heard that Bill Weber, who had been a salesman for many years with U.S. Steel Company, had an opportunity to purchase Southwest Tube Company from its parent company. Bill knew the industry, was well regarded by the customers, was very ambitious to get a large equity position in Southwest Tube and make enough money to substantially expand its operations. The original financing was as follows:

| | |
|---|---|
| Short-term bank loan | $ 550,000 |
| Narragansett Capital subordinated debentures | 1,300,000 |
| Narragansett Capital equity (50%) | 150,000 |
| Management equity (50%) | 150,000 |
| Total | $2,150,000 |
| Purchase price | $1,320,000 |
| Working capital | $ 830,000 |

Everything went well for a while; then Bill decided to put in welding equipment so that he could buy flat steel and make welded tubing instead of just buying steel tubing and drawing it to certain diameters and lengths for the industry. Part of the operation had been financed in the past through a $2 million municipal bond issue. When the expansion program was first approved, none of us realized that if the additional $3.6 million were borrowed over and above the original financing, the $5 million legal limit for such industrial revenue bonds would have been exceeded. The tax exemption would have been forfeited and the banks that owned these bonds could have sued us for damages. Fortunately, we discovered the limitation after we had entered purchase orders for the equipment but before we had closed the necessary bank loans to finance the expansion.

As a result, we had to change course suddenly and work out very expensive true leases for $1.9 million of the equipment with Chandler Leasing Corporation, a division of Pepsi Corporation. The total value of a true lease is not counted against the $5 million limitation on industrial revenue bond issues, although borrowed funds or lease financing of the type considered as debt would have been.

*ADVICE: If you are ever involved in revenue bond financing for land, buildings, or equipment be certain that the total amount of debt, including future expansion, does not exceed $5 million during any three-year period. This dollar limitation does not apply to large municipal bond issues when required for environmental or pollution control or for financing of docks and piers that have certain public usage. Recently the limit has been doubled.*

## CONSOLIDATED FOODS

To show how important it can be in business to play golf, the story of how Narragansett had an opportunity to finance six small businesses and permit the management to have a piece of the action is a good example.

In 1977, Bob Gunness, a friend of mine who is also a member of the United States Seniors' Golf Association, called me. He was formerly the chief executive officer of Standard Oil of Indiana. He said, "Roy, I would like to bring John Bryan, the chief executive officer of Consolidated Foods, to Providence for a game of golf so that you two can get to know each other. I'm now on his board." My son Arthur and I had a good game with them at Agawam Hunt Club. The next time John Bryan and I met and played golf was in the winter of 1978 at the Lyford Cay Club in the Bahamas. He had a group of his top executives there for a business get-together away from the telephone and other interruptions that would have occurred in Chicago.

I discovered that John's long-range plans involved selling off some of the smaller divisions of Consolidated Foods, which Nate Cummings, the company's founder, had accumulated during their rapid expansion period. As a result of these discussions we finally worked out contracts for Narragansett to finance six different divisions on a highly leveraged basis so that the management would have an opportunity to acquire a piece of the action at relatively low cost. The total package involved $30 million, with our close associated, Industrial National Bank of Providence, putting up all of the senior money.

There was one problem in this whole transaction, however, that caused us considerable difficulty. Some months before, Consolidated's public relations officer, in talking to a group of financial analysts, mentioned the fact that the company's long-range policy was to divest itself of many of its small, unrelated businesses and to concentrate more on the acquisition of large food companies. This publicity created a furor in many of the small divisions, and John Bryan had to calm them down by assuring them that he had no present intentions of any such divestitures. Since only about six months had elapsed, John felt that he could not run the risk of advising the managements of these divisions that Consolidated was considering selling them. Although we were given complete financial information, we were not permitted to visit the plants and talk with the divisional management. It was necessary, therefore, for Narragansett and Industrial National Bank to sign a firm contract to take over these six operations without any contact with the managements involved.

We had had so much favorable experience in the past in acquiring divisions of companies and in giving the management an opportunity to invest in them, that we felt that all the management groups at Consolidated would be most enthusiastic about our plans. However, when the announcement of the sale was made, all hell broke loose. The president of one of the divisions took it upon himself to try to create among the other divisional presidents a mutiny in the ranks. Fortunately, we were able to calm everyone down except the disorganizer, and worked out favorable arrangements for everyone concerned.

In the case of the mutineer, he set up a competing company to the division he operated, but we were fortunate in persuading the former owner, who sold that division to Consolidated Foods, to come back to the company and buy control of it with our assistance and that of the bank.

This was a case where things became so hectic at one stage that some of the staff people at Narragansett felt that we should find some way to walk away from the entire deal. I am delighted to say that my son Arthur, the present chief executive officer of Narragansett, had the courage to carry these plans through to a successful conclusion. I am convinced that all of these six companies will be very satisfactory money earners for Narragansett, and that the net result of the entire transaction should add about sixty cents a share to Narragansett's dividend.

*ADVICE: Don't ever buy any division of a company without having an opportunity to meet with the management and evaluate them and their facilities.*

*This whole Consolidated Foods transaction turned out to be what might be called a near miss. Fortunately we have salvaged it, but it could have been a real disaster.*

## SUMMARY

It is interesting to look back and see how Narragansett became so heavily involved in many situations by repeatedly putting up more and more money without realizing that we would ultimately reach our maximum before the venture was successful.

For example, in the case of Bevis, we got permission from the SBA to finally go to $5,551,000 after our initial $1,100,000 investment on February 1, 1961. We made a total of four equity investments and four debt investments before we finally stopped struggling with that one.

In the case of Codata, we got involved to the extent of $2 million from April 12, 1972, to the present time with one equity investment and thirteen injections of capital through subordinated debt.

One of the worst cases was Acrodyne, with our first investment made in September 1970, but with total investments of $1,903,-756.50 made through three equity investments and a total of thirty-one individual debt investments.

In the case of Masonry Systems, starting in August 1973, we ended up investing $810,000, with one equity investment and twenty-two debt investments.

In the case of Masslite, we made our first equity investment in May 1961, but made repeated advances of subordinated debt nine different times until we finally reached a total of $1,880,000.

Two other examples of continually putting good cash after bad are: (1) Sam Snead All-American Golf, which we started in September 1961, ending up with a total of three equity investments and putting up subordinated debt (believe it or not) thirty-four different times for a total of $2,990,000 before we finally threw in the sponge on that one; and (2) Texas Pepsi, where we made our first investment in November 1969, pouring money into that situation through subordinated debt financing ten times before that company finally became insolvent, and we had to let the Pepsi-Cola parent company sell off all of the franchises and liquidate the operation.

One of the basic problems involved in venture capital financing is knowing when to stop pouring money into a venture. We have had cases where we put money in at least a dozen times and finally turned things around, but we have had many more cases where we have completely failed after pouring good money after bad.

One particularly interesting case where we certainly would have taken a bath was in Photo Systems when in August 1973 we invested $2.1 million to buy these operations from KMS. This division had, in addition to three high quality photo labs that did developing work for professional photographers, a division that made unusually fine equipment for professional photographers who wished to do their own developing work. The name of that division was Unicolor. Here was a case where we paid too much for the company, an amount substantially over book value, so there was an unusually large amount of goodwill. In addition, the man who was to head the operation had been an officer of the selling company but had not been directly involved in this particular division's operations.

His involvement had been in acquisitions but with the parent company now liquidating divisions, he had been in charge of the sale of the operations. Since Photo Systems was the last division to be sold, he decided that he should head up the company that was to purchase that division. The total price that we paid was $4.6 million, and this was financed by $500,000 of equity, half by the management group and half by Narragansett Capital. In addition, Narragansett put up $1,750,000 of subordinated debt for a total investment of $2,000,000. Industrial National Bank put up $2,750,-000 to complete the purchase price.

This operation soon got in trouble and began to lose money. After looking at the current financial figures and the huge indebtedness, I was personally prepared to write the entire investment off and take our licking, but Bill Considine, who was on the board and is now chairman of the executive committee, didn't agree. He was certain that if he personally took on the supervision of this operation that he could turn it around.

Bill has done an amazing job reorganizing the Photo Systems operations. As a result of his efforts Industrial National loans have been paid off and Narragansett will some time in the future not only get its debt paid but will make some recovery on its equity investment.

*ADVICE: Don't throw in the sponge too soon on some investments. If you have a competent businessman like Bill Considine who is willing to tackle the job of rehabilitating a loser, give him a chance—he may perform a miracle the way Bill has at Photo Systems.*

Now let's summarize what has happened at Narragansett Capital since I started it in 1959, three years before retiring from Textron.

We raised $5 million in 1960 through a public offering, selling shares at $11 per share. Since then, Narragansett Capital has assisted in the financing of over 110 different companies. The total amount of capital that Narragansett has provided through debt and equity financing to these companies has amounted to approximately $100 million. Out of all of the companies that we have assisted financially, 46 of them have been unsuccessful, and we have lost a total of over $20 million. Many of our investments, of course, have been paid off and a few of our ventures have been successful, with the result that Narragansett's net worth in 1977 as determined by directors' evaluation was approximately $25 million. Up to then we had $40 million worth of successes, which added to our original $5 million capital equals $45 million, less our $20 million losses comes out to our 1977 directors' evaluation of $25 million.

This entire Narragansett Capital venture over nearly twenty years has been a great disappointment to me. I had assumed that with the many mistakes I had made personally and in Textron that I had the qualifications to run a venture capital company without duplicating my poor record. Alas, I was overoptimistic again! It is amazing that anyone with the wide experience that I had in business could have done such a lousy job for the stockholders as I have done at Narragansett Capital. Before my son Arthur took over as president and chief executive officer in the summer of 1977, the stock was selling below its original offering price.

I have certainly learned that trying to run a venture capital business is probably the most difficult way to make money for stockholders. The mortality rate on start-up situations is fantastically high. We found that many bright young entrepreneurs have brilliant concepts but have no administrative ability and prove to be poor managers. We found that the temptation is very great to keep pouring good money after bad and in retrospect, if we had been wise enough to stop putting more and more capital into some of the ventures we backed, we never would have lost a total of $20 million on the businesses in which we invested.

I must stress the importance of backing the right people. If it had been possible for us to have spotted those who had inherent management capabilities, and if we had limited our investments to those people, our results would have been far superior. There is no question that the most important thing in venture capital financing is people! people! people! just as the most important thing in real estate financing is location! location! location!

As a result of my most unsatisfactory record at Narragansett Capital, the company is now managed by my son Arthur D. Little, age thirty-five, as president who is ably assisted by Jim Robison as chairman of the board, Harvey Sarles as consultant, and Bill Considine as chairman of the executive committee, plus a very competent staff and board of directors.

Narragansett Capital has become a regulated investment company so that in the future if 90 percent of the earnings are paid out to the shareholders, it will pay no federal income taxes. The directors will have the option, however, of either paying out capital gains to the shareholders or retaining those earnings and having the corporation pay capital gains taxes.

Narragansett Capital, at the present time, has available close to $35 million to invest in the future. These funds are now in uninvested cash and certificates of deposit, in additional long-term subordinated government guaranteed debt, and in unused bank lines. I am certain that the present management of Narragansett Capital will not make the many mistakes that I did in the past and that these new funds will be invested more carefully in mature situations with competent management.

I doubt whether there will be many start-ups financed in the future, since our record with start-ups indicates that they are unusually risky and that nine out of ten will result in losses. In addition, our experience has indicated that when a start-up becomes highly successful, Narragansett Capital does not have the staying power with its present $2.75 million maximum investment limitation to carry a highly successful new venture through to maturity. It is therefore impossible to really cash in on the winners to the extent necessary to offset the many, many losers.

Under the present plans to operate as a regulated investment company (RIC), it will still be possible for Narragansett Capital to be a small business investment company and have all the advantages of both categories. With Congress's interest in assisting small business in the country, the size rules and regulations for qualification as a small business are continually being lifted so that more and more concerns can now qualify for financial assistance by SBICs. When the original act was passed by Congress the financial qualifications were limited to the following strict requirements:

Total assets—not over $5,000,000.
Total net worth—not over $2,500,000.
Average net earnings after taxes—$150,000 for the past three years.

At the present time it is proposed that these limits be raised to the following:

Total assets—$15,000,000
Total net worth—$5,000,000
Total net earnings after taxes—$500,000 for the preceding two years
 as reported to IRS.

In addition to the financial limits for determining whether a company is a small business, the final controlling factor is the number of employees. There is a tremendous variation in this final determinant, with a maximum of 250 employees in many industries, while in some cases the maximum is as high as 1,500. For example:

| | |
|---|---|
| Aircraft manufacturer | 1,500 |
| Cigarette manufacturers | 1,000 |
| Pulp mills | 750 |
| Glass containers | 750 |
| Pump and pumping equipment | 500 |
| Household laundry equipment | 1,000 |

There is no minimum requirement as to number of employees.

There are many other proposals before Congress that should encourage small business investment companies and make it possible for more small businesses to receive financial assistance.

Under the regulated investment company provisions of the law, an important amendment is in the works that will give the same protection to the stockholders of SBICs operating as regulated investment companies as the stockholders of real estate investment trusts have in the latitude granted for the payment of earnings and dividends.

Real Estate Investment Trusts (REITs) have a provision under the law that if for any reason the Internal Revenue Service decides that the REIT has not paid out 90 percent of its earnings to the shareholders and therefore imposes a heavy tax on the corporation for that failure, the REIT has relief. The REIT is permitted retroactively to correct the situation by paying out whatever amount is necessary after the IRS brings its action to correct the deficiency through the declaration of an additional dividend within ninety days of the IRS determination. This same provision has now been applied to the SBIC law by Congress. SBICs like Narragansett Capital will be adequately protected against a big deficiency tax that otherwise might have been levied.

To go the regulated investment company route, it was necessary for Narragansett Capital to readjust some of its investments. In some cases it was necessary to convert voting stock to nonvoting shares. It also means that in the future Narragansett will not have quite as close control over its equity investments as it has had in the past, where in many cases the stock ownership has been fifty-fifty and Narragansett has had, in effect, veto power on certain matters like salaries, capital investments, bonuses, mergers, and so forth.

On the other hand, these controls can be adequately provided for in the debt instruments where subordinated loans are made, and Narragansett can be protected by providing that after its debt is paid off the company be required to pay 25 percent of its aftertax earnings in dividends so that Narragansett gets some return on equity investment. Narragansett Capital should also have a put for another ten years of its equity investment to the company at the full book value any time it wishes to make it during that period.

Under these conditions, and with its competent new management and plenty of uninvested funds, Narragansett will avoid disastrous mistakes in the future and should be able to pay its shareholders over $2.00 a share in dividends in the future.

Since I am no longer on the payroll, Arthur has done a terrific job. The directors' valuation is up to $28.14 (June 30, 1978), the directors are already paying $1.60 in dividends, Narragansett has made many fine investments and will soon have the bulk of its available funds profitably employed. Even more important, the stock has sold for over $25. Some improvement over my record!

# Realty Income Trust

In 1959, Congress passed an act called the "Real Estate Investment Trust Act," which permitted trusts organized under this act to deal in highly leveraged real estate investments, which had not been permitted for pension trusts or other tax-free institutions since the tax law was changed in 1954. As soon as this act was passed, we realized that it would enable us to continue to make highly leveraged investments such as the Sixty Trust had made in the past but was no longer permitted to make. It required an organization of at least one hundred stockholders with no one stockholder owning over 5 percent of the outstanding shares.

At the time this act was passed, I was managing some twenty-nine different Textron pension and profit-sharing trusts. Our lawyers had advised us that each one could be counted as a separate entity so as to avoid the prohibition of any one owner holding over 5 percent. We had G. H. Walker and Company make a public offering of a couple of hundred shares at $1,000 a share to meet the legal requirements. The bulk of the capital was subscribed by Textron's various pension trusts.

As a result of this ownership it was possible for us to have two tax-exempt organizations back-to-back, since if 90 percent of a real estate investment trust's (REIT) earnings were passed through to its shareholders each year, no federal income tax would be payable. Since the bulk of the shareholders were tax-exempt themselves, no taxes would be paid in the future on any kind of nonleveraged real estate investments that the pension funds made or on any dividend received directly through the highly leveraged Realty Income Trust.

Through this vehicle it was then possible for this new REIT to borrow money from the banks to make investments without the trusts themselves guaranteeing such loans. Whenever the opportunities for investment required more loans than the credit of the trust would justify, the various pension trusts would subscribe to more shares, pay off the bank loans, and start all over again.

As a result of this new opportunity to make leveraged deals we now started a trend, which many other REITs later followed, of buying land under office buildings and other real estate properties and net leasing the land back to the owner with the ground lease being subordinated to the first mortgage. We always put in a provision that the first mortgage could never be refinanced for an amount greater than the original nor the maturity date extended, with the result that our ground leases would ultimately be superior to any new financing.

One of the most successful of this type of operation was at the Center Plaza development in Boston, directly opposite all the new government buildings. This was in the Redevelopment Agency area where old buildings had been torn down and developers were being given options to acquire land and build new structures on these sites. The Leventhal brothers in Boston had received such options but did not have sufficient capital to pay cash for the land as the options expired. Our REIT, Realty Income Trust, agreed to put up the cash on three separate occasions as they developed the property and to subordinate the ground lease to their first mortgage lenders on the buildings. Our net lease required a 10 percent return to us on the land investment plus an override based on their gross rents in excess of a specific amount in each of the three locations. This was typical of the sort of deal that we were making in our REIT before the deluge of financing that occurred in this field in 1969 to 1971.

When money got tight and the banks were having difficulty in providing mortgage financing for real estate developments at that time, they became aware of the advantages of setting up REITs that they managed through advisory companies raising capital from the general public through the sale of common stock and subordinated debentures. The law was so drawn that the advisor was permitted a fee of 1½ percent not only on all of the investments made by the REITs but also on all the commitments outstanding for which the money had not yet been put out.

The result of this outrageous fee structure was that everybody and his brother set up REITs all over the country. Through the sale of securities to the public plus huge borrowings from banks with high leverage up to 4 to 1 permitted, some $20 billion of new capital was injected into the real estate market within a three-year period. The greed of the advisors was so great and the capital available for investment so enormous that absolutely everyone who managed REITs made some fantastic mistakes by forcing capital out to unqualified borrowers at unprofitable spreads. Result—one of the worst financial debacles in the history of this country occurred in the last ten years because of these excesses.

The banks thought that by having huge advisory fees and using OPM (other people's money) they could earn more for the stockholders of the banks than they could earn if the banks made the loans directly to the developers. Because of this huge surplus of capital, the risks taken by REITs were unwarranted and the competition to put funds out was so great that the spread between the cost of money and the return received produced no profit to the lenders. In addition, most of the leverage was created through open lines of credit to the REITs at floating rates. On the other hand, the REITS were making largely long-term fixed rate commitments to their customers with this short-term money. When prime rates went to 12 percent in 1974, the roof fell in. Practically every REIT in the country was in serious trouble and many of them will never recover.

Since practically all of the leading banks in the country lent money to the REITs, aggregating even today many billions of dollars, the situation finally reached the stage where the banks could not foreclose their mortgages. They have had to be satisfied with work-out situations at low-interest rates requiring many years in the future to resolve.

I'm glad to say that one of the very few REITs that has come through this situation intact is Realty Income Trust, which has never missed an interest payment to its banks or to its debenture holders and is currently paying dividends at the rate of $1.40 per share. It is, I believe, the only REIT in the country that is currently paying such a high return through dividends on its total equity capital—approximately 9 percent.

The two young managers of Realty Income Trust, Ron Kutrieb and Rob Freeman, have done an outstanding job in an industry that has been nothing but disaster for practically every other REIT ever formed.

*ADVICE: For hundreds of years almost every generation has been tempted by greed to overspeculate in some promising new venture. When too much capital enters any new field prices rise too fast and disaster ensues. For example:*

> *South Sea Bubble*
> *Holland Tulip Boom*

*Ponzi Scheme*
*Florida Land Boom, 1920s*
*Stock Market, 1920s*
*Sugar Speculation, 1974.*

Although this impressive list of past speculative ventures cost investors hundreds of millions of dollars none of them can approach the disaster of REITs in effect upon the financial community with the exception of the stock market excesses of the 1920s.

A new, dangerous situation is occurring in California—the rapid sale and resale of homes—the warning flags should be flying! Also, by the time this book is published, the present overspeculation in Resorts International and other New Jersey gambling house shares should have run its course with that bubble bursting and causing enormous losses to thousands of unsophisticated investors.

## DUMAS MILNER

Dumas Milner, who lives in Jackson, Mississippi, and who had a principal office there, operated several Chevrolet agencies in various parts of the country: Miami, Florida; Jackson, Mississippi; San Antonio, Texas; and Seattle, Washington.

These operations were all what is known as Subchapter S Corporations, which meant that so long as he declared all of the agency earnings on his personal income tax return, the Subchapter S company paid no federal income taxes. To shelter this income from federal income taxes, Milner built up a large real estate operation by constructing many office buildings in various parts of the country, and getting the benefit of the depreciation on those properties to offset his Chevrolet agencies' income.

For many years we had a very close relationship with Milner and financed many of his office buildings in Mobile, Alabama; Kansas City, Missouri; Jackson, Mississippi; Midland, Texas; and San Antonio, Texas, as well as in Cincinnati, Ohio.

Milner would have come through almost any recession in general business when his income and cash flow from his Chevrolet agencies might have dropped off if he had confined his investments to prime office buildings. Unfortunately, he spread his activities to hotels like the King Edward in downtown Jackson and a hotel in Beaumont, Texas.

The El Tropicano, which he built in San Antonio anticipating expanding business there because of the World's Fair became a problem. In 1970, Milner got into real trouble. The recession that year seriously affected his income from his automobile agencies. In addition, his hotel operation in downtown Jackson was a disaster and a heavy cash drain. The El Tropicano, while it did well during the World's Fair, was now doing poorly since others had also over-built hotel capacity in San Antonio at the same time. Another serious blow came when American Telephone and Telegraph failed to renew its lease in the Kroger Building in Cincinnati and abandoned 100,000 square feet of floor space, which resulted in a loss of over $400,000 annual rent in that one location.

All of these misfortunes hitting him at once were too much for Dumas and he had a paralyzing stroke, so his affairs had to be handled by his lawyers and accountants.

Since we were one of his principal creditors and had made many very profitable loans to Milner, we hoped to help him solve his problems without requiring him to go into receivership. We forced him to sell all of the marketable securities he had in order to clean up indebtedness, and we took over and operated several of the office buildings as well as the El Tropicano Hotel. The final result of all this was that we did not enforce his personal guarantee and on the whole, the Milner situation will ultimately work out for us, and will leave Dumas Milner solvent.

*ADVICE: The primary reason that we backed Dumas Milner to the extent we did was that he had a net cash flow of about $1 million a year from his automobile agencies. We felt secure in making substantial real estate investments with him because of this tremendous cushion he had developed from investments outside of the real estate business. The advice here is: Don't count on the income from outside sources holding up forever in a recession year. That cash flow can dry up and precipitate a crisis for the entire operation. Furthermore, don't count on personal guarantees from aggressive real estate developers.*

## GALVESTON ISLAND

In the fall of 1969, I was in Houston, Texas, in connection with the affairs of the T. J. Bettes Company. We had lent them some money a couple of years before, but now they were in financial difficulties. Instead of putting Bettes into Chapter 10 or 11 all of the major creditors agreed to have a prominent local lawyer, Dan Arnold, negotiate settlements with each of the principal creditors.

This was a most equitable arrangement since it saved a lot of court costs and trustees' expenses that would have been involved in a receivership. Since there were relatively few creditors and they were all in for large amounts, it was much simpler for Dan to deal individually with us.

We had financed Bettes' housing sales by lending money at a high interest rate against his future payments on homes that had been sold. After about a two-hour negotiation, we worked out a satisfactory settlement. We improved the collateral on our loan, but did reduce the interest rate from the original 18 percent rate.

After finishing, I made the mistake of saying, "Dan, do you know of any other real estate people in the Houston area that we could help by lending them money?"

He said, "Roy, I know of a situation that needs the sort of help that you people could provide. The president's name is Welcome Wilson. His company is The Timewealth Corporation. He has acquired large acreage on Galveston Island down in the Gulf of Mexico, which is only half an hour's drive from Houston. It gets pretty hot in this part of Texas in the summer and a lot of our wealthy people are looking for second homes in that area to get the benefit of the nice cool breezes off the Gulf. Sales are going very well for him, but he does need more capital in order to put in sewer systems and other facilities so as to service the unsold lots which he owns that do not have such utilities."

I said, "Dan, I would certainly be obliged if you would put me in touch with this gentleman. Perhaps I can see him today while I am in Houston."

A meeting was arranged, and before I returned to New England, I had made an agreement with Welcome Wilson for Realty Income Trust to lend him $2 million, provided our first mortgage was on sufficient lots to give us a substantial margin in value over and above our loan. After we had people inspect the property, and lawyers check the title, we put the loan through.

Everything went quite well for a year or so until one of his principal banks in Texas went broke, and the receivers of the bank insisted on being paid off. This created an immediate crisis and feeling that this might force Welcome Wilson into receivership, we arranged to take title to all the lots plus an assignment of all the receivables that had been developed on the sale of the lots that we had originally financed. By so doing, we would not be involved if he later went into receivership.

Timewealth was a typical high-pressure land sales operation, as

we later found out. The salesmen were being paid a higher cash commission on the front end than the down payment of 10 percent received by the developer. The paper taken back on the lot sales ran for eight years with a 7 percent simple interest rate. As part of our arrangement, we were to continue to have his people sell our lots and we turned all of the paper over to a Houston bank to act as a collection agent for us.

Later, when I visited Galveston Island, I was surprised to find that because of hurricane danger all homes were built on stilts. Every house was on a waterway with its own boat. To protect the boats against hurricanes, they were hauled up on davits so that they were at least at the floor level of the house. Such construction, of course, meant that the cost of building was far greater per square foot for second homes in this area than in practically any other place in the country.

Unfortunately, the company did end up in receivership and has not been completely liquidated. Although Realty Income Trust has collected substantial amounts of receivables and has actual ownership of some fine Galveston Island property in case any one ever wants it, the recession of a couple of years ago certainly slowed down the sale of property in that area.

*ADVICE: Don't finance developers of second homes. There are enough problems financing developers of primary residences. The problems involved in developments like Galveston Island, which is subject to hurricanes, where the homes are used only on weekends or in the summer, greatly compound the developers' difficulties. This type of investment should be avoided at all costs.*

## KASSUBA

Walter Judd Kassuba, with his principal office in Palm Beach, had been most successful in building large apartment units in various parts of the country. Ten years ago he was expanding so fast that he was having difficulty in providing the equity capital needed to support the long-term debt on all of the new projects that he hoped to build.

We visited him in Florida and were much impressed with the organization he had put together and with his long-range plans. We indicated how he might get some equity on his existing properties by selling to a real estate investment trust the ground under the apartments and then leasing it back. This type of financing required that we subordinate our position to that of the first mortgage holders on the property. The result of transactions of this sort with Kassuba was that he could not only get his equity investment in the property back, but in many cases could draw down a substantial profit. Since he was expanding extremely fast, he was creating new depreciation all the time on new developments and, therefore, not paying taxes on the profit made from these sales.

We purchased land under some of his apartments in both suburban Chicago and Atlanta. In making these subordinated investments, we required his personal guarantee on the leases, which he readily gave us.

Everything went along fine for a few years until apartment building all over the country was overdone, and there was a surplus of unleased apartments in many of his new operations. Because he expanded too fast and overleveraged his properties, he was finally forced into Chapter 11. To our amazement, the court in Chicago handling the case permitted him to receive for his overhead expenses a large portion of the rental payments instead of applying it against the first mortgages and ground leases. Because of these diversions, millions of dollars were used by him in keeping his organization together in Florida. When the final settlements were made, most of the creditors took over the properties to operate them.

The result of this amazing receivership was that instead of getting any immediate benefit from the cash flow, the creditors are now working out their investments through direct ownership. Kassuba has probably come out of this transaction worth several millions of dollars.

*ADVICE: Don't count on receiverships under Chapters 10 or 11 in the future to wipe out the equity owners for the benefit of the creditors the way the courts used to in the past. There are many cases these days where the creditors take a beating and the equity owners come out whole.*

## SOUTHERN CALIFORNIA DOCTORS' BUILDING

In a town in southern California, not too far from Los Angeles, there was a very modern hospital, which was privately owned. In the eastern part of the country, most of our big hospitals are run as tax-exempt institutions to which contributions can be made for tax credits by the donors. There were relatively few operations of that sort at that time on the West Coast.

The doctors who were using this hospital felt it was necessary for them to have an office building on adjoining land conveniently located to the hospital. A group of them got together and made arrangements with a local developer to build the office building, and they protected him with long-term leases.

The developer, in turn, not wishing to own the building after completion but only to make a profit on its construction, obtained a complete take out from the Woodlawn Cemeteries, an organization that was in a very strong financial position. Because of the shortage at that time of construction loans in California, the builder was unable to arrange the bank financing necessary to cover the cost of this project.

Although this was not a Realty Income Trust project, I was involved some twenty years ago in negotiating the terms of this deal with the other parties for the tax-exempt lender. In financing of this sort, the lender provides the money to the builder through a specially controlled bank account. The bank requires the builder to provide certificates of expenditure before advancing cash on a progress payment basis.

We had an irrevocable take out from the Woodlawn Cemetery upon completion. The Woodlawn Cemetery had the long-term leases from the doctors, so that the cemetery was going to make a good return on the $2 million investment over many years in the future. The necessary contracts were signed, and from time to time we put up funds as required by the bank to make progress payments to the developer.

When our $2 million was finally expended we were advised that the developer had gone broke. When we and our lawyers on the West Coast checked into the situation we found that the contractor had filed false certificates with the bank and that our $2 million had been diverted to his housing development. He hadn't even broken ground at the hospital site. With his housing development in bankruptcy, there were no assets of any sort for us to get a lien on. This was one of the few mistakes I ever made with a 100 percent loss on an investment with no tax offset since the lender was tax-exempt.

*ADVICE: Even if you have a bank making progress payments, you should make sure that the bank or some representative visits the site periodically to see that the money is being used on site. Also, don't ever get involved in a transaction of this sort without completion bond coverage—which, incidentally, we had failed to require.*

## VILLE DE BROSSARD

In 1961, a group of Swiss investors wanted to buy 1,358 acres of land in Ville de Brossard, a little-developed community on the south shore of the St. Lawrence River directly opposite Montreal. A new bridge was to be built across the river, which would make it possible to get to the center of the city in twelve minutes from that small town.

The Swiss group figured that the land they were purchasing would become immediately desirable to developers wanting to build homes for commuters working in the city. There was no other land available so close to the heart of Montreal. Within three or four years the bridge would be completed and this land would become extremely valuable. How could they lose?

I was convinced this was a sound project and lined up $2,500,000 of mortgage money subject to purchase money mortgages of $1,-825,000. Every year, the new owners had to invest more capital in the venture to cover real estate taxes and to make further payments to the former owners.

After three years the Swiss got fed up with the project and refused to put up any more money. That's when we really got involved. We foreclosed the mortgage and took over ownership of the land subject to the purchase money mortgages. We arranged with a large Montreal bank to be our agent to collect the land rents, pay the taxes, and disburse the money required to meet the installments to former owners. This investment was the opposite of a "cash cow"—all the money kept going out instead of coming in.

After the bridge, which connected Montreal with the most direct highway to New York City, was finished, we were certain we would make 200 to 300 percent on our investment. We approached all the important developers in eastern Canada. To our amazement, none of them even made us an offer. Residential building was slow in the area and they all had huge land commitments elsewhere to get out from under, so we continued to hold the land and throw good money after bad.

In addition, we had made a deal with the town that we felt would ultimately increase the value of our land. The town could take over at no cost to it some of our acreage provided it was used for "public park purposes." Imagine our surprise when we learned that the bank representing us had turned over free of cost to Ville de Brossard one hundred acres of our valuable land for a municipal golf course. We hired a prominent law firm to sue the bank and attempt to recover several hundred thousand dollars. Our lawyers finally convinced us our case was hopeless. We had not put an acreage limit on the town's rights. In addition, wouldn't the local courts consider a municipal golf course a park? Furthermore we were "étrangers" and we would be suing one of Montreal's leading banks. We finally threw in the sponge, and in 1977 the Ville de Brossard property was sold for cash and notes. We had invested money in this land for sixteen years, it was within one mile over the new bridge to Montreal, Canada's largest city, so how could we have lost money in this real estate deal?

*ADVICE # 1: If you ever get involved in an agreement of this sort with a community, be certain your lawyers specify exactly what is meant by "park" and more importantly, state the maximum acreage to be involved.*

*ADVICE # 2: I have found from sad experience that purchasing large tracts of raw land is not the perfect inflation hedge. It isn't even a good investment, for two simple reasons. First, the payment of real estate taxes and the loss of cash flow income on the investment amount to more per annum than the land will increase in value. Second, and even more important, there is a greater spread between the bid and asked prices on land than on any other commodity. When you insist on buying land from someone who really doesn't want to sell, you are probably paying a price that the land may be worth on a forced sale ten or twenty years hence. Unless you can afford to be very, very patient for the next twenty years, stay away from undeveloped land purchases.*

## WILLIAM ZECKENDORF

The name Bill Zeckendorf is well known to many people in this country. For years, he was the genius behind many new real estate developments that were creative, well planned, and profitable. For example, he was responsible for the rejuvenation of the center of Montreal, with his Place Ville Marie, and also for the Denver, Colorado, Mile High development, both of which included office buildings, hotels, and other center of the city improvements. He also assembled all of the land required for the development of the United Nations complex. In addition, many of the large housing projects in New York City were financed and built by him. Without question, Bill Zeckendorf was one of the most imaginative and creative real estate people in the country during his lifetime.

In our real estate operations we had many successful investments with Zeckendorf, and as is usual with most expansionist developers, he always gave us his full personal guarantee on any transactions we had with him. In addition to creating new real estate projects, Bill also expanded his operations into hotel ownership. Shortly after World War II, he purchased four of the leading hotels in New York City: the New Yorker, the Commodore, the Roosevelt, and the Biltmore. During the war, all construction of hotels and office buildings had stopped. Therefore, with the postwar boom, there was a tremendous shortage of hotel rooms in New York City.

At the peak of this period of prosperity, Bill sold these hotels, which were operating at over 90 percent occupancy, at a very fancy price based on their high current earnings, and leased them back on a net lease basis for a long period. When we heard about this transaction, we told Bill that in our opinion this transaction might ultimately cause him to go broke, since he had taken on enormous long-term lease commitments that were based on hotel occupancy rates far above anything that would be normal. When the four hotels returned to normal occupancy, he would never be able to pay the net rental required by the transaction. We also told him that if he needed money from us in the future we would make no further loans. We would consider buying land that he might require for future developments if we felt the price was right, and lease the land to him.

As a result of this decision on our part, we did not get involved in the very complex reorganization that took place when he went into receivership. We canceled the lease on the land that we had purchased and were able to resell it promptly at a price that got our money back.

*ADVICE: You might call our Zeckendorf transactions a near miss. When you are dealing with a real estate developer who appears to be getting overextended, don't lend him any more money directly, but protect yourself by owning the property and leasing it to him. Don't count on personal guarantees from real estate expansionists. They won't be worth a damn.*

# *Amtel*

On April 15, 1964, Herman Goodman of Franklin Corporation and Narragansett formed a new corporation called Amtel, and in May, two companies that had been financed by two SBICs some years before were merged into it. Janesville Cotton Mills of Janesville, Wisconsin, was a producer of seat cushioning material for the automotive trade similar to the Burkart Division of Textron. Janesville batting was made primarily from cotton linters, cotton waste, and sisal. Prior to the advent of synthetic foam cushioning, none of the auto manufacturers made their own product of this sort, relying instead upon about half a dozen independent suppliers. Janesville had been a very successful small company, extremely profitable, and primarily dependent upon General Motors for its principal business.

The other company merged into Amtel was Lawson Machine and Tool Company with a new single-story plant on Route 128 in Danvers, Massachusetts. Lawson had been very successful, supplying high-precision parts for United Aircraft's Pratt and Whitney Engine Division. The quality work this shop did assured them of continuation as a supplier for Pratt and Whitney so long as the engine business remained strong. So, in effect, the two companies we put together were largely dependent upon their success in supplying two huge corporations.

On July 13, 1964, Amtel entered into an agreement with the Prudential Insurance Company of America to borrow $2.5 million, maturing June 1, 1979, at 5½ percent. The loan was contingent upon the sale of 250,000 common shares in a proposed public offering. Without using an underwriting firm, the money was raised by a unique device. Through a prospectus dated July 17, 1964, Amtel offered to the holders of outstanding common stock of Franklin and Narragansett nontransferable subscription privileges to buy Amtel stock at $5 per share. One share was offered for every nine shares of Narragansett and every twelve shares of Franklin. An additional subscription privilege was granted to all those who took up their original rights with any oversubscription being prorated. The prospectus showed the following pro forma sales and earnings:

|  | 1961 | 1962 | 1963 | 5 Mos May 1964 |
|---|---|---|---|---|
| Sales | $9,366,902 | $10,444,394 | $12,139,848 | $5,323,294 |
| Net Income | 412,801 | 432,989 | 640,478 | 300,138 |
| Earnings per Share | .57 | .60 | .89 | .42 |

The stock offering price was about seven times the last three years' average earnings. In addition to the 196,460 rights being offered to the SBICs' stockholders, 53,540 were being taken down by three key employees.

Amtel's condensed balanced sheet (unaudited) as of May 29, 1964, showed the following position:

| | |
|---|---|
| Cash | $   810,767 |
| Accounts receivable | 771,444 |
| Inventories and prepaid items | 2,010,123 |
| Total current assets | $3,592,334 |
| Net fixed assets | 2,464,041 |
| Misc. items | 196,007 |
| Total assets | $6,252,382 |
| Total current liabilities | $1,390,273 |
| Deferred liabilities | 179,200 |
| Long-term debt: | |
| 6% Notes payable to bank | 517,212 |
| 8% Subordinated notes payable to SBIC's | 2,445,000 |
| Total long-term debt | $2,962,212 |

Stockholders' equity—720,000
    shares                                       1,720,697

| | |
|---|---:|
| Total liabilities and equity | $6,252,382 |
| Net working capital | $2,202,061 |
| Book value per share about | $2.40 |

The $1,200,000 raised from the sale of shares and the $2,500,000 from the Prudential loan enabled Amtel to pay its bank loans totaling $517,212, and the Narragansett and Franklin subordinated notes totaling $2,445,000, and to add over $700,000 to its cash position.

These transactions raised Amtel's net worth to over $2,900,000, or $3 per share. In addition, the wide ownership resulting from the public offering enabled the company to use its stock for several important acquisitions. Our timing couldn't have been better. In December 1967, our price earnings ratio exceeded 30 so in rapid succession we were able to acquire in December of that year Madison Industries for 120,000 shares; Monroe Forging for 300,000 shares; Fenn Manufacturing Company for 750,000 shares; and in September 1968, Goldfarb and New England Toy for 319,000 shares. On January 27, 1969, Amtel common was listed on the New York Stock Exchange, and in September 1969, Continental Screw Company was acquired for 631,427 shares.

In a little over five years, we had built Amtel's sales from $11,-734,000 in 1964 to $110,600,000 in 1969, its profits from $436,000 to $3,944,000, and its net worth from $2,824,000 to $28,499,000. But we made several bad mistakes.

## MEDICAL OPINION AND REVIEW

During this period of rapid expansion, we noticed that the stocks of publishing businesses were selling at an unusually high multiple, and, although we had had no experience whatsoever in the publishing business, we thought it might improve our multiple if we bought a couple of businesses in that field.

The first one that was brought to our attention was *Medical Opinion and Review*, which was owned by two individuals. They had built a very profitable operation providing the doctors in the country with up-to-date information on all medical research and other medical information in summary form so that the doctors could get this information without having to read all the complicated medical journals and other sources.

They built up pretax earnings to $1 million, but since they had no fixed assets and only receivables from the drug manufacturers who were supporting the operation with their advertisements, the company had very little net worth. In October 1969, we made arrangements with the owners to buy their stock for $4.5 million in cash, or approximately nine times aftertax earnings. The sellers had to pay capital gains taxes on the transaction, but they both ended up as millionaires. We had hoped, of course, that they would work as hard in the future as they had in the past and that our investment would prove to be a successful one.

Unfortunately, the partner who did the editorial work providing the important information for the publication decided that he wanted to retire. The other partner, who handled the distribution and solicitation of advertising, was left without a competent editor. As a result, the advertisers discontinued using the publication to reach doctors and *Medical Opinion and Review* suddenly became a loser instead of a winner.

Since our experience in the past had been primarily with manufacturing operations, we had no one in the organization competent to rehabilitate that division. After that disaster, we practically gave the business back to the remaining former owner and took our loss.

*ADVICE # 1: Don't get involved in the publishing business if your principal business has been manufacturing—particularly if you have made the former owners wealthy.*

*ADVICE # 2: (This second bit of advice applies to all types of acquisitions.) Be very careful not to buy businesses that have earnings but no net worth. If the earnings evaporate, you have no escape route to recover any portion of your investment.*

## *BARNES AND NOBLE*

Amtel again ventured into the publishing business by purchasing the old, established firm of Barnes and Noble, which became available after Mr. Barnes died and his estate was in the hands of the United States Trust Company, which administered matters for his widow.

The company was well known throughout the country because of its various successful operations in selling secondhand textbooks to students, colleges, and universities that preferred to save money by purchasing secondhand books rather than new ones. Barnes and Noble's source of supply, of course, was those students who had just completed courses and who had purchased books to comply with the requirements of the various courses they were taking in college.

This business had been profitable for many, many years. The Barnes and Noble name was extremely well established. At the time we had purchased the business for $4,370,000 in November 1969, the young man who had been brought in as president to take over the operation for the widow and the estate came up with what appeared to be a brilliant idea. Why couldn't Barnes and Noble do something as a result of their tremendous sales coverage, which was relatively new to the industry. Why couldn't they bring out a complete series of paperback textbooks to compete with the hardcover textbooks and thereby reduce the cost to the students for the book requirements for their various courses? Barnes and Noble had made arrangements with many of the textbook authors to write the copy for this new type of distribution that would greatly expand the volume of books sold since they would not enter the secondhand market. Sales might run four or five times the total volume of hardcover textbooks.

We went along with the project, hoping that it would be successful. The ultimate long-range results could have made Barnes and Noble far more important in the publishing business than if restricted to the sale of secondhand books in universities and special stores in large cities.

This new concept led us to hope that we could triple or quadruple Barnes and Noble's sales and earnings within the next five years. Unfortunately, this new idea was a complete flop. As a matter of fact, the whole concept, had it been successful, would have put Barnes and Noble's basic operations out of business since paperbacks would have replaced hardcovers and there would have been no market for secondhand textbooks. We discontinued this operation in 1971 with a loss of approximately $6 million.

*ADVICE: The people who took over the Barnes and Noble operations from us promptly abandoned the paperback project and have greatly expanded Barnes and Noble's original concept of retail bookstores. Their current full-page ads in various cities indicate profitable business. We just didn't have the right management, and we got involved in something we knew little about. That was our first mistake. Worse than that, however, was the fact that when Barnes and Noble's earnings for the six months prior to acquisition dropped drastically, I didn't have the courage to walk away from the deal. Whatever you do, don't feel obligated to sign a purchase contract if the most recent financials indicate an earnings trend far below what was represented.*

## AN UNUSUAL AMTEL ACQUISITION

Amtel purchased a company in September 1968 from a small group of stockholders. The principal shareholder became a millionaire as a result of the sale since we issued common stock with a market value of $6,619,250. The following year, pretax profits were $1,178,000 on $11,152,000 sales.

The company did not manufacture anything but was primarily a large distributor of a wide variety of products made in the Orient and sold to gift shops and chains like J. C. Penney and Woolworth. It was a volume business, primarily because of the low cost of production in places like Hong Kong, Taiwan, and Japan. In effect, what this company did was to search the market for novelty products that were made in high-cost areas and redesign them to be made in low-cost areas. As a result of the time needed to have these products made in the Orient, it was necessary to carry very substantial inventories in order to make fast deliveries to the retail distributors who purchased from us.

One of the principal problems was that if an item was particularly successful, the long lead time for reorders prevented really cashing in on the hot new products developed. Conversely, if large quantities of items were purchased in the Orient that later proved to be unsalable, there were always losses from inventory writedowns and disposal at discounted prices.

Again, this was a business in which we had no prior experience. Our expertise was primarily in manufacturing—not in distributing. We soon had a problem. The former owner came to us and said that he was going to leave. He found that he could not adapt to working for a large corporation. We were left without the leadership and management we had expected. Basically, this is the kind of business that should be owner-managed. It should not be a division of a large publicly owned company.

This whole operation became a serious problem.

Several years ago we uncovered the worst case of defalcation in the operations that I have ever experienced in my sixty years in business—and I'm sorry to say I've seen all kinds. There was a complete conspiracy among all the officers of this division to defraud the company over the past four years. They were so clever that even our public accountants failed to uncover their schemes. To show the breadth of their deceit here are some of the ways these individuals stole from the company:

| | |
|---|---:|
| Duplicate payments | $139,669.99 |
| Fictitious salesmen | 14,088.38 |
| Various business enterprises owned by officers doing business with company | 506,185.29 |
| Excess commission payments | 212,435.00 |
| Unsupported checks | 13,866.00 |
| Unauthorized gratuities | 10,843.49 |
| Funds diverted to relatives | 5,622.00 |
| Unauthorized payments to management's trading companies | 28,500.00 |
| Unauthorized family trips | 3,215.09 |
| Unreported payments to nonemployees | 118,050.49 |
| Payments to treasurer's family | 2,259.67 |
| Unauthorized bonuses | 93,524.00 |
| Unauthorized travel allowances | 1,500.00 |
| Unauthorized sale of auto | 4,499.00 |
| Home improvements for officer | 1,000.00 |
| Sales commissions paid on phony billing | 4,697.21 |
| Checks issued without support | 20,056.07 |
| Unauthorized hiring of officer's relative | 63,782.09 |
| Unauthorized excess salary to treasurer | 190,230.53 |
| Unaccounted for inventory shortages | 1,644,921.89 |
| Bad debt loss on excessive credit granted to officer getting "kickbacks" from customers | 697,141.46 |
| Kickbacks and payoffs to vendors and customers | 274,734.58 |
| Excess contingency payout | 156,500.00 |
| Total | $4,207,322.23 |

Amtel filed this enormous claim with its insurance company to cover all losses sustained, which has recently been settled for $2,500,000.

*ADVICE: If you are a large publicly owned corporation, don't ever buy a business that can only be successful if operated by an owner-manager.*

*EXTRA ADVICE: Whatever you do, don't take a chance of getting along without fidelity insurance. Place plenty of coverage on every one in the organization including yourself.*

## CATHY LORD

We knew that there were many successful schools to train girls for important business assignments after being graduated from high school. There are so many girls in the country who never have an opportunity to go to college that there has been a tremendous demand for one- and two-year schools that train girls for high paid secretarial jobs and other positions for which women are particularly well qualified. Some examples of these schools are: Katherine Gibbs, Sawyer, Berkeley, Bryant College, Dean Junior College, Chamberlayne Junior College, Newberry, and Fisher Junior College.

A small group of investors in Providence had financed an operation of this sort called the Cathy Lord School, which gave courses primarily in advertising, promotion, and retail selling. They had seventy-eight students at the time Amtel took it over in June 1970.

We felt that this was an excellent opportunity, if this first school was successful, for Amtel to start a chain of schools under the Cathy Lord name all over the country and develop a most important new divisional operation for Amtel. We continued to finance this operation for a couple of years before we finally threw in the sponge and decided that we had better take our loss before the operation became a disaster.

*ADVICE: The mistake we made in this case was trying to run a school of this sort in a small community such as Providence, where the demand for girls of these qualifications was limited. The graduates were all getting excellent jobs, but this was a case where the operation was successful but the patient died.*

*This, again, is the type of business that has been most successful when run by owner-managers. Most of the successful schools have been so operated by men and women who were primarily entrepreneurs. Again, Amtel lost money by diverting its capital and efforts into a field in which it had no prior experience.*

## PUBLIC LIABILITY AND PRODUCT LIABILITY

The directors of Amtel received a shock in 1977 when the insurance companies got together and raised the premiums for public liability and product liability insurance to five times what it had been the year before. We had been paying approximately $250,000 for all of this coverage with no minimum exposure to the company. Our record had been excellent; our total claims for the last five years had been only $400,000. Suddenly this year the insurance company quoted us a price of $1,250,000 with $250,000 deductible for the same type of coverage. This seemed to be outrageous, but we could not get any other insurance company to do better. We finally had to rearrange our whole program to reduce the premium to $830,000. It was necessary for us to take the first $3,000,000 in losses ourselves and then reinsure with another company for any disasters within that $3,000,000.

The problem that this big increase in insurance has caused small businesses is fantastic. Many small companies have been quoted premiums that would wipe out their entire earnings and, as a result, quite a few have liquidated their operations and gone out of business rather than subject themselves to these exorbitant charges.

*ADVICE: In order to avoid such outrageous charges, particularly where experience has been as good as it was at Amtel, the only way that this problem can be solved is to have about twenty companies of Amtel's size that have had equally good records to get together and form a mutual company to cover these risks. The thing that has happened to Amtel and other companies with good experience is that, in effect, they are paying through these exorbitant premiums for the bad experiences of other companies throughout the industry.*

*In our opinion, if the primary insurers continue to raise premiums to the extent they did in 1977 they will force industry groups to self-insure by organizing mutuals.*

In spite of all the costly mistakes I made in Amtel, Jerry Ottmar, president and chief executive officer, did an excellent job in turning things around. Sales in 1977 were $407,114,000, with earnings of $7,009,000 for 16 percent return on the year's starting net worth. Not bad for a little company that was created in 1964 by putting together two small operations whose combined sales were $9,300,-000 with $412,000 in earnings in 1961 on a pro forma basis!

## SUMMARY

I have been asked many times why we chose the name Amtel for the company when we started it. You could never guess the answer—so I'll tell you.

With Textron starting with "T," I had to wade through three or four financial pages in the *New York Times* to find the price of the stock on the New York Stock Exchange. I decided that the next time I founded a company, its name would start with "A"—that would solve that problem. I also wanted a short name that could not be mispronounced. Herman Goodman suggested "Amtel." Fortunately, American Telephone and Telegraph had not preempted the use of that name.

Some years ago, before Jerry Ottmar came aboard at Amtel, and I was unsuccessfully trying to run the business, I got the company overextended financially. The banks threatened to withdraw their lines of credit, and we were afraid that everything was going to go down the drain. When our Hartford bank pulled out of the line, a crisis arose.

Our other banks finally agreed that if we would raise $2 million by selling common stock to build up equity, they would continue to support us.

The stock was selling for $22, but the situation was so urgent that there was not time for a registration statement. The banks therefore suggested that perhaps some of the directors might put up the money.

Herman Goodman, the co-founder of Amtel, and I agreed to place privately 100,000 shares at $21 to raise $2,100,000. The directors approved the plan and the money was raised. Then came a bombshell! The New York Stock Exchange (on which Amtel was listed) advised the company that it would be necessary for Amtel to call a special meeting of stockholders to approve the sale, since two of the buyers were directors and therefore there might be a possible conflict of interest.

Four months later, the stockholders approved the plan. By that time the price had dropped to $15, but Herman and I were committed to pay $21. Since then, the stock has sold as low as $4. From the company's point of view our rescue operation was satisfactory—but *we* didn't do so well!

*ADVICE: If your company is listed on the New York Stock Exchange, don't count on any transaction being permitted without special shareholder approval if there is any possibility of a conflict of interest being involved.*

On November 10, 1977, AMCA, the wholly owned subsidiary of Dominion Bridge of Canada announced a $15 tender offer for all Amtel shares. The Amtel board, on which I had not served for some months, settled the matter by agreeing to recommend a $16.50 price to the shareholders. This event provides me with a wonderful good news–bad news story. The good news is that the average cost of my personal stock was $16.90 so I did not have to pay any income taxes. The bad news is that I've been sued in six separate class action cases. Although I can see no merit in any of these complaints, I'll probably be involved in depositions and court actions for the next couple of years. I predict that the legal bills just through depositions for all defendants alone will exceed $1,000,-000. But it's nice work for the lawyers—all fourteen firms of them!

*ADVICE: If you don't enjoy being sued, my advice is: Don't get involved in publicly owned companies the way I have—stay private. I'll guarantee that if you are active in business for sixty years as I have been and are an officer or director of a public company, sooner or later you'll be involved in some kind of class action or derivative suit. Just relax and enjoy it—it's all part of the free enterprise system!*

.

# *And Other Valuable Advice*

# Directors

*A*s a result of many years' experience, I have very definite ideas about the composition of boards. Never have more than two management representatives—the chief executive officer and the chief operating officer. Other management directors are worthless. They don't dare speak if they disagree with the boss and therefore contribute nothing. If they do speak out in disagreement, the outside directors wonder whether the boss is really in control.

In a diversified company such as Textron, never have a division president on the board—don't put the chief executive officer in a position where someone reporting to him is, as a director, his boss. If possible never have commercial bankers or investment bankers on the board—it restricts your options when you need capital.

Never have suppliers or customers on the board. Don't invite your company lawyer to join. You'll have no trouble with your auditors since none of the large firms permit board memberships.

Where then do directors come from? With every large company I have always arranged to have a professor from the Harvard Business School on the board. They are tops, they do their homework, and they don't hesitate to ask embarrassing questions when needed. Most companies now insist that their chief executive officers serve on at least three or four outside boards to broaden their experience. There are also many brilliant businesswomen who haven't yet been tapped.

Take a thorough look at your stockholder list. You may find some large owner who would make an ideal director. With mandatory retirement for management at sixty-five and directors at seventy-two, former chief executive officers from other companies can provide seven years' worth of the most capable ability available for board service. Above all, pay your outside directors well for the responsibilities they assume; otherwise, you may not attract the quality you need.

*"Then it's moved and seconded that
the compulsory retirement age be advanced to ninety-five."*

Comment: Royal Little is on twenty-one boards and commit-
tees—but then he's only eighty-three.

One plan that I developed, which has not been adopted by
others, may be of interest. To simplify the problem of getting
directors to resign at seventy-two and also to give them an incentive to do so, we offered, in effect, a small pension for retired board
members. Any director could retire between sixty-five and seventy-
two, but must retire at seventy-two. He could then receive a lifetime annual consulting fee from the company equal to $20 for
every month of past service. By this means, future income for life is

provided to these important individuals at a time they will need it most.

One further bit of advice. You may be doing your retiring chief executive officer a disservice by asking him to remain on the board. If he's in good shape mentally and physically, he'll be much happier getting involved with new, exciting projects rather than remaining as an eunuch, so to speak, on the board of a company where he had formerly been the decision maker.

Although Textron had many directors who were most helpful and performed valuable services, I would like to give special credit to one man who, in my opinion, was the outstanding director of Textron while I was with the company. That was Jack Bierwirth, the former chief executive officer of National Distillers. My first contact with Jack came when our Kordite Division, which made finished products out of polyethylene film, purchased raw material from him and extruded and converted film.

There were two transactions Jack and I were involved in that were far beyond the call of duty as far as he was concerned. Jack told me in the spring of 1960 that the entire government operations at Bell Aircraft might be sold and that Lockheed was considering buying them. After Lockheed backed out because they wanted only the helicopter operations in Fort Worth, Texas, Jack and I negotiated with Dave Milton who controlled Bell through his Equity Corporation holdings and worked out a deal. The transaction was set up with a cash payment of approximately $32 million and leases of all the real estate for thirteen years with very low renewal options thereafter.

Textron was attracted to this opportunity since we had very little government work and felt it was time that we got our proportionate share of this business. The negotiations moved along reasonably well while we visited the different facilities, but I found that Dave Milton was impossible to deal with. He kept changing his mind every day. Finally, I got Bill Miller into the act and told him that it was up to him to get this transaction through because I was afraid I would tell Dave Milton to go to hell if I continued to be involved in the final nitty-gritty with him and the lawyers. Without Jack Bierwirth being on the board, we would never have known about this opportunity, and I must say, in retrospect, that the timing on the Bell acquisition was superb. Their huge Buffalo facility had very little work so it took considerable courage to buy that part of the business. When I visited that plant, there was hardly anybody working. The total business of the three Bell operations in 1959 was about $100 million.

The method of acquisition was unusually attractive since government work was subject to renegotiation. It was particularly advantageous to rent all of the floor space, since rents would be allowed as expense. If we had borrowed millions of dollars to buy the real estate, the interest would have been disallowed for renegotiation purposes.

Then in 1963, when Jack, as a director, knew that we were interested in ultimately disposing of our remaining textile business he was also director of Deering Milliken's huge textile business. Roger Milliken had proposed to their board that they should build some new plants in the Carolinas to expand their operations, but Jack convinced him that it would be far better to buy Textron's very modern facilities in the same area rather than expanding capacity by building new mills and causing overproduction in the market.

With Jack Bierwirth's assistance, Textron received its full net worth, approximately $45 million, for its Amerotron Textile Division, which had only been earning $6 million a year before taxes. Within the next eighteen months, Textron put that capital to work buying unrelated businesses that earned 25 percent pretax on our investments.

And, speaking of directors, Ken Lindsey deserves special commendation for his acumen in spotting my many mistakes. After his frequent diatribes I always said: "Ken, if you had your way, Textron would still be a small textile business in South Boston." One of his memos to the directors was typical:

3rd June 1957

The disparity between the forecasts of Textron's earnings and the results actually achieved is a subject which must be of concern to the Directors. The figures for the first quarter of the current year reveal how over-optimistic we were a year ago. The earnings for 1956—again after high hopes—amounted to only $6,502,592. In the years 1949 to 1956 inclusive, the average earnings per year on the Common Stock were 60 cents.

There must be a reason why a Company which engenders so much excitement as Textron, and which so confidently proclaims the wonders it is about to perform, so invariably fails to meet expectations.

In the opinion of the writer of this memorandum the explanation of this unhappy record is that too much is expected of the Chairman. Granted that he is the creator of the Company and the person to whom alone credit is due for bringing it from its humble beginnings to its present size, and, acknowledging his quite exceptional mental powers, the fact remains that except for those years in which conditions were abnormally favourable he has never been able to translate his brilliance into anything commensurate in the way of earnings; but for the shareholders these, in the long run, far transcend in importance the pleasure they may derive from witnessing feats of virtuosity on the part of the Chairman.

Mr. Little, in fact, has the defects of his qualities. To the same extent that he is bold and imaginative, he is impulsive and unpredictable. He moves with great speed and determination, and on many occasions the Directors have been presented with what were, in effect, *faits accomplis* which they have accepted through acquiescence rather than conviction. The resultant mistakes have been on such a scale that they have more than outweighed the successes, and this has been repeated so regularly that it has formed a pattern.

The moral of the tale is that the Directors must take a more positive and critical attitude towards the conduct of the business. They must not assume that because a new project is recommended to them in persuasive terms that all is for the best in the best of worlds. It should be an invariable rule that no proposal be adopted without the unanimous consent of the Board, and if any single member expresses disapproval, or even doubt, it should be immediately dropped. This does not mean that Textron will ever be a quality Company for its limitations are becoming increasingly clear, but at least it should be possible to avoid a repetition of such farcical situations as the S.S. LEILANI.

What is suggested above is only a defensive measure. If anything of a more constructive nature could be devised that would be an additional source of strength to the Company.

As you can see, Ken was one of my staunchest supporters. When he visited with company officers, he invariably opened the conversation with, "How's our peerless leader doing today?"

The following letter was written by Ken to Eliot Farley who was then chairman of the board of Textron:

1st April 1948

Dear Eliot:

Thank you for your letter of March 23rd and I was most interested to have your impressions of Puerto Rico.

Regarding the second and third paragraphs of your letter, it is as well that the real facts should be stated. Far from being ready to tell me at lunch that he was against the $5 per share issue, Royal's opening words to me were to the effect that it *was* going through and at that time that was his intention. He changed his mind on one of the following days, and the only reason which he gave me over the telephone for so doing was that because of the rights of conversion the result might be that there would be four million shares outstanding.

There was therefore no misunderstanding on your part of the essential fact of the situation, which was that Royal would have cheerfully gone ahead with the idea, to the great detriment of the interests of existing shareholders, if other considerations had not caused him to drop it. It was and remains a thoroughly upsetting incident, not only in itself, but in its wider implications.

If you prefer to ignore realities and live in an imaginary world, you are free to do so, but it seems to me that one should learn something from experience. Among these things are that Royal, while a likeable person with unusual abilities, has a positively Rooseveltian delight in treating his position as an amusing personal hobby. For him business is one exciting adventure after another, and he experiments, improvises and goes off at any tangent that occurs to him. The effect of this on the fortunes of his shareholders is to him purely incidental, and he has not the slightest hesitation in sacrificing them to the passing whim. No one has had more experience of this than yourself.

The one important and useful function which you could perform, because of your position and long years of association with Royal and the business would be to give leadership to the responsible members of the Board, such as Hutchins, Weld, Hoskins and Leeson, and support the younger ones, such as Dyson and Rawle so that some coherence is maintained in the Company's policies. As it is, you seem to feel a sense of shame in defending your own interests, or for that matter, those for which you are responsible. If you are feeling too old or unwell to face up to these responsibilities, I should understand it if you said so frankly, but as it is it grieves me to see you display so consistently such pitiable weakness when you could so easily be a source of strength.

As to the place for offering Londsale rights, I do not understand the $3 per share being on the basis for two or three times earnings per share, and had thought the earnings were much higher. Perhaps some further explanation will make this clear; at any rate, it is a less awful idea than the last one.

Yours sincerely,<br>Ken

Eliot Farley's answer to Ken Lindsey's letter is, in itself, an example of this man's great sense of humor:

April 5, 1948

Dear Ken:

Your very courteous and understanding letter of April 1st received.

For once I think you will have to admit you are wrong. The old custom on April 1st was to make fools out of others.

Sincerely yours,
Eliot Farley

# Management Compensation

## DEFERRED PROFIT-SHARING PLANS

In the past the tax law permitted payments made from deferred profit-sharing plans in a lump sum on retirement to be treated as capital gain. This is no longer possible, so that deferred profit-sharing plans are not as attractive for the employee as they used to be.

In Textron, we had a deferred profit-sharing plan called the Market Square Trust that was self-administered. The payments into the plan covered only Burkart Division, Dalmo-Victor Division, the textile division called Amerotron, and the home office. The formula for determining the contributions to the plan were, of course, based on earnings; but under the law could not exceed 15 percent of the payroll of those participating. The company received a tax deduction for the payments made into the plan for the benefit of the employees, but the participants paid no tax on the contributions and had the advantage of a tax-free investment fund during the rest of their years of service with the company. No taxes were paid by the trust or by the beneficiaries on the earnings accrued for their benefit during their employment.

After having applied this plan to our textile division and our first two diversified acquisitions we found that the older management people were most enthusiastic about the plan. However, since it was possible to put the plan into effect only if all salaried employees in a division were included, the younger executives with children in school told us that they would much prefer to have cash incentives paid to them as earned rather than being deferred until they retired. As a result, the Market Square Trust was not used to put deferred profit-sharing plans into any other divisions.

When we first set up such a plan in our textile operations, it provided that after ten years' service the employee could get full payment out of the plan if he quit and went to work somewhere else. Subsequently, we changed the provision so that the money was paid out only on death, complete disability, or retirement at age sixty-five. Formerly, we had lost a number of excellent people who took their benefits and started a small business or joined a competitor. We had no problem with this concept until Textron sold the entire Amerotron Textile Division to Deering Milliken in 1963.

Although I had retired both from any executive capacity in the company and also from the board of directors in 1962, I had continued to manage the pension and profit-sharing fund investments. I was personally involved, therefore, in the hassle that developed when the employees who were transferred to Deering Milliken found that their profit-sharing trust funds did not travel with them. Under the indenture, they became creditors of the trust with no return on their capital until death or retirement when their benefits would finally be paid out.

As a result, a group of former Amerotron employees sued the trustees demanding distribution of the funds. This was an interesting case since the trust instrument governed what the trustees could do and gave us no latitude to pay out any funds to retired persons until they reached age sixty-five or died. This suit lasted several years and was completely deadlocked. It would have obviously been unfair to the remaining beneficiaries of the Market Square Trust if all that money had been paid out to the Amerotron employees, when the trust instrument did not permit it. The trustees were really in the middle on this one and finally, with the court's approval, the case was settled by retaining the Amerotron employees' funds in Market Square Trust but granting them cumulative interest on their accounts.

*ADVICE: As a result of this unfortunate experience, I advise amending all profit-sharing trusts so that in the event that an entire division or subsidiary of a company is sold the employees shall either receive annuities or have the funds representing their vested interests transferred to a plan set up by the company acquiring that unit.*

## OPTIONS

Options used to be a very good device for attracting top management. Originally, a qualified option could be granted at market price at the time of issuance, provided such a plan was approved by the shareholders. The employee receiving such options could take them down and sell them after six months and make a substantial profit after capital gains tax, with a minimum of risk. This proved to have real disadvantages since the employee could then cash in his chips, go to another company, and get another option.

The law was then changed so that to qualify for capital gains treatment, the employee had to hold those shares for three years before selling. This solved the first problem, but created an even worse one. When key employees borrowed money, as was usually necessary, to pick up options, to get favorable tax treatment, they were required to hold the stock with heavy indebtedness for three years before selling. The result was that in recession years like 1974 and 1975, executives who had exercised options at high prices a couple of years earlier with borrowed money at extremely high interest rates were faced literally with bankruptcy. Many individuals were wiped out during this period.

To avoid further disaster many corporations, over the objections of their stockholders, bailed out their top management by lending them money to pay off their bank loans, and, in effect, financed the purchase of the shares for the individual without prior shareholder approval. Changes in the tax law have made qualified options much less attractive than they originally were.

*ADVICE: With qualified stock options no longer attractive tax-wise, large corporations should provide net worth incentive plans for key management, generous pensions (which since 1976 are treated as earned income when received), and stock purchase plans as described later. For small companies there is nothing like "a piece of the action" with management owning shares in a highly leveraged company.*

## NET WORTH AND ASSET INCENTIVE PLANS

Having observed many types of management incentive plans, we decided that it was unwise to pay incentives to divisional management in Textron based on some percentage of the total earnings that the division made. We found that this type of incentive tended to encourage the aggressive manager to get more and more capital from the home office to expand his operation, regardless of whether that would increase the rate of return that he was making on the total capital involved in the division. Under a percentage of earnings plan, division management could greatly expand bonuses through the use of more capital even though the overall return on the divisional net worth was being reduced.

So we adopted a basic plan that involved incentive being tied to the return that the company earned on the divisional net worth. Our plan required that there would be no bonus unless the management made at least 10 percent pretax on the divisional net worth and that the maximum bonuses could be reached if an unusually high rate of return was made. Under the maximum bonus, the divisional president could earn 100 percent of his base salary, the second group could earn 75 percent; the third group 50 percent; and the next group 25 percent. It was our feeling that these plans should go far enough down in the organization so that everyone who had an opportunity to make or lose money for the company as a result of their decisions should be included.

When we first instituted this plan, we used to get ten or a dozen of the participants in the group together and explain to them how they could increase their bonus by such simple things as getting their supplier to give them more frequent drop shipments instead of loading them up with big chunks of inventory at one time; by getting the customers to pay the receivables more promptly; by increasing the efficiency in the manufacturing operations; and by decreasing sales and advertising expense without hurting volume or price. In many cases when long-term money was available at 6 percent or less, it was to the management's advantage and also to the stockholders to have someone else build our new plants and lease them to us at these low rates. The result of this type of plan put the management in exactly the same spot as the stockholder, namely, what percent is being made on total investment?

There is one possible defect with this plan, which we found a way to cure. Some managements might miss opportunities to expand or diversify the division's business through the production of new products that required substantial engineering and development expense. We handled this problem by capitalizing those total development expenses for the purpose of determination of net

worth incentive and then writing off that cost over a reasonable period of time. In that way, management was not discouraged from
developing new products and expanding.

In Textron's case, and that of other large companies that were
not overly highly leveraged, the incentive is based on the percentage return on the divisional net worth. However, this plan does not
work well for highly leveraged companies where equity may be
only 10 or 20 percent of the total capital investment involved. In
those cases, we have developed a similar plan where the bonus is
paid based on the return on average total assets over a full year. It
is obvious that the net worth incentive plan would not be productive in a highly leveraged company since the total equity could
double in the early years and management's bonus would be reduced. A typical return on assets plan is shown in this chart.

### INCENTIVE COMPENSATION PLAN

To determine incentive compensation: (1) start at left scale with Bonus
Return, as defined in Plan; (2) read across to intersection with diagonal
line; (3) then read down to bottom scale which shows per cent of base salary payable as incentive compensation for each group.

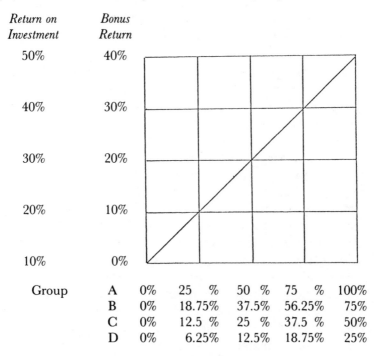

| Return on Investment | Bonus Return |
|---|---|
| 50% | 40% |
| 40% | 30% |
| 30% | 20% |
| 20% | 10% |
| 10% | 0% |

| Group | | | | | |
|---|---|---|---|---|---|
| A | 0% | 25 % | 50 % | 75 % | 100% |
| B | 0% | 18.75% | 37.5% | 56.25% | 75% |
| C | 0% | 12.5 % | 25 % | 37.5 % | 50% |
| D | 0% | 6.25% | 12.5% | 18.75% | 25% |

*Incentive Compensation as Per Cent of Base Salary*

## STOCK PURCHASE PLAN

Many years ago, Textron felt that stock options should be restricted to the top officers in the company. Many companies were spreading them throughout the organization but we felt that was not wise. We also had discovered that deferred profit sharing, while particularly good for the high-salaried older executives, was not motivating for the rest of the employees since the need for cash was more immediate and they discounted the value of something that might be received twenty or thirty years hence.

As a result, Textron set up a stock purchase plan in 1960 for all employees who were not members of a union bargaining unit. Since the unions considered any such plan as within their jurisdiction to negotiate, it was not possible to voluntarily put in a plan of this sort for union employees. It had to be restricted to nonunion members unless at some future date the union required that a stock purchase plan be negotiated as part of their settlement. We felt that the advantage of this type of plan would be most attractive since it gave all of the eligible employees an opportunity through weekly or monthly payroll deductions to participate in the ownership of the company for which they worked. In our case, the plan provided that the employee could put in up to 10 percent of his salary and the company would match up to 50 percent of the employee's contribution. In addition, any employee could put up an additional 10 percent of his salary without the company matching it if he wished to have a larger interest in the company.

The beauty of this program is that the trustees have to invest the funds in the open market in Textron common stock as fast as the money comes in. They are given no discretion to try to outguess the swings in the market. In effect, the employee is dollar averaging his purchases of Textron stock at two-thirds of the market over the entire period in which he is employed and participates. The other feature that makes this plan attractive is that all of the dividends received are reinvested in Textron common stock. The company gets a tax deduction on its federal tax return for all of the contributions made for the benefit of its employees, but the employee pays no tax on that contribution, nor on the dividends received for his benefit in the plan until he retires.

When the plan was originally put into effect, an employee on retirement received in stock, tax-free, all the money that he had put in and, in addition, all of the shares received from company contributions and dividends accrued were reported by the employee as capital gain. Moreover, any appreciation in the value of the shares in the trust over and above the employee's proportionate cost was received completely tax-free, subject only to capital gains tax at the time the employee finally sold his shares. This plan has been phenomenally successful at Textron, where 14,524 employees are participating; the trust owned 5,293,927 common shares, or 17.05 percent of Textron's entire outstanding capitalization on June 30, 1978.

In Amtel, the plan finally owned 10 percent of the total common stock. I have been amazed that more companies have not used this plan to encourage their employees to have a greater interest in the company for which they work and to have greater incentive to personally do a better job to make their shares more valuable. Although there have been some changes in the 1976 tax law making part of distribution subject to ordinary income rather than capital gains tax, the stock purchase plan is still one of the most attractive ways for the employees to participate and to feel, in effect, that they have "a piece of the action."

## PENSION PLANS

In 1945, we recommended to the Textron directors that we set up a trust with an individual trustee to invest our pension funds in the future and obtain a much better return on investments than we were currently receiving. Our funds were with an insurance company which, at that time, was allowing us only 2½ percent return on our contributions. In 1945, 1946, and 1947, the company contributed a total of about $1.2 million. We had employed Larry Green, a very competent tax lawyer at Hale and Dorr in Boston, as sole trustee to manage these funds under conditions that we specified. The salaried employees' fund was called the Sixty Trust because Larry's address was 60 State St., Boston. We advised Larry that we did not want to have the funds invested in common stocks without our approval. We felt that there was a great opportunity as a tax-exempt trust to make relatively high yield investments in mortgages and special loans at far higher rates than common stock dividends would return.

In 1948, the Cleveland Pneumatic Tool Company in Cleveland, Ohio, one of the principal suppliers of landing-gear struts for the aircraft industry, became available because Walter Shott, the owner, had been advised by his doctors to lighten his business activities because of a heart condition. The company was earning about $1 million a year after taxes and had $3 million of surplus cash in it, so that Mr. Shott also had the problem of undistributed surplus. Larry Green and I discussed this situation and asked Textron's lawyers whether there was any way that the company could buy it. We were told our articles of association were so limited that there was no way that we could purchase a business outside of the textile industry. When we suggested a wholly owned subsidiary, that also was turned down.

We therefore decided that this acquisition was so attractive that the Sixty Trust should buy Cleveland Pneumatic Tool. The price was $6.7 million, which was only a little over six times earnings. If the Sixty Trust purchased it, the trust could withdraw the $3 million in surplus cash without paying any taxes since it was tax-exempt. This meant that for the trust the price was a little over three times earnings. Although this was a most unusual investment for a pension trust to make, the lawyers advised us that there was nothing in the tax law at that time that would prevent our doing so.

To raise the purchase price, Larry Green borrowed a large portion of it from the Cleveland Trust Company. Then the Textron directors lent the trust $900,000 to make up the difference. When the transaction was completed, Textron permitted one of its key employees, Sam Mullen, to move to Cleveland and be the company's chief executive officer. Larry Green went in as chairman of the board and after paying out the $3 million in dividends, reduced the bank loans.

We then found that General Tire Company's pension fund was being operated very much the same way Textron was managing its funds. They were looking for high yield, good cash flow investments. Larry sold all of the fixed assets of Cleveland Pneumatic Tool at the depreciated book value of $1,100,000 to the General Tire Pension Fund and leased them back under a contract that provided a rental payment of a small percentage of sales until they had received $1,500,000. Thereafter, options ran for many years to lease the fixed assets at $50,000 a year. The $1,100,000 was also paid out to the Sixty Trust and used to reduce bank indebtedness. With earnings continuing at $1,000,000 a year after taxes and no need for these funds in the business, the Sixty Trust was able to pay off all its debt in about two and a half years

When the Sixty Trust purchased Cleveland Pneumatic Tool, the company had no real incentives for management and all other employees. Larry set up a plan for all of the employees, in which the company would pay a percentage of pretax earnings into a deferred profit-sharing trust each year so that a substantial amount of funds would be available for the employees upon retirement. After having recovered the entire purchase price of Cleveland Pneumatic Tool, Larry felt that it would be advisable to sell that company at a very substantial profit and diversify the investments in the Sixty Trust. Sam Mullen and the union people were violently opposed to being sold to another company. They asked Larry to negotiate a price with them so that the company's own profit-sharing trusts could buy 100 percent of the shares. Obviously there were not enough liquid funds in their trusts to accomplish what they wished. Larry had received several cash offers of very substantial amounts, so he felt that if the Sixty Trust were going to take back paper the price would have to be very high.

He and Sam finally worked out a plan whereby the company's profit-sharing trusts paid $2 million down toward a total price of $13 million, with the balance to be payable at $1 million per year without interest for the next eleven years. Since Cleveland Pneumatic's contributions to its profit-sharing trusts were in excess of $1 million a year, Larry felt secure.

As a result of dividends paid in 1948, the Sixty Trust now had so much income (the $2 million paid as a down payment in 1951 and all subsequent payments were pure profit) that Textron until 1977 never had to pay one cent toward the funding of its pension plan for its own salaried employees, except for those of the Bell Aircraft Division.

The return from mortgages and all other investments were averaging over 8 percent every year on the total capital in the trust. This cash flow was so much greater than the benefits being paid out that the compounding effect of reinvesting these surplus funds at high rates made it possible for Textron, when they acquired new businesses starting in 1953, to merge the purchased companies' pension funds with the Sixty Trust and eliminate any cost whatsoever for future pensions for all of the salaried employees in all of the newly acquired divisions. The Bell operations were an exception because the insurance company handling their funds was unwilling to transfer them to the Sixty Trust. After Larry Green's death in 1952, the new trustees made an occasional exception to the basic edict against investing in common stocks.

In the early days of Textron diversification, when few investors believed that the program would work, the Sixty Trust purchased hundreds of thousands of shares of Textron common stock at about one-tenth the price they realized later when they sold them. We now had three trustees, always including me, who managed these funds and we never really deviated from our basic investment plan. We believed that with a tax-free pension fund it was far better to get immediate high cash flow than to invest in common stocks in competition with millions of others. Why hope that a very low dividend cash flow plus possible future appreciation in market value might make up the difference? This policy worked so well that whenever Textron took over a company they not only had no future cost for their salaried employees' pensions, but the actuaries were willing to give us credit for a 6 percent return on some twenty-nine other nonsalaried pension plans that we inherited when acquiring businesses.

In all cases we cleaned out the portfolios and followed our standard investment procedure. The actuaries previously had allowed only a 4 percent return on funds invested by institutions. It was as a result of our record that they allowed us to figure a 6 percent return on these new funds. We invariably cut Textron's contributions to all their nonsalaried plans in half as soon as our trustees took over.

When I retired from Textron as an employee in 1962, I also retired from the board of directors. The board, however, asked me to continue, with a small staff, to run the investments of the pension and profit-sharing trusts—some thirty in all, with a couple of hundred million dollars involved. In spite of the wild stock market and the new issues that were coming out during this period in the early sixties, the trustees stuck completely with our basic philosophy and avoided all common stock investments except for a couple of times when stock yields were unusually high.

However, in 1968 the directors decided that I was missing the boat. They thought that my policies were not protecting the employees in the pension fund against inflation. At the height of the market, all of the trust departments of banks were changing their policy and going to a higher and higher percentage of common stock and a smaller percentage of fixed income securities. The board of directors asked me to drop my staff of bright young people who had worked with me for some years, and all $200 million worth of pension funds were turned over to the trust departments of the banks that were involved in the company's lines of credit.

They also suggested to the banks that they put the entire funds into common stock as soon as possible, and liquidate most of the investments that we had previously made. The result was that within the next few years the market collapsed and at the low point these funds had shrunk $40 million in value.

It wasn't long thereafter that Bill Miller persuaded the board to take back the Sixty Trust and Market Square Trust investment responsibility with a well-trained group of company employees in charge. The funds have now been built up substantially. Bill saved the situation just in time.

As a result of my experience in running pension trust investments, all of the companies that I have been involved with have adopted the policy of high cash flow investment in well-rated bonds and practically no investment in common stocks. The thing that most trust departments of banks do not realize is that high cash flow for tax-exempt pension trusts is the surest way to protect against inflation. The surplus income over distributions is reinvested in more high yield situations.

In one of the situations that I am presently involved with, our cash flow is four times our benefit payments. The company's contribution plus the reinvestment of surplus cash flow builds up these funds at an astonishing rate. It not only saves the company money in contributions but also gives the employees far greater security in the long run by reassuring them that their pensions are safe.

One thing that has bothered me very much in the last twenty years is the tremendous accumulation of capital in the nation's pension funds. Under normal trust department investment policies, these funds are being invested primarily in the securities of the several hundred largest companies in the country. Actually, a very small portion of these funds go directly into the capital of these companies. The money is used to buy out some other shareholder so that the $250 billion now in private pension funds is not being used in any way to build up the smaller businesses in this country to help them become bigger and more competitive with the larger firms. Most people do not realize that, overall, the large corporations in this country have fifty cents invested in pension funds for every dollar of equity capital that the company itself has. To me that is sterilized capital that can no longer finance the future entrepreneurs of this country.

*ADVICE: If your company has $50 million or more in pension funds, you should seriously consider managing the investment of this capital with a com-*

*petent group of employees. You will not only do a better job for your employees, but you will be able to reduce company contributions if you invest in high yield bonds.*

# A Piece of the Action

With our objective of helping entrepreneurs to start or finance small businesses, Narragansett Capital has assisted these entrepreneurs in acquiring a substantial piece of the action in various types of businesses.

Many of the smaller businesses in this country can be more efficiently managed if the key people involved have a substantial equity interest in them rather than if the businesses remain tiny divisions of huge conglomerates. For the past few years, most large diversified companies have been disposing of enterprises with little growth even though they have had good earnings and could be considered "cash cows." A "cash cow" is a business that throws off substantially more earnings than will be required in the future to support its operations.

Narragansett Capital has given many managements of such companies an opportunity to become stockholders. By setting up new corporations with highly leveraged financing, we have been able to pay cash to the seller and permit the management group to invest in the new venture and acquire a substantial piece of the action. The enthusiasm created by this plan is fantastic. With their own capital at risk, performance improves immediately. This is the free enterprise system working at its best. As a result of this activity at Narragansett, I have been spending most of my time lately deconglomerating the conglomerates.

Here are a few specific examples of how it has worked:

## OLD FOX

One of my younger golfing friends, who was a lawyer in Providence, told me one day that he thought he would prefer to become

BOOTH

*"Honeywell knows what makes people tick."*

active in a business and give up the legal profession provided he was given an opportunity to purchase some of the equity. As one of the members of the Narragansett Redevelopment Agency, I'd worked closely with Bernie Buonanno, who is the secretary of the agency, and had been very much impressed with his ability and personality. As a result, when the owners of the Old Fox Chemical Company wished to sell their business, we paid the two of them $2 million for the company and permitted them to purchase 20 percent of the stock of the new company of the same name provided they would stay on for three more years and train Bernie Buonanno to take over the management. Bernie put up $40,000 for 25 percent of the stock and a few other management people purchased 5 percent to bring the total, including former owners' holdings up to 50 percent, with Narragansett having 50 percent. This purchase was made in 1970. Narragansett has been pleased with the way Bernie and the former owners operated the business. With the former owners now retired, Bernie is president and chief executive officer. Narragansett recently sold its shares to the company at a substantial profit. Bernie has picked up a few more shares so that today he has control of a company that has earned money every year of its existence with a total investment of only $40,000. Bernie is only forty years old and if he continues to do as good a job in the future as he has in the past I'll be very proud of him.

## MAIN LINE FASHIONS

Back in the mid-sixties the owner of a garment business called Main Line Fashions died, and his wife was liquidating the estate. At the time we heard about it, there was practically nothing left except the cutting tables, the designers, the sales force, and a reputation for fine quality, low-priced women's coats sold directly to the retail trade. It was impractical for Narragansett to finance this acquisition unless we could find a qualified garment manufacturer to head it up who would put some of his own money into the venture.

Bill Margolis was president of a men's wear division at BVD, earning a substantial salary, doing an excellent job, but owning no equity in the company. He agreed to leave his highly paid position and put up $112,500 for 45 percent of the shares and rebuild the company.

As usual, the operation was highly leveraged with long-term bank debt and subordinated debt as follows: The closing date was February 21, 1968, and Main Line was purchased for $151,438. The bank loans and Narragansett Capital loans totaled $1,300,000 with management having 45 percent of the equity and Narragansett Capital owning 45 percent. The bank's SBIC owned 10 percent.

Bill did a fantastic job. He ran a tight operation, and since he subcontracted the sewing and controlled only the designing, cutting, fabric purchasing, and distribution, the company had only $30,580 invested in fixed assets with loft space in the garment district in New York. Bill made money every year, and after building up a net worth of a couple of million dollars, he became anxious to get some money out of the business.

Since a garment business is impossible to sell at a fancy price, we came up with a whole series of plans to accomplish what Bill wanted—but all of them had some disadvantage or unusual tax liability. We finally conceived the idea of setting up a new Main Line Fashions Corporation, which purchased at book value all the assets and liabilities of the old corporation, leaving it with nothing but cash as an investment company. Bill used part of that cash to purchase a 35 percent interest in the new, highly leveraged corporation. More cash was used to purchase the old company shares held by the bank and Narragansett. This left Bill with substantial cash free and clear in the old corporation without paying any capital gains tax personally, since the company has not been liquidated. Since assets were sold at their tax basis, the old company paid no taxes on the sale. Bill was then able to sell some shares in the new venture to three or four of his key people so that they would have some future equity.

Narragansett arranged the necessary financing with the Industrial National Bank for the senior money and with itself for the long-term subordinated debt as follows:

| | | |
|---|---|---|
| *Voting* | | |
| Margolis Investment Co. | 35% | $87,500 |
| Narragansett | 35% | 87,500 |
| | 70% | 175,000 |
| *Nonvoting* | | |
| Margolis Investment Co. | 8% | 20,000 |
| Management Shareholders | | |
| (excluding Margolis) | 22% | 55,000 |
| | 100% | $250,000 |

| | |
|---|---|
| Loans: | |
| Bank Loans | $750,000 |
| Narragansett Capital Loans | 550,000 |
| | $1,300,000 |

The Main Line Fashions business was purchased on March 31, 1976, for $1,904,027. This transaction was possible only because of the small investment in fixed assets, and also because prior to the transaction, Bill had paid off all his previous long-term debts. If he had sold his stock, he would have paid capital gains tax and could have, under present tax regulations, purchased only 20 percent of the new shares.

In addition to buying divisions of large companies, it is often possible to set up highly leveraged companies to buy out owners of small businesses such as we did with Old Fox and Main Line.

*ADVICE: Many business owners do not realize that it is possible for them to solve their own estate tax problems by this means. If they are willing to let* *someone like Narragansett set up a new corporation to buy all of their assets and liabilities for tax basis net worth, they can reinvest in the same enterprise as minority stockholders, and manage it for the new owners. They can have "a piece of the action" with a relatively small investment in a highly leveraged\* company, and yet get complete liquidity in their original business.*

## MD PNEUMATICS

Several years ago, I got a telephone call from a man named Earl Fester. He said, "Mr. Little, I understand that you are interested in helping the management of divisions of big corporations acquire an equity position when operations are sold. Mr. Little, I'm running the MD Pneumatics Division of Rockwell Industries out in Springfield, Missouri. They have told me they are going to dispose of it."

I said, "Why do they want to sell if you're currently making money?"

He replied, "We have a huge plant here from which they have moved at least half of the equipment, consolidating it into another division. What they have left me with did only $2,796,000 in sales the past twelve months [1971–72], and, therefore, is too small for that $3 billion corporation to be interested in. The plant is an excellent one, well equipped, and with all the idle floor space we have room to expand the business substantially in the future if we can buy it now."

"Earl," I said, "get on a plane and fly to Providence—we're interested in talking with you to see whether it's practical to set this operation up on a highly leveraged basis with you and your key management group." After thoroughly investigating the situation and feeling that it was viable, we arranged the purchase price of $2,808,627 with the following capitalization:

| | |
|---|---|
| Debt: | |
| Bank term loan | $1,000,000 |
| NCC subordinated term loan | 1,100,000 |
| | $2,100,000 |

* High leverage means financing companies with a maximum of debt and minimum of equity. For example, Narragansett has often capitalized companies with 90 percent debt and 10 percent equity so that management could afford to buy 50 percent of the common stock for 5 percent of the total purchase price.

| Equity: Management (50%) | 200,000 |
|---|---|
| NCC (50%) | 200,000 |
| | $2,500,000 |

The balance of the purchase price was paid out of accounts receivable, which were purchased by MD Pneumatic, and the closing date was March 31, 1972, with fourteen employees purchasing shares.

This operation, which started with $400,000 net worth, has made money regularly ever since, and now has a net worth of $1.5 million. On March 31, 1976, MD Pneumatic paid off in full Narragansett's long-term $1.1 million subordinated term loan.

Here is another case where Earl Fester, owning 31 percent of the stock, will build up a nice nest egg if he works until retirement.

MD is currently being sold to Bevis, whose large loss carry-forward will permit it to pay a fair price on an installment sale basis to MD shareholders over the next five years. Since Earl is sixty, this deal solves his retirement and financial problems extremely well.

## GALILEO ELECTRO-OPTICS CORP.

C. B. Sung, a Bendix officer, arranged the sale to Narragansett of their Fiber-Optics Division in 1973. We were very much impressed with Jim Oglesby, George Batchelder, and the rest of the management group at the plant in Sturbridge, Massachusetts. We paid $3.3 million cash for the business, setting up financing as follows with several members of the group.

| Debt: | |
|---|---|
| Bank loans | $1,500,000 |
| NCC loan | 1,500,000 |
| | $3,000,000 |

| Equity: Cash | | |
|---|---|---|
| Management (50%) $150,000 | | |
| Narragansett (50%) 150,000 | 300,000 | |
| Purchase price | $3,300,000 | |

This company was doing $3,745,669 in sales the year it was purchased although it had lost a substantial amount of money in prior years. When this able group of entrepreneurs put their capital into the venture, it was turned around fast. The audit for the year ending September 30, 1976, showed sales of $8,878,978 and a net worth of $1,616,139. Not bad!—an increase of over 500 percent in equity in three years.

This small company might some day become one of America's leading business enterprises when glass replaces copper and other materials for transmitting sound and light.

## GREENVILLE TUBE

We heard that Emerson Electric was planning to sell its Greenville Tube Division, which had been part of their heater coil operations at Weigand. Greenville had supplied Weigand with stainless steel tubing in addition to selling surplus capacity to the trade. At this particular time, part of the equipment at Greenville had been transferred to Weigand's plant at Murphreesboro, Tennessee, so that division became completely integrated and no longer dependent on Greenville. Although it had been unusually profitable in the past, averaging at least 16 percent pretax on sales, Greenville no longer fitted into Emerson's future plans. Hearing that this operation was for sale, I called Chuck Persons at Emerson and asked him whether he wouldn't prefer to have Narragansett set up a new Greenville Tube Company so that Art McGonigal, who had done such a wonderful job at Emerson, could have an equity position in the new company, which we would establish. He told us that Art was a terrific operator and had done an excellent job for them, and that he would certainly prefer to let Art participate in a new venture of this sort rather than sell to someone else.

The original price was $5.5 million, including taking over the $1.3 million long-term lease obligation on the new plant in Clarksville, Arkansas. The original financing was as follows:

| | | |
|---|---|---|
| Debt: | | |
| Bank loan | $2,500,000 | |
| Narragansett loan | 1,500,000 | |
| | 4,000,000 | |
| Equity: | | |
| Management (50%) $250,000 | | |
| Narragansett (50%) 250,000 | 500,000 | |
| | $4,500,000 | |

This acquisition was made January 11, 1974, for $4,780,485. Art put up $125,000 for 25 percent of the stock, and other management people bought an equal amount. So that in effect, the operators of the company purchased 50 percent of the outstanding shares for about 5 percent of the total purchase price.

With his own money in the company, Art McGonigal has done a fantastic job. It is now part of Bevis, the loss carry-forward problem child that caused Narragansett's biggest loss. Art and the other shareholders will get a substantial price for their stock through this installment sale if management can keep the earnings up.

## AIRBORNE MANUFACTURING COMPANY

C. B. Sung recently brought to our attention at Narragansett Capital a company in Elyria, Ohio, called Airborne Manufacturing Company, owned by a small group of stockholders—some of whom wished to get their money out, and some of whom wished to continue the business. Airborne is the principal producer of fuel pumps for the civilian aircraft industry. They also had gone into the sump pump business and a medical testing business, both of which were losing money. The overall operation seemed to have some future potential and we were impressed with Herb Kaatz's enthusiasm and ability. As a result the following highly leveraged plan was worked out:

| | |
|---|---|
| Debt: | |
| Bank loan | $1,600,000 |
| Narragansett loan | 1,200,000 |
| | 2,800,000 |
| Equity: | |
| Management (50%) (shares retained) | |
| Narragansett (50%) 150,000 | 150,000 |
| | $2,950,000 |

Airborne was an unusual case. The money that Narragansett put up was lent to the company so that those stockholders who wanted "out" could sell their shares to the company and get cash.

Recently, Herb has taken on a small company in Denver that makes air conditioning equipment for helicopters and light planes, which he thinks has real opportunity for expansion. They also have started a vertically integrated operation to make their own parts, which are made of mechanical carbon, by taking an expert in that field and setting him up to produce this material. Although Airborne is a relatively small operation, it is making money on its fuel pumps, it has disposed of its medical testing division, and hopes to sell the sump pump business. Now concentrating on their aircraft business, Herb Kaatz and his group of entrepreneurs should build up a very substantial equity position by the time they retire.

To protect the entrepreneurs and Narragansett Capital in these situations, we require the companies to take out very substantial life insurance on the chief executive officer. In addition, to protect the management group from being taken advantage of, the company itself gives the group the right to sell their shares to the company upon death, complete disability, or retirement at age sixty-five at the full book value of the shares. Since any successful, highly leveraged small business pays out very little in dividends, the net worth is increased every year by retained earnings after taxes.

## BURRO CRANE

A couple of years ago, the Federal Sign and Signal Company decided to sell its Burro Crane Division. This operation is the principal manufacturer of self-propelled on-track cranes for use on railroads, particularly in repair work and maintenance of rights of way. The company had not done too well in the past, but it seemed as though with huge amounts of government money to be spent by Conrail and other railroads on their rights-of-way, particularly with the new method of welding tracks to eliminate the joints, this looked like a worthwhile small business to finance—provided we could get the entrepreneurs to head it up. We were fortunate in finding Leland Boren, president of Avis Corporation, and Dick Doermer, president of the Indiana Bank and Trust Company of Fort Wayne, Indiana. These two gentlemen had participated in a business venture in San Francisco that became successful, and they decided they should join up as partners in other deals that were available. Leland took a good look at the operation and decided that there were some savings to be made and that young Ron McDaniel, a Burro executive, could, with his guidance, make an excellent manager. He has done a terrific job.

We were worried about the fact that Boren was the chief executive officer of a company doing over $100 million in sales, and we wished to be certain that he had clearance from his board and stockholders to enter into outside activities of this sort without any conflict of interest.

As a result of our questioning, Boren sent the following report:

International Bank ("IB") has effective control of the Avis Company through stockholdings totalling directly and indirectly 100%. At present, IB is involved in a proceeding before the Board of Governors of the Federal Reserve System (the "Board") to contest determinations of the Board to the effect that IB is a bank holding company. The staff of the Board has advised IB that, in the absence of Board approval, it would view an acquisition or engaging in an additional business activity by IB or its subsidiaries or affiliates as a willful violation of the Bank Holding Company Act. Since the Company is a subsidiary of IB, this position would also apply to the Company. IB has announced that it intends to dispose of the banking properties that are the subject of the Board proceeding.

Since Avis could not make any acquisitions itself, there was no conflict of interest problem for Leland so long as his involvement was primarily that of an investor.

On February 3, 1976, Burro's operations were purchased from Federal Sign and Signal for $3,514,000, and the financing was arranged as follows:

| Purchase price: | | |
|---|---|---|
| Inventory | $2,388,000 | |
| Fixed assets | 1,126,000 | $3,514,000 |
| | | |
| Capitalization: | | |
| Bank term loan | 1,500,000 | |
| Working capital— | | |
| Line of credit | 500,000 | |
| Subordinated term | | |
| loan Narragansett | | |
| Capital | 1,100,000 | |
| | | |
| | $3,100,000 | |
| Equity: | | |
| Management (50%) | $ 200,000 | |
| NCC (50%) | 200,000 | |
| | | |
| | $ 400,000 | $3,500,000 |

Leland and Dick each put up $100,000 for a total of 50 percent of the common shares and, therefore, had a big piece of the action. They have done a fantastic job in tightening up the operations, making them more profitable. They have also been fortunate in building up a substantial backlog from the railroads for their on-track self-propelled cranes. By the summer of 1978, Burro had paid its entire long-term debt.

As a result of the success of this operation, we have financed Leland Boren and Dick Doermer to have a substantial equity position in two other companies.

# Shoestring Financing

This country must encourage its entrepreneurs. We must find ways to help the creative people who wish to develop their new ideas, processes, and products. There are not too many sources of capital for start-up situations available today. The reason this is so important is that we must plant the seeds of our future important businesses today to reap the benefits of their expansion and growth in the future.

Most readers may feel it unusual that Textron could have built up a $3,000,000,000 business from its humble beginning in 1923 with a $10,000 bank loan and no equity capital—not even a shoestring. People do not realize that practically every large corporation in the country was originally started by some entrepreneur with very limited capital. Many of our large corporations today resulted from mergers during the 1920s when the stock market was booming, but if one could go back to the origins of these companies we would find that some entrepreneur started with very limited capital to create the original business. The replies I have received to my inquiries from these companies indicate how frequently this has occurred. It's true, however, that one could not start a railroad, a public utility, or a steel mill on a shoestring.

Since no one has yet published a summarized list of who started many of today's billion dollar corporations and how they were financed, I would like to. I have received some most interesting information from sixty-one companies that were started on a shoe-string, each with current sales in excess of $1 billion. However, because of space limitations, I am limiting the story to sixteen.

## AVON

David H. McConnell started Avon in 1886 with a $500 loan from a friend. In 1977, sales were $1,648,000,000 with profits of $191,000,-000. The total market value of the company as of August 15, 1978, was $3,486,000,000.

## CAMPBELL SOUP

Campbell Soup was founded in 1869 in Camden, New Jersey, as a partnership of Joseph Campbell and Abram Anderson, with no specified capital. In 1977, sales were $1,769,000,000 and earnings were $107,000,000. The market value as of August 15, 1978, was $1,213,000,000.

## COCA-COLA

An Atlanta druggist, Dr. John Pemberton, produced the first Coca-Cola syrup in 1886, and he had earnings that year of $50. In 1977, sales were $3,560,000,000 and profits were $326,000,000. The market value as of August 15, 1978, was $5,510,000,000.

## DIGITAL EQUIPMENT

Kenneth H. Olsen, his brother Stanley, and Harlan E. Anderson started Digital Equipment when American Research and Development Company purchased 70 percent of the stock for $70,000 in August 1957. In 1977, sales were $1,059,000,000 and profits were $108,000,000. The market value as of August 15, 1978, was $1,941,000,000.

## DU PONT

Eleuthère Irénée du Pont organized the company in 1802 with eighteen shareholders providing $36,000 equity. In 1977, sales were $9,435,000,000 and profits were $545,000,000. The market value of the company as of August 15, 1978, was $6,152,000,000.

## EASTMAN KODAK

Eastman Kodak was founded by George Eastman a few days before Thanksgiving in 1880, with a $3,000 investment. In 1977, sales were $5,967,000,000 and profits were $643,000,000. The market value of the company as of August 15, 1978, was $10,625,000,000.

## FORD MOTOR

Henry Ford and eleven associates filed incorporation papers for Ford Motor on June 16, 1903, with only $28,000 in cash invested. I was amazed to learn that on October 26, 1909, General Motors offered to purchase Ford Motor Company for $8,000,000, with $2,-000,000 down and the balance in the future. Henry Ford held out for all cash, and since William Durant was unable to raise the money, that acquisition fell through. In 1977, sales were $37,842,-000,000 and profits were $1,673,000,000. The market value as of August 15, 1978, was $5,513,000,000.

## GILLETTE

On September 28, 1901, King Camp Gillette founded Gillette with $5,000 of equity. In 1977, sales were $1,587,000,000 and profits were $80,000,000. Market value as of August 15, 1978, was $896,000,000.

## GOODYEAR

Frank Seiberling started the Goodyear Tire and Rubber Company on August 29, 1898, with $13,500 of borrowed money. Sales in 1977 were $6,628,000,000 and profits were $206,000,000. The market value as of August 15, 1978, was $1,277,000,000.

## HEWLETT-PACKARD

In 1939, William R. Hewlett and David Packard invested their personal savings of $538 in Hewlett-Packard. In 1977, sales were $1,360,000,000 and profits were $122,000,000. The market value of the company as of August 15, 1978, was $2,486,000,000.

## McDONALD's

In 1954, Ray Kroc obtained the exclusive franchise rights from the McDonald brothers to start hamburger drive-ins, using their name, throughout the country. Since then, Kroc has built McDonald's into the leading fast-food business in the country. In 1977, sales were $1,406,000,000 and profits were $137,000,000. The market value of the company as of August 15, 1978, was $2,366,000,000.

## PEPSICO

Caleb Bradham originally incorporated Pepsi Cola in North Carolina in 1902, and produced the first drink in his drugstore. He had no equity capital. In 1977, sales were $3,546,000,000 and profits were $187,000,000. On August 15, 1978, the market value of the company was $2,779,000,000.

## PROCTER AND GAMBLE

William Procter and James Gamble organized the company on October 31, 1837, in Cincinnati, with equity capital of $7,192. In 1977 sales were $7,284,000,000 with profits of $461,000,000. The market value of the company on August 15, 1978, was $7,311,000,000.

## SEARS, ROEBUCK

Richard Warren Sears started the company in the fall of 1886 at North Redwood, Minnesota, to sell watches. In 1977, sales were $17,224,000,000 and profits were $838,000,000. On August 15, 1978, the market value of the company was $7,846,000,000.

## SINGER

Isaac Merrit Singer, with $40 in borrowed capital, invented the first practical sewing machine in 1850. In 1977, sales were $2,285,000,000 and profits were $78,000,000. Market value of the company's shares on August 15, 1978, were $327,000,000.

## XEROX

Xerox Corporation was founded in 1906 in Rochester, New York, by Joseph C. Wilson, Sr., and three other businessmen under the

Haloid name. In 1977, sales were $5,077,000,000 and profits were $407,000,000. The market value of its shares on August 15, 1978, was $4,931,000,000.

*ADVICE: After reading about all these shoestring-financed companies, don't say, "That all happened in the past. It can't be done again." Under our free enterprise system, it will continue to be possible for entrepreneurs to duplicate in the future what has been done in the past; but it will just be more difficult to do so. It's up to the young people of this country to have the vision and determination to accomplish it. More power to them—they'll need it!*

# *Vacations*

I have always felt that it was advisable for businessmen with great responsibility to take long vacations, particularly to get away from the telephone and do exciting and stimulating things that would get one's mind completely off business problems. I probably took more time off for vacations than almost any other businessman in the country. I had to travel a lot when I was at work, and it was very difficult for me to stop thinking about business problems when I was near the office and even at home. It was most important, therefore, to take unusual vacation trips far away from the office.

For example, in the middle of July 1954, at the height of our fight to gain control of American Woolen, I took off with the family and some friends for a long-planned trip to Bayreuth for the Wagnerian operas and sightseeing in that part of Germany. When we returned, I was well rested and in good shape to handle the final negotiations for that complex merger.

Again in 1957, the family took an eight-week trip around the world. Each member of the family was to pick some place during the trip where we would spend two weeks. My wife picked Japan; my daughter Augusta, India; my son Arthur, the Fiji Islands so that we could do some snorkeling and spear fishing. My choice was a two-week photographic safari in East Africa to take movies of the wildlife. A good friend of mine, Bob Stone, had been on a photographic safari in 1930, spending six months taking superb black and white movies of wildlife. That was before Kodachrome or any other color film was available. When I saw his pictures, it made me wish to go to East Africa someday to see the animals. It was twenty-seven years before we had the opportunity to do so. On this particular trip we were fortunate in having Syd Downey, a partner of Ker and Downey, the famous outfitters and white hunters in Nairobi, as our personal guide. We had a marvelous experience. We've since gone back with friends and members of the family for a total of thirteen trips and have taken over 120,000 feet of color movies.

It was the practice in our family to take long summer vacations and alternate between going to Europe and visiting national parks in different parts of the United States. Late in the summer of 1944, when all parks were closed during the war to conserve gasoline, Augusta and I took a three-week pack trip through Yellowstone. Just before entering the park, we stopped at Two Ocean Pass and saw a small stream come down the mountain then split in two with one branch going west into the Snake and Columbia Rivers to the Pacific Ocean and the other half going east into the Yellowstone, Missouri, and Mississippi Rivers to the Gulf of Mexico. This was an entirely natural phenomenon, probably the only place in the world where such an unusual thing occurs. At Hart Lake, we were fortunate enough to see a large flock of the rare trumpeter swan. At that time I believe there were fewer than two hundred still in existence. Of course we visited Old Faithful and many of the other geysers and hot springs, and during the trip we saw pronghorn antelope, elk, moose, and bison. The amazing thing was that we did not see a single bear. Since the park was closed, the bears no longer had garbage dumps in which to scavenge, and therefore had to go back and live in the wild without panhandling the public.

One day, when we were crossing a large meadow near a mountain, a large herd of elk cut directly across our group, running for the high country up to the left. This spooked our pack horses and they ran off in every direction—bucking and throwing off their packs so that we lost some of our food and all the eggs were broken. It took some time to round up the horses and get organized again. On the last day of our trip, we headed into the Lamarr Valley and suddenly saw a herd of a couple of hundred bison grazing ahead of us. Since the rangers normally herd them into corrals when winter

comes, this group decided to head for the hills, so we saw a wonderful stampede of both the older bison and the young calves loping through the high grass up into the mountains.

While my daughter and I were on this trip there was a severe hurricane along the New England coast and our home on the beach at Narragansett, Rhode Island, was pretty well smashed up. A two-hundred-pound boulder was hurled by the force of the waves through the picture window in the front of the house twenty feet across the room and into the fireplace. We had to saw the house in half and move it up onto a higher sand dune and protect it from future storms with a huge terraced bulkhead.

One winter in 1935, we went on a skiing trip to Switzerland and Austria. Our first stop was St. Moritz. There we were most fortunate in getting as our ski guide Peter Gabriel, a most attractive young man whose family owned the small inn at Sils Maria nearby. We skied at St. Mortiz, Davos, and at St. Anton in Austria. This was a great opportunity for me to improve my skiing, since before then I had trouble in making turns, particularly in deep snow. I had actually started skiing with toe straps back in 1911 and had gone on the so-called snow trains that the Boston and Maine Railroad ran Sundays to New Hampshire in the late twenties, but I had never had adequate training. Peter Gabriel persuaded us to return the next summer and do some mountain climbing. We returned the next summer on the *Hindenburg*.

## THE HINDENBURG

It was an August evening in 1936. The giant airship *Hindenburg*, leashed to its mast at the Navy's lighter-than-air base at Lakehurst,

New Jersey, hung in readiness for its nonstop trip to Frankfurt, Germany. It was already dark as the passengers entered the dirigible up a gangway that had been lowered to the ground. Once aboard, everyone was amazed by the appointments in the lounge, including, of all things, a grand piano.

After being assigned to staterooms, we returned to the grand salon to lean out the windows, wave good-bye, and chat with friends twenty feet below. At 10 o'clock, without any prior notice, the figures on the ground suddenly became smaller and smaller, the voices stilled, and with an eerie feeling we rose into the darkness of the night. When we gained an altitude of 1,000 feet, the voyage really began as the engines were started.

Over a bit of New Jersey heading for New York City, the craft created a bright spot half a mile in diameter with its huge floodlight shining directly below that illuminated like a movie screen all the towns, farms, and houses that we passed; an enchanting way to travel at night. Upon reaching New York, with the top of the Empire State Building as the hub, we circled Manhattan Island twice. On that brilliantly clear evening, a spectacle of rare beauty lay before us, one that few had ever seen before while traveling by air—greater New York's millions of lights a thousand feet below.

Bidding farewell to the city, our course headed eastward along the Connecticut coast. With the aid of the powerful searchlight illuminating everything in its spot, it was easy to identify the cities and other well-known places quietly sliding by: Bridgeport and its factories; New Haven and Yale University; the Connecticut River near Essex with its boatyards; New London, with the Thames River and the Coast Guard Academy; and soon after midnight, Providence. With only its street lights shining, Providence seemed sound asleep except for one brilliantly lighted building that turned out to be my own Franklin Rayon plant—a twenty-four-hour textile operation—whose early morning shift had already come to work. We next passed over Boston and circled the State House with its resplendent gold dome before continuing up on the coast over Nahant toward Maine.

After a very short night's rest in a tiny 12 x 8 stateroom with folding aluminum upper and lower bunks, we passed over St. Johns, New Brunswick, at daybreak, with the fishing fleet going out to sea, and steam rising from some of the small factories along the shore. Continuing along our great circle route, many farms and pastures lay below us. We were amazed to see all the horses, cows, and other animals stampede around the fields when they saw this huge 800-foot-long monster pass overhead, terrified by the sight of something they had never seen before.

After leaving New Brunswick, we went over Moncton, Nova Scotia, and shortly thereafter passed Prince Edward Island in the Gulf of St. Lawrence. Again we saw the same stampeding of animals. The chickens, flying around in panic, apparently thought some gigantic bird of prey was about to descend upon them.

Then came the Magdalen Islands, situated in the middle of the Gulf of St. Lawrence—a remote and lonely spot. A man, with his horse and wagon, was collecting seaweed on the beach. The horse took one look at the ominous shadow passing overhead and ran away. The owner, legging it as fast as he could, never did catch up while still within our view. A short time later, we passed over an isolated home. A man and his wife rushed out the front door, took one look at the huge airship, and ran off into the woods to hide. The inhabitants of the Magdalen Islands were in such a remote part of the world that they had never even heard of the *Hindenburg*.

Late that afternoon as we were cruising over the Straits of Belle Isle, between Labrador and Newfoundland, the skipper noticed a huge iceberg below and circled it for a few minutes so that we all got a bird's-eye view of that massive chunk of floating ice. Along the coast of Newfoundland were its windswept rocky shores, heavily timbered interior, and salmon streams—a sparsely settled, undeveloped land. From there to our next landfall, Ireland, were 1,900 miles of open ocean—uneventfully covered during the night.

Early next morning, while still over the Atlantic, we were invited to visit the command gondola. We proceeded on a narrow catwalk through the center of the airship about 100 feet forward of the main lounge. Amazed to find that the entire interior was not filled with gas as we had assumed, we passed many long, cylindrical gas-tight containers in which the hydrogen was stored. These so-called cells did not fill over half of the total cubic area, so that the complete aluminum inner structure around which the outer fabric was tightly stretched was visible. While on the catwalk, one realized that a misstep would drop one through the fabric and into the sea below. The command gondola protruded from the main structure and was entered by descending a gangway. In the compartment the steersman facing forward operated the rudder wheel, and the helmsman on the port side controlled the elevator wheel. The latter had in front of him a large level, with a bubble in it, so that he could always tell whether the ship was on an even keel.

That afternoon I had the opportunity of sitting in on a conference with Commander Rosendahl, who was the United States Navy's commanding officer of all of its lighter-than-air operations, and Captain Ernest A. Lehmann, who was the *Hindenburg*'s captain on that voyage since Dr. Hugo E. Eckener, the original skipper, had not come that trip. The discussion between the two was most interesting—the German claiming that hydrogen, although inflammable, was much safer for airship operation than helium, which was used by the Navy. The Germans were especially careful about fire. Passengers were not permitted to take matches or lighters aboard. Anyone insisting upon smoking was escorted to a small room lined entirely with asbestos. Rosendahl maintained that, since helium was not inflammable, it was therefore the only safe lifting gas to use. Lehmann pointed out that the reason the United States had lost the *Shenandoah* and most of its lighter-than-air ships was that helium had far less lift than hydrogen. Therefore, when the American craft got into a storm center with a down draft there was insufficient lift to prevent the ship from being dashed to the ground. Lehmann further stated that the Navy made a mistake in plotting their flight course from one point to another on a direct line, which took them through rather than around low pressure areas. Captain Lehmann explained that the German flight technique was to use the high velocity winds at the edges of both low and high pressure centers to avoid going through the middle of storms. Although the mileage was greater, the Germans actually cut down their flying time by passing to the right of low pressure and to the left of high pressure to take advantage of the favorable wind conditions.

By this time, we had been a day and a half in flight, always at

approximately 1,000 feet above sea level, and at an air speed of 80 knots. Because of its 800-foot length and the fact that the course was never through storm centers, there was absolutely no motion—either pitching or rolling—during the entire voyage. Late in the afternoon of the second day, we passed Ireland to our left, and learned from the German crew that they were not permitted to fly over Ireland, England, France, or Belgium since these countries were worried that the Germans might take pictures of military and other important installations. After passing south of England, it was necessary, therefore, to fly up the English Channel and then turn easterly again over Holland. As we passed cities and towns in the Netherlands, thousands of people rushed out into the streets and cheered the *Hindenburg* as it went overhead. The noise was so great that it could be heard clearly over the four quiet diesel engines. Little did the Dutch realize that a few years later German planes would bomb and devastate their major cities.

Our course then followed the Rhine, the latter part of the trip being in darkness, and when we came over the airfield at Frankfurt a large ground crew rushed out and grabbed the landing lines, which had been lowered to guide the great ship into the hangar. It had taken us just forty-two hours and fifty-three minutes to complete this most comfortable, fascinating trip. Within a few minutes we had passed through customs and joined our good friend Peter Gabriel who was waiting with a car to drive us to Switzerland for our vacation of mountain climbing.

During several delightful weeks in Switzerland and Austria, we climbed Piz Palu in the Engadine, near St. Moritz; Austria's highest mountain, Grossglockner; and the Jungfrau from the upper railway station.

We returned to Frankfurt for the trip home on the *Hindenburg*.

Again we flew at 1,000 feet and 80 knots, using the high velocity winds of the high and low pressure areas to accelerate the ground speed, arriving uneventfully at Lakehurst in late September. The whole trip was most comfortable and so interesting that we decided never again to go to Europe on a steamship. This was the ideal form of travel. After our arrival, the *Hindenburg* was flown back to Friedrichshafen and stored in its hangar for the winter.

In early May of 1937, the *Hindenburg* again started its first of many planned round trips to America. Then on May 6, 1937, as it was being guided to its mooring at Lakehurst, it happened. The *New York Times* headline of May 7, 1937, read:

# HINDENBURG BURNS IN LAKEHURST CRASH
## 21 KNOWN DEAD 12 MISSING 64 ESCAPE

## *MOUNTAIN CLIMBING*

While we were in Switzerland, before we climbed Piz Palu, I wondered whether it would be possible for me to make it to the top. In spite of Peter's many reassurances, I had my doubts. However, that evening six German climbers and their guide showed up at the mountain hut. They sure didn't look like they were in as good shape as I was in, so that sold me. About three o'clock the next morning, with each of us carrying a little lantern with a candle in it, we headed for the mountain. After about an hour, we passed the Germans, who were all out of breath and sitting down to regain their strength. It was a beautiful day and a relatively easy climb— no rocks—just a good long uphill walk over slightly crusted snow. When we got to the top, I was really hooked and decided to do some more climbs with Peter. Coming down that day we really set a record. Because of the slightly crusted snow, it was possible to run without sliding as one's feet broke through the crust just enough to give a good purchase. I must have looked very much like a tame bear on a lead as I led Peter down the mountain with him holding me in check at the end of the rope. It had taken us about three hours to go up but, because of the ideal conditions coming back, we did it in twenty minutes—running all the way.

We went into Austria and decided to climb the Grossglockner, the highest peak in that country. Again, we started about two in the morning, and again we were roped together. It was necessary to go down about five hundred feet from the inn, across a wide glacier, and then climb the mountain. At the top there was one peak separated by a hundred-yard narrow ridge of snow from the main mountain, on top of which had been erected a huge wooden cross. The path was about eighteen inches wide and level, but there was a drop of at least three thousand feet on either side. I didn't dare walk across, so I sat down astride the ridge and inched my way over. Halfway over, Peter said, "Mr. Little, the last time I was here my friend lost his balance and fell off to the left, so I jumped down to the right and we got hung up on the rope and nobody got hurt."

When we descended and reached the glacier, I was really exhausted and the lodge was still five hundred feet above us. Right on the edge of the glacier was an Austrian farmer who was collecting wood with a tiny donkey. I tried to persuade him to take me back up to the inn on his donkey, offering what I thought was a substantial fare—this he turned down. Then I tried to buy his donkey at what I thought was a phenomenal price—he also turned that down. Peter was really in stitches during these negotiations.

We finally made it back to the inn and after resting for a while, we got in the car and drove down to Kitzbuhel and went to Praxmair's Cafe on the main street where there was a wonderful group of yodelers and *schühplattler* dancers. After having some supper and seeing the fabulous show, Tony Praxmair came over to our table and said, "You are Americans, aren't you?" Then he told us that he had taken his troupe to England every spring for a most successful tour, but had never been to America. We thought it would be a wonderful idea to bring Tony and his group to Providence.

By midnight, although we were complete strangers, the group had agreed that seven of the men would make the trip if we sponsored them. They arrived via Hamburg-American Line and gave many delightful performances at ski clubs and in water sports carnivals at Boston Garden and Madison Square Garden. Their trip was so successful that we brought them back again in 1952 and several other times, and finally Sol Hurok brought a large group of twenty-four or more Austrian boys and girls over for a concert tour to some thirty-six cities in Canada and the United States.

## SKIING—THE AVALANCHE

In March 1945, Tom and Virginia Cabot, Dan Brown, five other friends, and I went skiing in the Canadian Rockies. We stayed at Temple Mt. Lodge, north of Lake Louise, and had marvelous powder snow. Our guide was Herman Gadner from Obergürgl, Austria, and an instructor at Grey Rocks Inn in the Laurentians, north of Montreal. After two weeks of climbing all the nearby mountains with seal skins on our skis—there were no lifts of any sort—we had a disaster late in the afternoon of our last day. On our way down the trail to the lodge, we saw a slope to the right with perfect powder and less than a thousand-foot climb. We decided on just one more run. Climbing to the top of the long ridge, Tom, Herman, and I led the way down. We then headed for the lodge but stopped on a high spot to watch the others. One of the girls was having trouble handling the deep powder and called to Herman to help her. He started to traverse his way back up when WHOOSH, the entire mountainside avalanched with a roar. Hundreds of thousands of tons of snow came tumbling down as Tom and I watched, horrified.

All the rest of the party were being swept off the mountain. Virginia was the only one with the presence of mind to throw herself on her back and hold her arms and skiis high so they wouldn't get buried. Herman and one of the girls had completely disappeared, and one of the men was buried to his arm pits. We found the ring of a ski pole and dug frantically to release the girl from New Orleans who had partially suffocated but recovered consciousness when dug out. But where was Herman? We found one of his ski poles on top of the snow. He had apparently thrown it up in the air just before being engulfed. Concentrating in that area we used skiis to probe six feet into the snow, but no luck. We then asked Virginia to ski back to the lodge for a toboggan and help. It was late afternoon and would soon be dark. Digging six-foot-deep holes in the snow, and probing from that level we finally struck Herman's head with a ski. Then digging frantically we finally cleared his face, which was that frightful orange color of suffocation. Giving mouth-to-mouth resuscitation while others dug his body out, we got his blood flowing again and his face color became normal although we could not detect breathing. We thought we had saved him, but it was getting dark and cold. The toboggan had not arrived so four of us, each with an arm or a leg, tried to ski down in the deep powder trying to carry him. We kept falling, picking him up again, falling again and again. The color had now completely left his face and we knew we had lost him. That was a very sad ending for our ski trip.

*ADVICE: Don't ever take an advanced ski tour without a local guide. The avalanche had been caused by six feet of snow on a slate base—no bond of any sort. During the Canadian Mounted Police investigation we were told that no Canadian guides ever skied that slope—it was too avalanche prone.*

## PACK TRIPS AND FALTBOATING

One summer the family took a pack trip on the John Muir Trail along the highlands of the Sierras, including riding horseback all the way up to the top of Mt. Whitney, the highest mountain—14,-595 feet—in the continental United States. (Mt. McKinley in Alaska is 20,000 feet.) This was a thrilling experience. The weather was perfect, we slept out without tents every night except one, had some excellent fishing, and I don't believe I thought about Textron once on the entire trip.

Another interesting pack trip was from Banff to the foot of Mt. Assiniboine. We passed many beautiful glacier lakes and camped in tepee-type tents right near the small glacial pond at the foot of the mountain. Every evening as it got cold and the water, which melted during the day, froze, great chunks of ice fell off the glacier and dropped with a crash into the lake thousands of feet below. What a marvelous vacation that was—and no telephones!

Another interesting pastime in vacations was faltboating. In the early thirties, I had seen these kayak-like boats on the Rhine River near Basel. They appeared very safe and maneuverable, being made of rubberized canvas stretched over wooden frames, decked over with a small open cockpit. The boats were maneuvered with a double-ended paddle. When we came back to Providence, we interested some of my younger friends in taking up this new sport. It was particularly exciting to run through so-called white water in heavy rapids. In the spring, when the water was high, we arranged to do many of the good streams in various parts of New England. In 1938, Alec Bright, Smithy Jackson, and I went up to Rapid River, Maine, the outlet of the whole Rangely Lake system running from Lower Richardson Lake down to Lake Umbagog. So far as we knew, this river had never been successfully run before, although there was a legend that some Indians had done it many years ago. Although this stream is only two and a half miles long it has an extremely rapid current, dropping almost two hundred feet. With the large volume of water, it attains a speed of up to fifteen miles an hour in the rough spots. We finally finished the run, although it took us two days to do it because it was necessary to scout the river time after time before running the worst rapids. Fortunately, there was a tote road alongside the river, which enabled us to get the boats back and forth.

The reason that this stream is so good in summer is that the dam at the end of the Lower Richardson Lake, called Middle Dam, can be controlled to hold back the high water in the spring and then let water out in the summer to run the textile plants on the lower Androscoggin River. This trip proved to be such a challenge that in 1939 we organized the first White Water Championships in America. Over sixty boats of various kinds showed up, and we had state police along the river with ropes to rescue overturned boats. Because the state of Maine was interested in promoting this event, they arranged to have the newsreel people present to record the race. As I recall, sixteen boats were completely smashed up and very few people finished.

As chairman of the committee, I made a special rule that any contestant would be considered to have finished even if he tipped over so long as he hung onto his boat when he crossed the finish line. Guess who won that first White Water Championship—I tipped over fifty yards from the finish line but hung on to the boat!

Since then the White Water Championships have been held on the upper Arkansas River in Colorado, a stream much more accessible than Rapid River.

*ADVICE: I am convinced that it is most important for business executives to take at least four weeks' vacation every year. This is vital in my opinion—to get away from the telephone and any contact from the office. If you can find something exciting, so much the better. It will take your mind off business. To show how important this idea is, since 1971, Bill Miller of Textron has required every division head and every principal officer of the company to take a three-month sabbatical every five years. If a busy executive is going to be able to work at a high performance level for many years, it is most important that he take a diversionary vacation of this sort.*

# Old Age

If all of your grandparents lived to be ninety, you're certain to live to a ripe old age, with four provisos: First, don't smoke (I never smoked a cigar, pipe, or cigarette in my life). Second, don't be a heavy drinker (I gave up all hard liquor over thirty years ago). Third, don't let yourself get overweight. Many people eat too much and then spend thousands of dollars on special diets and reducing plans. Here's a very simple program that costs no money whatsoever: Weigh yourself every morning and if you are up even one pound, eat a fruit salad for lunch. Fourth, don't divorce your wife in latter years and marry some twenty-year-old chick. I was divorced twenty years ago and so far have resisted that temptation.

Besides the don'ts there are a number of most important dos: As you get older, try to walk at least a couple of miles a day. My former home is on the beach at Narragansett, Rhode Island; a round trip of the beach is about two and one-half miles. I also still play a lot of golf, usually three days a week in the summer, and very often walk the full five miles around the Point Judith Country Club course when the weather is good. When I go to the office I walk about a half a mile in the morning to meet the bus and another half mile from the bus terminal to the office and back. In addition, it's approximately a half mile from the office up a steep hill to the Hope Club for lunch and back.

Pick young doctors, dentists, and executors. If you select people in those categories older than you are, you are certain to have the problems that I have had. So far, I have had four different doctors and am about to take on a younger one for my regular semiannual physical check-ups. My first doctor was a delightful older man who was the father of one of my closest friends. He was a general practitioner and most satisfactory as far as my requirements were concerned, except that he died when I was about thirty. Next I picked a brilliant specialist about my own age, with whom I became great friends, but unfortunately he committed suicide—I hope it wasn't

because he couldn't put up with me any longer. The next one was an excellent diagnostician who took care of my regular check-ups and had some forty years of my cardiogram tapes, but he had a stroke and died a couple of years later. The fourth one was a friend with whom I played a lot of golf and who was one of the finest diagnosticians I had ever known, although he was really a country doctor. Unfortunately, he retired.

The next problem was with dentists. When I lived in Brookline, Massachusetts, I had an excellent dentist who took good care of me, but unfortunately, he finally decided to retire and sold his practice to another man in whom I did not have the same confidence. For some reason, whenever a single tooth was giving me trouble, he would send me to a specialist who would pull the tooth out. In spite of my imploring him to save these teeth, he still continued the same program until he finally had all my wisdom teeth out. That was the last straw! I decided that his primary interest must be to remove all of my teeth so that he could, as a specialist in making artificial teeth, fit me with a beautiful set of false teeth costing several thousand dollars. So I gave him up and found an excellent dentist in Providence who agreed with me that his main objective was to keep as many teeth as possible in my head instead of pulling them out. To give this new dentist some real incentive, I made him the following deal. At the end of December every year, we count the number of teeth I have left, multiply it by $25 and give him a year-end gift for his good work. As a result of this program, I've lost only one tooth in the last five years and he received a check for $625 last December.

Another problem is with executors. I made the mistake of starting off with a lawyer friend my own age. That didn't work because he died some twenty years ago. Next I picked a good friend and

able lawyer fifteen years my junior, a man who was in such marvelous physical condition that I was certain he would surely outlast me. He dropped dead on the tennis court about five years ago so I had to make another decision. This time I went to the other extreme. I picked a young lawyer who had left his firm and had come to work for one of the companies in which I was interested. He is now thirty-four years old and if he doesn't outlast me, I'm going to give up.

I'm convinced that it is absolutely essential for older people to keep mentally active. I've seen too many chief executive officers of large corporations retire without having planned mentally stimulating things to do after retirement. The chief executive officer who lets the board of directors persuade him to keep a secretary and an office at the company soon gets completely frustrated. Prior to retirement, he had been the decision maker in the company, now no one asks his advice. That's tough to take. As a matter of fact, when I retired from Textron in 1962, I even resigned from the board since I had picked two very able younger men to succeed me, Rupe Thompson, who was ten years my junior, and Bill Miller, who was thirty years younger. Since I had complete confidence in Rupe as chairman and chief executive officer and in Bill as president and chief operating officer, I felt that it was most important that they be permitted to run the company in the way they wished. I'm sure that as the founder of the business I would have been a real pain in the neck to them if I had stayed on the board. That decision on my part was one of the smartest things I ever did.

For many years I've observed with interest among my friends who have been chief executive officers of large companies what happens to them after they retire, and I am convinced that those who do not get involved in projects that really use their brain, wither on the vine real fast and die early. On the other hand, those who make long-range plans ahead of time to continue to be active, provided of course that their basic health is good, certainly tend to live longer.

I was expounding these theories to some of the editors of *Fortune* some years ago and they asked me to write a story for them on this subject. The title of the article I wrote was "Don't Let Your Brain Go Down the Drain."

I have recommended that as you get older—provided, of course, that your grandparents all lived to be over ninety—that you start in your fifties and sixties developing close friendships with congenial and interesting people at least a generation younger than you are. A good example of this is the wonderful relationship that I have developed with Jim and Jan Robison, both of whom are young enough to be my children. Jim, as you will recall, was the young man who headed up Indian Head Mills when it was spun off by Textron in 1953. Since I served as chairman of the board of his company for a number of years, I became a great admirer of his, both as a businessman and as a fine human being. Outside of business, we played a lot of golf together and very often when in New York I spent the night with them at their Armonk home.

When I moved my winter vacation activities over to the Bahamas, I joined the Lyford Cay Club when it was first organized in 1959. This club, built by Eddie Taylor, the prominent Canadian industrialist, was beautifully designed, with an excellent golf course, tennis courts, marina, and was right on one of the finest beaches in the world. I soon persuaded the Robisons to join the club and use its facilities.

A few years ago, when Eddie Taylor built eight most attractive duplex clubhouses that were to be available to members under long-term leases, I persuaded Jim and Jan to join me in taking one of the apartments. This arrangement has been particularly advantageous to me since Jan has taken care of all of the interior decoration and household chores and made it a great place for the three of us to stay at when taking time off in the winter to relax and play golf. We just recently sold the apartment and bought a house on the golf course. I am now a permanent resident of the Bahamas.

Jim and Jan have a winter ski lodge at Stowe, Vermont, where they spend most of their winter weekends. Unfortunately, they did not take up skiing until after I had given it up, otherwise we would have had many wonderful experiences at famous ski resorts of the

The pleasure of the company of

is requested
at a Bicentennial Birthday Ball
by

| Jan Robison | 60 |
| Jim Robison | 60 |
| Roy Little | 80 |
| | 200 |

to be held at the St. Regis Roof
Fifth Avenue and Fifty-fifth Street
New York City
on Sunday evening, February twenty-ninth
Nineteen hundred and seventy-six

Cocktails at seven                Dinner at eight
Music by Lester Lanin from eight to twelve o'clock
Leap Year - Ladies may cut in

No presents                Black tie

*"Today, on a vote of seven to five, the board of directors
wished me a happy birthday."*

world. When I was seventy and had not broken a leg or arm, I decided to give up skiing, since I found that whenever I took a hard spill I would lie on the ground wondering what the hell I was doing there. Last winter, however, I did go cross-country skiing.

March 1, 1976, was to be my eightieth birthday, and I discovered that Jim and Jan Robison were going to be sixty at just about the same time. Since 1976 was the bicentennial year, we decided to give a bicentennial birthday ball. The invitation is on page 318.

The party was held on leap year, February 29, 1976, and was organized so that everyone should arrive early so that the music could start at 8:00 and end promptly at 12:00 with Lester Lanin playing "Happy Birthday" at 12:01. As we moved from the cocktail lounge into the St. Regis ballroom, I was horrified to see a large sign in red letters saying it was unlawful for more than 250 people to be in the room. Two hundred and fifty-two of us had arrived for the party, not counting Lester Lanin's orchestra or the St. Regis's waiters. Fortunately, no one from the fire department showed up that night so we all had a marvelous time. About quarter of twelve, Jim Robison suggested that since everyone was having such a good time we ask Lester Lanin to stay on for another hour. I vigorously vetoed this suggestion. I have found from experience at big parties that it is most important to stop them when everybody is having a wonderful time. In the past, whenever I have paid the orchestra to stay over an extra hour, the whole affair would go into a tailspin and not end up the success it should have been.

In the summer of 1977, Jim and Jan took a most exciting boat trip down the Colorado River with a group of about twenty on a huge rubber raft. They tried to persuade me to accompany them, but I passed up that trip. Since Jan has always enjoyed camping trips that don't particularly interest Jim, Jan has joined me and other friends two or three different times on wonderful camping safaris in East Africa. Among the various activities that I have enjoyed since retirement have been a total of thirteen photographic safaris to that part of the world.

These trips to East Africa gave me the opportunity to get to know many of the government officials and trustees of national parks, directors of national parks, and other conservationists like Dr. Bernhard Grzimek, who has done so much for the preservation of wildlife in East Africa. Knowing that the New York Zoological Society was interested in the preservation of all wildlife, I worked closely with them in assisting the East African governments in plans to increase the national parks in those countries.

Financial assistance was given to the Tanzanian government by the New York Zoological Society in creating the Ruaha National Park—a wonderful game area. Because this was heavily wooded country, it did not have the huge concentrations of wildebeest, zebra, and other plains animals normally seen in the Serengeti National Park. On the other hand, it had the rare roan and sable antelope, greater and lesser Kudu, many elephants, hippo, leopard, cheetah, and a wide variety of other game. Although one assumes that creating a national park will preserve the status quo and that the game in the area will remain in balance because the predators keep the antelope and other game at a constant level, this assumption proved not to be so. Since man is the only predator of elephant and hippo, and since the Tanzanian government had moved 150

*One of the greatest thrills I had on safari in East Africa was taking movies of Amhed — the world's most famous elephant — who died of old age four years ago at Mt. Marsabit Game Reserve in Northern Kenya. His tusks were nine feet long and weighed 160 pounds apiece. He died just three days before I arrived at Marsabit to take more pictures. This is one of my favorites. He is now mounted in the entrance hall of the National Museum in Nairobi.*

native families out of the Ruaha who had been poaching for a living, we were amazed to find that within five years the elephant population in Ruaha had tripled. Apparently, the elephants had passed the word around for hundreds of miles outside the park that there was now a sanctuary at Ruaha. For protection, elephants migrated into the park from areas where hunting was permitted.

Since elephants eat all types of vegetation—grass, leaves, branches, and the bark of trees—a problem occurs when too many elephants live in an area; or rather, when more elephants live in an area than the habitat can comfortably support. Elephants strip the bark off trees, and once that has been done the tree dies. The same problem occurred at Murchison Falls in Uganda when it became a national park. The elephants are powerful enough to push over medium-size trees as well as destroy the bigger ones by stripping off the bark. In Kenya, in the eastern section of Tsavo National Park where there have been as many as twenty thousand elephants, the same thing occurred. Some believe in annual culling to keep the population in proportion to the habitat, as they have had to do in Murchison with elephants and in the Queen Elizabeth National Park with hippos. This problem is one of the most serious involved in the management of wildlife in the national parks in East Africa.

Another situation that needed attention was the Masai Game Reserve at Amboseli. It is a marvelous game area with tremendous variety of species right at the foot of snow-clad Mt. Kilimanjaro, Africa's highest mountain at 19,340 feet. The problem at Amboseli was that the land was owned by the Masai, a nomadic tribe of cattle raisers. The only year-round source of water in the area was a series of swamps and lakes at the foot of Mt. Kilimanjaro, fed by the underground streams that come down from the glaciers and snow fields on the mountain. These swamps have been used by the Masai to water their cattle and, of course, the wildlife was also dependent on this supply.

About eight years ago, David Western, a young British zoologist who was studying wildlife in Amboseli, suggested a plan to solve this problem. But he needed help to finance a scheme to pump water out of the swamps into drinking troughs where the Masai could graze their cattle so that it would not be necessary for them to drive their herds ten miles a day to drink.

We began working with the Kenyan government through its Ministry of Tourism and Wildlife and with the Masai through their Kajiado District Council to see whether they would put a couple of hundred square miles of the Amboseli Game Reserve into the national park system if such a plan could be financed. We finally persuaded the Masai to turn over 150 square miles of this area provided they were supplied with adequate water and grazing as compensation. The New York Zoological Society then agreed that they would raise the necessary funds for this project, up to one-half of the total cost, which at that time was estimated to be £100,000 or $280,000. Fortunately, we put a limit on the Society's commitment of $140,000. Since this project took many years to get approval from both the Masai and the government, the estimated cost of the project skyrocketed. It was therefore necessary to get the World Bank involved. One hundred and fifty square miles have been donated by the Masai to the national park system, and at the present time water is being pumped to numerous drinking troughs, each of which is at least three miles outside the park boundary. After eight or nine years of negotiation, the water project is in operation.

I have gone into considerable detail about projects in which I have been involved since retirement hoping that it may suggest to those of you who are either about to retire or actually retired the sort of activities from which you might get great satisfaction.

Another activity that I recommend for everyone, even before retirement, is bridge. It is undoubtedly the world's most popular card game and is actually played almost everywhere. I took the game up before going to college and, as a result of playing cards practically every evening instead of studying, achieved the distinction of being a dropped freshman and on probation at the end of my first year at Harvard. "Neither snow nor rain nor heat nor gloom of night stays these players from the swift completion of their appointed games."

In 1921, while I was living in Brookline, Massachusetts, a group of us formed a bridge club with two tables and a total of eight players. Our plan was to get together at least twice a month, having dinner at various members' homes before playing twenty-four hands of so-called party bridge. After four hands the winning couple moved to the other table and switched partners with the losers. This club was expanded to three tables and a total of twelve members shortly thereafter. The amazing thing is that this bridge club is still going strong. There are four of us who were in it at the start and we still adhere very closely to our original format. We get together for cocktails at 6:00, dinner promptly at 6:30, bridge at 7:30, play twenty-four hands, and wind up at 10:30. We do not play for money. The host is permitted to buy a prize for the leading man and woman each night, but the cost cannot exceed $1.00 apiece— the price has been the same since 1921. The winner for the year is the one whose average score is highest.

Those of you who are bridge players will get a kick out of this hand—32 honor count out of a possible maximum of 37. I opened six no trump. Seven diamonds is a lay down, but how do you get there? The lead was four of clubs which was taken by the eight.

With no possibility of establishing diamonds in dummy, all the high cards were played hoping that the spades would split three-three, or that the jack would fall. No such luck! As a result, a photograph of the hand now hangs on the wall of the card room at the Point Judith Country Club, Narragansett, Rhode Island with this caption:

LITTLE BID SIX NO TRUMP
DOWN ONE!

*North*

| Spades | 8, 3, 2 |
|---|---|
| Hearts | 7, 4 |
| Diamonds | J, 8, 6, 4, 3 |
| Clubs | 10, 7, 3 |

*West*

| Spades | 7, 6 |
|---|---|
| Hearts | J, 5, 3, 2 |
| Diamonds | 10, 9, 7 |
| Clubs | Q, J, 9, 4 |

*East*

| Spades | J, 9, 5, 4 |
|---|---|
| Hearts | Q, 10, 9, 8, 6 |
| Diamonds | 5, 2 |
| Clubs | 6, 5 |

*South*

| Spades | A, K, Q, 10 |
|---|---|
| Hearts | A, K |
| Diamonds | A, K, Q |
| Clubs | A, K, 8, 2 |

Alan Truscott wrote an article in the New York *Times* about this hand, entitled "Savoring the Rare Feast of a 32-Point Hand," in which he said 32 high-card points occurs about seventeen times in 100 million deals, so an average player playing once a week could expect to pick up a 32 point monster once in four thousand years.

Actually, the hand can be made. It's an easy solution after seeing all the cards. To every reader who mails me the correct answer I will send a $1.00 bill, but not more than one prize per family. As a result of this generous offer I will at least find out whether you have read the book this far.

Royal Little
La Colina
P.O. Box N 7776
New Providence, Bahamas

As I write this book, the realization occurs to me that never before in my life have I really looked back at the past. There have been so many fantastic opportunities that my concern has always been for the future. Perhaps this change in itself is a symptom of old age. Ultimately one has to plan even for death and I sure have done that.

Considered unconventional in life, no one is going to be disappointed with my plans: No funeral—a barbaric institution. No religious service. No cemetery burial—why waste all that valuable real estate. No undertaker—not necessary where I'm going. No memorial service—hope my friends will just think I've taken a long trip. Please have the body delivered to the Harvard Medical School. Incidentally, under most state law the only thing one cannot dispose of by will is the body—that law should be repealed. My children have agreed to sign the necessary legal documents. I have written Harvard to be expecting me. After whatever they do in medical schools is done, please cremate what's left over and flush the ashes down the john.

As one gets older, the principal worry is senility and becoming a burden to everybody and no longer making any contribution to society. If inability to remember names is one of the first indications of such a condition, then I'm well on my way. Also, if your friends start saying, "Roy, you haven't changed a bit in the last five years" don't be flattered—that's a sure sign you're slipping.

*ADVICE: I have a perfect solution to this problem. Get one of those cyanide pills that the CIA give to their people who embark on particularly dangerous missions, with instructions to swallow it and die within seconds rather than be captured. Now when you become completely senile and a burden to your family, just swallow the pill and end it all. The only trouble is when you get that senile, you'll forget where you hid the damn pill!*

# America and the
# Future

*I*n the summer of 1974, I was convinced that 1975 was going to be the worst recession year since World War II. All our leading economists and most businessmen were certain that double digit inflation was the problem of the future—hardly anyone else foresaw what was going to happen. In October 1974, when we had full employment, double digit inflation, a prime interest rate of 12 percent, and soaring commodity prices, I made certain forecasts about 1975 in an article that was subsequently published by *Fortune*. I predicted that unemployment would exceed 8 percent, that the rate of inflation would be reduced, that the prime interest rate would drop to 6 percent, that commodity prices would collapse, and that the stock market would boom.

How was it possible for me to have been so accurate in indicating what the future held in store? After World War I, when price controls were removed, I went to work for a small synthetic yarn producer and lived through an extraordinary inflationary period in 1919–1920. Many commodity prices tripled, labor became scarce, interest rates went to 12 percent, lead time for new equipment was up to two years, manufacturers' backlogs were enormous, and corporate profits were unusually high. Living through that experience made a lasting impression on me, particularly when the entire bubble burst in 1920 and many of our leading companies lost their entire working capital when commodity prices collapsed that year.

In 1974 I saw all the same danger signs: skyrocketing commodity prices, labor shortages, the prime interest rate at 12 percent, and excessive backlogs and profit. The stage was set for a repeat performance. There were probably only a handful of other active businessmen in 1974 besides myself who had survived the 1919–1920 boom and bust. That is why I stuck my neck out and predicted what was going to happen in 1975.

Now I'm tempted to make some very long-range comments about what may occur in the United States in the next century— no short-term predictions this time! All great civilizations in the past have always ultimately peaked out. It may be some decades before we really level off, but I'm convinced that our rate of growth as indicated by the gross national product is already slowing down.

During the two decades at the turn of the century, no industrial country on earth had a rate of population growth equal to that of the United States because of the millions of immigrants who were attracted by the opportunities in this country to run its factories and work its farms. As a result of this influx and a longer life expectancy, as well as the high birthrate, we had 203 million people in 1970, compared with 63 million in 1890.

During the two decades of high immigration ending in 1900 and 1910, the average increase in population was about 22 percent in each decade compared with 7.3 percent growth in the decade ending 1940, which reflected the effect the depression of the 1930s had on family planning. The rate increased to 18.5 percent for the ten years ending in 1960 but dropped to 13.4 percent in the next decade and is falling below that for the current period that will end in 1980.

The extent to which childbearing has fallen becomes dramatic when it is realized that it took only 35 million young women to produce 4.3 million babies in 1957, while 48 million women bore only 3.2 million babies in 1976. Although the Census Bureau estimates that the growth rate will drop drastically in the future, we may be rapidly approaching zero population growth, which will mean less need for expanded services and products.

Census Bureau charts graphically indicate population trends in this country compared with two opposite extremes: Sweden, with a zero birthrate, and Mexico, across an imaginary line on our continent, with one of the world's highest birthrates.

Why is the country approaching zero population growth so rapidly? More married women than ever are working full time. Over 50 percent of them are now working at least part time outside the home and no longer wish to have large families. In addition, contraceptives are more effective than in the past so that family size is no longer a matter of chance. Information on sterilization indicates an important new trend. A survey sponsored by the National Institute of Child Health and Human Development has found that sterilization is now second only to the pill as the birth control method favored by American married couples. Use of the pill has remained stable since 1973, declining only among older women, but sterilization has risen sharply, from 8.8 percent of all married

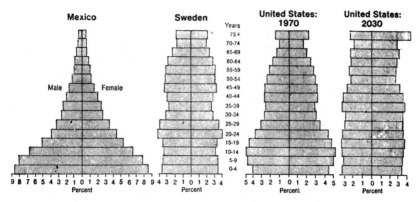

| Mexico | Sweden | Years | United States: 1970 | United States: 2030 |

FIGURES ARE FROM THE TAX FOUNDATION, INC., 50 ROCKEFELLER PLAZA, NEW YORK, NEW YORK 10020. DESIGN COPYRIGHT © 1977 BY THE READER'S DIGEST ASSOCIATION, INC.

couples in 1965 to 31.3 in 1975. By 1975, a total of 6.8 million couples of childbearing age had chosen sterilization, against 7.1 million who used the pill.

Zero population growth is a certainty during the next century— probably far sooner than the Census Bureau expects. The effect of this trend will be devastating to many businesses and, of course, on the rate of growth of the GNP.

In the past seventy years, the rate of increase in our farm and industrial production has exceeded that of any other nation. From $33 billion in 1909 to $1.397 billion in 1974, our GNP has gone up 42-fold, now exceeding the combined GNP of Western Europe and Japan. No longer will any such increase in the rate of growth of the GNP be possible.

Probably the most potent reason our growth rate and standard of living will not increase as fast in the future as it has in the past is that too many people are not providing services or making products that are included in the GNP. Over 30 percent of the adult population of this country is nonproductive for GNP computation purposes, and this percentage is increasing. In this group are the employees of towns, cities, counties, states, and the federal government, including all the bureaus and armed forces, the millions of unemployed, the millions on private pensions and social security, and the millions on welfare. With a lower population growth rate the average age will increase and the percentage of nonproductive persons will go up. In a democracy, there is no hope for governmental agencies to be cut back.

The Tax Foundation charts show the trend, with local governments increasing twice as fast as the federal government.

Another reason that the future growth rate will be dampened

# OUR
# EXPLODING BUREAUCRACY

American government is out of control. The total of
civilian employes on federal, state and local payrolls is
today <u>228</u> percent of what it was just 25 years ago.
Currently, there is one such employe for every 4.5 workers
in the private sector. And the increase in salary costs
has been even more staggering. These costs – for federal,
state and local civilian employes – are an astounding
<u>886</u> percent of what they were in 1950.
And the end is nowhere in sight.

**Increase in Employes**

| | | | |
|---|---|---|---|
| 5.7 Million | 7.9 Million | 11.35 Million | 13.03 Million |
| 1950 | 1960 | 1970 | 1975 |

**Increase in Annual Payroll**

| | | | |
|---|---|---|---|
| $17.2 Billion | $38.8 Billion | $95.4 Billion | $152.6 Billion |
| 1950 | 1960 | 1970 | 1975 |

is that an increasing number of our citizenry, particularly the younger ones, really don't want further expansion of our industries. The environmentalists and others are doing everything in their power—and they are very powerful—to block nuclear power plants, pipe lines, oil refineries, strip mining, and other urgently needed facilities. These people want to stop the clock and prevent further expansion. They are dissatisfied with present conditions and don't want any further deterioration in the environment. The Three Mile Island accident will strengthen their case.

Another reason that the GNP will not increase as rapidly in the next century is that the world can no longer afford to have major wars—a nuclear war would be so devastating that no nation will be crazy enough to start one. The United States has had a major war about once every generation—just far enough apart to get an unsuspecting youth to accept it, until Vietnam. Then the young ones were far wiser than their elders and recognized what a waste of life and assets that dreadful mistake caused. We must realize, however, that World War I, World War II, and the war in Vietnam put an enormous strain on our productive capacity and greatly increased our GNP in those war years. Hopefully we'll never have that kind of surge of industrial activity in the future.

I'll make two other predictions. So long as our present form of democratic government exists, and so far no one has ever invented a better one, we'll never have a balanced budget again. A constitutional amendment requiring a balanced budget is not the answer. While municipalities can be required to operate on a mandatory balanced budget basis because of fixed income from real estate taxes, I see no possibility for the federal government to develop equally consistent sources of money. There is no way that the huge fixed costs of Washington can be met year after year from our present principal sources of funds—widely fluctuating corporate and individual income taxes. Also we'll never control inflation below an average annual rate of 5 percent.

If the outlook for the long-term future growth of the GNP for the United States looks uncertain, and we continue to have inflation, unfavorable trade balances, and unbalanced budgets, why is capital from other industrial nations of the world pouring into this country at the rate of billions of dollars annually to buy many of our businesses? Those who control capital in the rest of the world are convinced that the United States will be the last place to go socialist. They want investments here since their own countries are well on the road to socialism already. Why will the United States be the last major industrial nation to go that route? For one reason and one reason only. Whereas the unions in other industrial countries have supported socialism, most of the unions in the United States are still strong proponents of the free enterprise system because, unlike other countries, their members have a vast stake in it through their pension funds' $250 billion ownership of equities in American industries.

There is one serious defect in our free enterprise system and we must correct it. We must find a way to eliminate the disastrous cycles that occur in business, which create our recessions and throw millions of productive workers out of jobs. Since World War I, we have had recessions in 1920, 1932, 1938, 1946, 1949, 1954, 1958, 1961, 1970, and one of the worst in 1975; and will probably have one in 1979 or 1980. We can no longer justify losing forever the output of services and products that 8 million unemployed could have contributed to the GNP during the last recession.

In the future, the private sector must not overexpand its productive facilities or overcommit for raw materials during every upswing in business the way they have in the past, for to do so will only accentuate our business cycles and create recessions and unemployment. The free enterprise system will not survive if 8 percent or more of its prime producers are unemployed and non-productive. Even the United States will then drift toward socialism.

Among the worst problems facing this nation are drugs and crime. With 25 percent of our young people and over 40 percent of black youths unemployed, this problem must be solved. Recent legislation extending mandatory retirement age from sixty-five to seventy will accentuate the problem by increasing the number of young unable to find jobs. We must find ways to provide meaningful employment for this segment of the population, otherwise they will continue to feel frustrated and bitter about the free enterprise system in which they are not permitted to participate. Without purpose in life, they will continue to resort to drugs and crime. If this situation isn't corrected, I can assure you that this country will be faced with conditions far worse than socialism.

While businessmen in the future will face far more problems than I did in the last sixty years, particularly from excessive government regulations and controls, nothing is going to stop the entrepreneurs of this country from creating new products and services so long as the free enterprise system survives.

# If I could live my life over I'd make the SAME MISTAKES but I'd start SOONER